Unauthorized Love

UNAUTHORIZED LOVE

Mixed-Citizenship Couples Negotiating Intimacy, Immigration, and the State

Jane Lilly López

Stanford University Press
Stanford, California

STANFORD UNIVERSITY PRESS
Stanford, California

Printed in the United States of America
on acid-free, archival-quality paper

Library of Congress Cataloging-in-Publication Data
Names: López, Jane Lilly, author.
Title: Unauthorized love : mixed-citizenship couples negotiating
intimacy, immigration, and the state / Jane Lilly López.
Description: Stanford, California : Stanford University Press,
2021. | Includes bibliographical references and index.
Identifiers: LCCN 2021007419 (print) | LCCN 2021007420
(ebook) | ISBN 9781503629318 (cloth) | ISBN 9781503629721
(paperback) | ISBN 9781503629738 (epub)
Subjects: LCSH: Intercountry marriage—United States. |
Foreign spouses—United States. | Foreign spouses—Legal
status, laws, etc.—United States. | Family reunification—
Law and legislation—United States. | Married people—
Legal status, laws, etc.—United States. | Citizenship—United
States. | Emigration and immigration law—United States.
Classification: LCC HQ1032 .L67 2021 (print) | LCC
HQ1032 (ebook) | DDC 306.84/50973—dc23
LC record available at https://lccn.loc.gov/2021007419
LC ebook record available at https://lccn.loc.gov/2021007420

Cover design: Susan Zucker
Cover art: Sandra Hutter | Shutterstock
Typeset by Motto Publishing Services in 10/15 Sabon LT Std

to all who have dared to love beyond borders
and to Lilly and Luca, whom I love boundlessly

Contents

Preface

In 2009, Camille, Juliette, and I fell in love with non-US citizens. Camille and Giovanni, whose parents brought him to the United States from Guatemala when he was just six years old, felt a spark as soon as they met. Although Giovanni's parents and siblings had been able to obtain a legal immigration status, he was too old to receive permanent residency automatically with his parents and still had no authorization to live in the US when he and Camille fell in love. Camille was not too worried about it; she figured that once they married, he would automatically qualify for citizenship through her. Tenoch, Juliette's partner, came into the US without authorization in his early twenties, shortly after his mother died. In Mexico, he had been studying at university to be a chemist. In the US, he began working in construction to help support his father and eleven siblings back at home. My boyfriend, Ramón, still lived in his Mexican hometown conveniently situated on the border with California. He had a tourist visa and could travel back and forth regularly to the US as needed, although Mexico remained his country of residence.

The first, and only, time all six of us were together was at Juliette and Tenoch's wedding in July 2010. Camille and Giovanni, newlyweds themselves, danced the night away. As Camille swayed and turned across the dance floor, I could see hints of her twenty-week "baby bump" through her long, flowing dress. Juliette and Tenoch glowed, with huge smiles beaming from their faces all night long. The warm evening was filled with laughter, song, and possibility. We all felt like our lives were just beginning as fate beckoned us toward a future full of promise.

By the time I began my doctoral program in 2011, Camille and Juliette were both married with babies, and I was newly engaged. In some ways, we all felt like we were heading down the same, happy path. But our partners' different legal statuses were already pushing our lives in divergent directions. Police had arrested Giovanni in late 2010 on a warrant after pulling him over for speeding. (He had missed a mandated court appearance, which triggered the warrant for his arrest.) He spent a year in jail and was slated for deportation as a result. Camille gave birth to their baby boy alone, and now she was fighting off depression and caring for her newborn while exhausting every possible lead that could help cancel or delay Giovanni's deportation.

Juliette experienced stress and anxiety as she adjusted to her new life "in the shadows" as part of an unauthorized immigrant family living in the US. She had nightmares that police were pounding on their door, calling out Tenoch's name, waiting to arrest and deport him. Most days felt "normal"—as normal as life with a newborn can feel—but Juliette also carried with her a new, never-ending worry that quietly gnawed at her peace of mind. Every day she wondered, Will today be the last day our family can be together?

And yet everything for Ramón and me seemed straightforward. We could marry when we wanted and live where we wanted (which, for the time being, would be in Mexico). We both traveled freely between the US and Mexico, building ties as a couple with family and friends in both countries. The world was as wide open as we wanted it to be, our opportunities seemed endless, and we felt uninhibited in charting our future together.

As I began my graduate studies, I sought answers to explain how Camille, Juliette, and I—all US citizens, all in love, all equally "deserving" of family success—could already be traveling along such varied trajectories because of our partners' (non)immigrant statuses in the US. Our three stories, and our very different experiences within the US immigration and family reunification system, have grounded this research from the beginning, setting me on my path to understand why US immigration laws have made it relatively easy for some families, like mine, to succeed while making it nearly impossible for other families, like Camille's and Juliette's, to survive.[1] This book is my attempt both to answer these questions and to bear witness to the consequences of US immigration policies on families, a record of our (un)authorized love.

Acknowledgments

I conducted my first interview with a mixed-citizenship couple during the spring of 2012, just as the presidential election season was getting into full swing. In June 2012, President Obama signed an executive order that made applying for family reunification less of a risk for unauthorized couples living in the United States; in 2013, the US Senate passed a comprehensive immigration reform bill and repealed the Defense of Marriage Act, giving married same-sex couples access to family reunification for the first time. In the early months and years of this project, many mixed-citizenship couples I met felt optimistic about the future of family reunification and immigration policy in the US. Although they all confronted challenges, they were still hopeful. I was, too. My husband and I had just begun our own mixed-citizenship marriage, and we felt certain that both of our countries also supported our cross-border union.

To say that things changed does not capture how dramatically our hope transformed into despair over the next eight years. The comprehensive immigration reform that seemed possible in early 2013 became very clearly impossible by the fall of that year, when the House of Representatives failed to pass the bill. This policy failure marked a shift in the political and social mood around immigration and immigrant families from concern to disinterest to disdain, culminating in the 2016 presidential election. The new administration's obsession with criminalizing immigrants and closing every door to legal immigration gave the stories I share in this book an urgency I had never felt before. Of course, the punishments mixed-citizenship families face were written into the law long before the 2016 election, but the Trump administration's attacks on immigrants and their families laid bare the stark vulnerabilities of both immigrants and citizens under the law. In this legal, political, and social context, it is both my duty and my honor to amplify the voices and experiences of mixed-citizenship couples and bring their lives and their love back into the immigration narrative.

In this book, I am able to tell love stories that we have not heard before because of many brave and generous couples who shared their love and lives with me. All of the couples I interviewed exposed themselves to some level of risk by speaking with me as they discussed openly, many for the first time, the burdens they have borne as families subject to US immigration laws. I am so grateful for them, for their willingness to share their lives with me, for their examples of passion and commitment, and for their audacity to choose to love beyond borders. I am inspired by them and the beauty they have created, even in the face of relentless opposition from the US government, and I feel it is one of the great privileges of my life to be able to share their stories with the world. I am especially grateful for Camille and Juliette, whose experiences inspired this research and whose determination and fearlessness continue to inspire me.

As I began to envision this book, I dreamed of publishing it with Stanford University Press, where most of my favorite ethnographies about immigration and the law have been published. I am so thankful to Marcela Cristina Maxfield for making that dream a reality and for providing me with the editorial guidance and support that I needed in just the ways that I needed them. I am thankful, too, for the production, marketing, and design team—including Marcela, Jessica Ling, Paul Tyler, Stephanie Adams, Sunna Juhn, and Susan Zucker—for taking my words and transforming them into a tangible thing of beauty, and for helping me share it with the world. I also extend my heartfelt thanks to the anonymous reviewers whose helpful suggestions have made this book better and whose enthusiasm for its message encouraged me to keep pushing forward when I needed it the most.

Indispensable funding for this project was provided by the National Science Foundation, the University of California Institute for Mexico and the United States (UC Mexus), the UC Consortium on Social Sciences and the Law, the Center for US-Mexican Studies, and the UCSD

Chancellor's Research Excellence Program. I am also grateful for the UCSD Division of Social Sciences Robert S. Koenigsberger Chancellor's Fellowship, which supported me through almost all of graduate school and, as such, indirectly funded much of the research I conducted for this project.

Unauthorized Love developed as I was living a life across (between?) borders, with the University of California San Diego anchoring my intellectual life in the US. At UCSD, I received boundless guidance, encouragement, constructive criticism, support, and just plain educating that made this project what it is and made me a better person and scholar. I am grateful and forever indebted to my mentors, Kwai Ng and David FitzGerald, for guiding me through every stage of this project. They have pushed me forward with the perfect combination of high expectations and encouragement, and their belief in my ability to succeed is what kept me going through the darkest days of data collection, analysis, writing, and revision. I thank them both, for teaching me through their examples how to be an effective academic and mentor, and for supporting me as a whole person, not just a scholar. I extend that same gratitude and high praise to other advisors—among them, Jennifer Chacón, John Evans, Nancy Postero, Gershon Shafir, John Skrentny, and Christena Turner—whose advice, enthusiasm, and examples of mentorship will continue to motivate and improve me as an individual and as an academic. I am grateful, too, for Isaac Martin, who invested so much time and patience to train me as a researcher and who, in the process, taught me the meaning of compassionate leadership, service, and scholarship. I express my thanks to the countless others at UCSD—students, faculty, and staff—who created such a strong community of scholars and made room for me to belong there.

I have been blessed to have moved directly from one nurturing academic community to another, and I am grateful to my colleagues and friends at Brigham Young University for welcoming me with open arms into such a supportive, collaborative, generative work environment. I have felt encouragement, motivation, and genuine care from all of my colleagues in the sociology department and many more friends and mentors working across the university. I thank you all so much! I am especially grateful to Curtis Child, Jon Jarvis, and Eric Dahlin for letting me invite myself into your writing group and giving me the feedback and encouragement I needed to take the abstract concept of this book and make it a comprehensible reality. I am grateful, as well, to Laura Walker for being such a caring and supportive mentor and friend. I have also had the privilege of working with wonderful student researchers, including Claudia Soto, McKay Zuñiga, Paige Park, and Faith Williams, whose hard work and diligence directly contributed to this book in ways both great and small, and for whom I am very grateful.

My mind and my heart have been nourished and enlarged by the scholarship, mentorship, friendship, and examples of many great minds, and this book is a direct product of that influence. I am so grateful for the work of scholars like Leisy Abrego, Debbie Boehm, Heide Castañeda, Joanna Dreby, Angela García, Ruth Gomberg-Muñoz, Cecilia Menjívar, and Natalia Molina, for their examples of scholarly excellence, and for the willingness of many of them to mentor and encourage me in my own work. Academia has also connected me with wonderful, loving, brilliant friends who have made my life and my work better in so many ways, including Hayley Pierce, Lauren Olsen, and Lindsay DePalma. I would not be who I am today without your steadiness, enthusiasm, and true camaraderie. And to my intellectual soulmate and dearest friend, Rawan Arar, thank you for giving all of your heart and your incredible mind to helping make me and my work stronger, deeper, and truer.

This book would not exist without the village of supporters rallying around me at home, too. I express my deep gratitude to all of our friends and family in Tecate who have loved, supported, and encouraged me and who have provided essential friendship and care for our family. I am especially grateful to our extended and adopted family in Tecate— including my *suegros*, Anita and Ramón, and brother-in-law, Marcos; Joaquin, Mari (Mana), Cesar, and Moisés Noriega; and Ema and Carlos Tom—for always making room for us in your homes and in your hearts. A special thank you, too, to Jen Rey, for being our home away from home in San Diego, and Riley and Ilya Lorimer-Reznik for being our adopted family in Utah.

I am grateful to my mother, Janis Lilly Werth, for being my advocate, interview recruiter, therapist, and copyeditor extraordinaire. Her confidence in my ability to succeed at everything has kept me going even through the bleakest moments of life. Thank you, Mom, for your tireless listening ear and your unfailing faith in my ability to accomplish every worthy goal. Thanks, too, to the rest of our San Antonio family—Aunt Jen, Uncle Kyle, Lainey, Scott, and Howdy—who have supported and encouraged me/us in many ways, great and small.

My father, John Lilly, has been gone a long time now, but I still hear his voice in my ear from time to time questioning why I chose sociology instead of a more lucrative discipline and asking when I'll ever finish writing that book. I hope to have honored his legacy by believing in myself, forging my own path, and never taking no for an answer.

Finally, I thank my husband, Ramón, for daring to love me and for encouraging me to chase all of my dreams. Thank you for keeping me grounded during this wild ride, for making me stop and smell the roses, for your willingness to start new adventures together, and for your patience and long-suffering as we have endured our own family reunification saga. Above all, thank you for our Lilly Ana and our Luca, who are my inspiration and my motivation and my distraction and my joy. My life is everything because the three of you are in it.

*　*　*

Some parts of chapter 2 were published in article form in "Redefining American Families: The Disparate Effects of IIRIRA's Automatic Bars to Reentry and Sponsorship Requirements on Mixed-Citizenship Couples," *Journal on Migration and Human Security* 5(2): 236–51. I am grateful to *JMHS* for allowing me to republish portions of that article here as part of a broader legal analysis of the US immigration laws that have redefined love and family for mixed-citizenship American couples.

Unauthorized Love

Introduction

"SO, HOW LONG BEFORE they become a citizen? It's automatic, right?" You would be hard-pressed to find a US citizen married to a non-US citizen who has never been asked this question. Many Americans believe this is the case. I certainly did. That is why I was baffled—then appalled—when my dear friend, Camille, called to tell me that the US government was deporting her husband, Giovanni. "How could this happen?" I asked. "You're a US citizen!" Camille's citizenship, it turns out, was not enough. Not enough to help Giovanni become a citizen. Not even enough to save him from indefinite banishment from the United States.

The US Supreme Court confirmed this unfortunate truth in *Kerry v. Din* (2015), stating unequivocally that there is no "constitutional right to live in the United States with [one's] spouse."[1] Yet "family reunification"—an entitlement in US immigration law that enables US citizens and legal permanent residents to extend legal immigrant status to some immediate family members—has served as the foundation of US immigration policy since its inception.[2] Hundreds of thousands of US citizens successfully sponsor their spouses for legal immigration status (with a pathway to citizenship) every year. Why wasn't that true for Camille, too?

Over nearly a decade of searching, I have come to learn that, rather than being an exception, an accident, or an anomaly, Camille's experience of governmental rejection and family separation is as central to US immigration policy as family reunification.[3] Every year, the US government rejects the reunification requests of thousands of mixed-citizenship American couples based on "disqualifying" traits of the citizen, her partner, and/or their relationship. From the state's perspective, though, excluded *families* have not been rejected, nor have any of their citizen members. Family reunification denials only affect "unworthy" or "unqualified" *individuals*, precisely because (non)citizenship and (un)authorized status are, technically, individual-level statuses. In matters of citizenship and immigration, the state deals with individuals, not families. As the majority in *Kerry v. Din* declared:

> There is a "simple distinction between government action that directly affects a citizen's legal rights, or imposes a direct restraint on his liberty, and action that is directed against a third party and affects the citizen only indirectly or incidentally."[4] The Government has not refused to recognize [the US citizen's] marriage to [the noncitizen], and [the US citizen] remains free to live with her husband anywhere in the world that both individuals are permitted to reside. And the Government has not expelled [the US citizen] from the country. It has simply . . . denied [the noncitizen] admission into the country.[5]

Rooted in the individualistic logic of modern citizenship, this decision declares that the citizen's rights have not been affected, as she continues to have free access to her country and her spouse. But the implication of this decision—one that is never explicitly stated—is that a citizen in this circumstance is unable to live *in* her country of citizenship and live *with* her spouse at the same time. Although the US Supreme Court has confirmed the citizen's right to residence in US national territory[6] and all individuals' (citizens and noncitizens) right to marriage,[7] it maintains that those rights are not mutually inclusive. According to this logic, denying a spouse legal entry to the US (or legal status and protection from deportation once living inside the US) does not preclude the citizen's access to her country and all the individual-level benefits of her citizenship, nor does it prevent her from being able to live with her spouse. The government has "simply" exercised its right to prohibit an individual from legally entering its territory.

This rationalization, grounded in the individual boundaries of citizenship, isolates identities and relationships that, in everyday life, cannot be separated. The conflict that arises from this policy focus on individualism rather than interdependency creates problems for both families and the government. Mixed-citizenship couples' position at the crossroads of immigration, citizenship, and family law reveals the limits of our individualistic formulation of (non)citizenship and its consequences, which jeopardize the stability of the state, mixed-citizenship families, and society at large.

Mixed-citizenship couples embody a basic, yet infinitely consequential, conflict for the modern nation-state. On the one hand, states need families. Families continue to serve as the central organizing unit of society, a key locus through which a state's members are cared for, socialized, counted, and controlled. It is therefore in the state's best interest to recognize and support families whose members include citizens.[8] Excluding a family with at least one citizen member could generate multiple problems for the state, primarily because the state's responsibility to its citizen remains in effect even if she has been excluded from the country (literally or figuratively) alongside her family.

On the other hand, states want as much specificity as possible in determining which individuals "belong"—in other words, who they are willing to claim as their own. In an increasingly globalized and interconnected world, states' long-term viability depends upon their ability to identify their members and distinguish them from nonmembers.[9] This is particularly important given states' increasing obligations to their citizens, including a growing list of civil, political, and social rights they promise their members.[10] Using family (rather than individual) status to determine state membership could lead a country to formally acknowledge and accept responsibility for individuals it otherwise would not choose to claim. But accepting only some family members, and limiting the reach of the related rights and protections granted to those individuals, jeopardizes the well-being of citizens and destabilizes the family unit upon which the state remains wholly dependent.

The United States has tried both approaches to resolving the individual-family citizenship conflict. Spanning from the mid-nineteenth to the early twentieth century, US citizenship law prioritized family over individuality in determining citizenship, automatically granting citizenship to the noncitizen wives of US citizen men. (For a shorter span of time, the US government also automatically stripped the citizenship of US citizen women married to noncitizen men.)[11] This approach to citizenship ensured that all family members had the same citizenship status, effectively eliminating the mixed-citizenship couple problem.[12] During this time, adult males were generally the only citizens who could make a direct claim on the state; thus, the wholesale acceptance or rejection of a family based on the male head-of-household's citizenship followed the logic of the citizenship regime at that time.[13]

Women's suffrage and other equal rights movements pushed the US (and other nation-states) to expand citizenship rights and extend them directly to women and children.[14] This expansion of rights proved to be a double-edged sword for mixed-citizenship couples.[15] Once every family member could make a direct claim on the state for their citizenship rights, the meaning and content of citizenship shifted, prompting a significant change in the way the US government deals with mixed-citizenship families. Where noncitizen wives once automatically obtained citizenship through marriage, now mixed-citizenship couples must apply for legal status benefits through family reunification. For couples that choose to apply, the citizen, noncitizen, and their marital relationship undergo scrutiny to determine their "worthiness" before they can access legal status. For couples that choose not to apply, the citizen's family relationship and its effects on her life remain invisible—and irrelevant—to the state.[16]

The individuation of citizenship changed the legal (and philosophical) relationship between the American state and its members, creating a direct line between citizen and state where once the family served as an official intermediary.[17] While this direct connection to the state brought many significant improvements for newly acknowledged citizens, it did not actually alter the role of the family in mediating the citizen-state relationship. The family remains paramount in shaping individuals' physical, economic, educational, and social opportunities and experiences. But the individualistic framework of citizenship no longer contemplates the family, despite the ongoing role of the family in organizing individuals' daily lives. A citizenship regime founded on the principles of individuality and autonomy, one that actively denies our endless interdependencies—including those of the family—destabilizes society and leads to policies and legal decisions grounded in an impossible fiction.[18] In turn, mixed-citizenship families are rendered "impossible": forced to navigate laws and statuses as "individuals" while embedded within and affected by familial relationships deemed legally irrelevant.[19]

Part of the impossibility of mixed-citizenship families stems from the fact that citizenship is a "legal fiction," an invented concept established in law to create a distinction where one otherwise would not exist. Governmental authorities invented citizenship when they created laws and signed treaties delineating state membership based (generally) on one's presence in a territory at birth (*jus soli*) or one's claim on territorial membership through descent (*jus sanguinis*).[20] While the concept of citizenship may seem natural to us today—and the way it orders our lives and the world may seem inevitable—there is nothing natural or inevitable about it. Citizenship is a fiction, an invention, and it represents only one of many potential arrangements through which the relationship between states and their members could be legally recognized. We cannot lose sight of this as we consider the consequences of (non)citizenship—(un)equal access to rights, safety, territory, life—which, while far from fiction, are equally unnatural and evitable.[21]

For mixed-citizenship couples, the problems created by their different citizenships unnaturally interfere in the otherwise natural evolution of their relationships.[22] In most cases, citizenship has little to do with these couples' motivations to form families together. Their partnerships result from the same forces driving other couples' relationships: love, necessity, hope in the future, practicality, whimsy. Yet mixed-citizenship couples face myriad questions, hurdles, and complications simply because they officially "belong" to different countries. Their efforts to satisfy basic needs, such as finding a place in which they can live together, frequently prove exhausting and even futile. While citizenship generally plays little or no role in the initiation of these couples' relationships, it often becomes the central issue dictating their daily opportunities and threatening their relationships' long-term viability.

In the United States, family reunification law exists to address the legal and practical complications of mixed-citizenship relationships. By opening access to legal status and citizenship to some immediate family members of US citizens, family reunification offers the promise of family togetherness without the threat of separation. But what most outsiders to this process do not understand is that both noncitizens and their citizen family members must *earn* their successful family reunification. For some families, this means the investment of significant time and money as they wait for months or years for the government to accept their demonstrations of "worthiness" and approve their family claim to reunification. Other families face certain failure, as their "unworthiness" has been predetermined.

For every US citizen in a mixed-citizenship family, the strain of mixed-citizenship status—whether temporary or long-term—generates multiple levels of conflict. It creates conflict between the citizen and her spouse as they struggle over whether and how to subject themselves to the scrutiny and uncertainty inherent to the family reunification process. It creates conflict between the citizen and her state as she confronts daily reminders of her country's antipathy toward her family. And it creates conflict between the citizen and herself as she is forced to constantly question her identity, her allegiance to spouse and country, her value as a citizen and as a human being. These conflicts yield multigenerational consequences that endure far beyond families' (un)successful reunification bids, outcomes that directly challenge the assumptions of untethered individuality undergirding modern conceptions of citizenship and national belonging. Mixed-citizenship families underscore our "radical dependency" upon one another—both within families and in society at large—and their experiences highlight the failings of a citizenship regime that ignores the reality of these ties.[23]

The consequences of the legal fiction of citizenship and the impossibilities it creates for mixed-citizenship families fall most heavily on the families themselves. But the effects of these consequences reach far beyond mixed-citizenship families to the heart of society, warping social conceptions of national identity, social interdependency, and who "belongs." In the chapters that follow, I detail how US immigration laws—and mixed-citizenship couples' engagement with them—create (un)authorized families whose opportunities and outcomes directly stem from their family-level legal status. I argue that, rather than some other unique quality of the couples I interviewed, it is the imaginary categories and statuses established in the law—(non)citizen, (un)authorized— that produce the drastically different trajectories couples follow. Mixed-citizenship couples' experiences show unequivocally that our current individual-centered citizenship regime is incompatible with the family. Utilizing data from interviews with fifty-six mixed-citizenship couples, I show that (non)citizenship status has family-level consequences that significantly affect the experiences and opportunities of *all* members of mixed-citizenship families. And those experiences and opportunities, in turn, redefine the meaning of citizenship and belonging for citizens and noncitizens alike. (For a detailed description of my research methodology, see Appendix A. For brief background information on each couple, see Appendix B.)

In chapter 1, I briefly describe five mixed-citizenship couples' relationships *before* law intervenes. As they meet and fall in love, their stories seem as familiar and unremarkable as those of other American couples. There is nothing in their "love stories" that would suggest why some of these couples will face endless obstacles to their continued existence while others will find the doors of opportunity opened wide to receive them. Inequalities in law, both as written and as applied, set couples on these divergent paths.

Chapters 2 and 3 examine the laws and legal processes, respectively, that determine couples' "worthiness" for family reunification and their subsequent family reunification outcomes. In chapter 2, I take a deep dive into the three laws that currently drive US family reunification policy regarding mixed-citizenship couples. Each of these laws has contributed its own modification to the definition of the "American family," drawing narrower boundaries around who and what qualifies as "family," what "legitimate" marriage looks like, and which kinds of individuals and families get to be "American." Collectively, these three laws have changed the nature of American mixed-citizenship families by redefining them, and they have altered American society in the process. But couples' actual legal outcomes do not perfectly adhere to these legal definitions. Chapter 3 examines why many couples who, according to the law, should (not) qualify for family reunification, do (not). When, why, and how couples choose to apply for family reunification affect their likelihood of success. Like a high-stakes game of poker, couples' timing, strategy, and expertise—in addition to the "cards" they were dealt—all contribute toward determining whether or not they ultimately hold a "winning hand." The law-as-written, the law-in-practice, *and* couples' orientation toward those laws and their enforcement all contribute to families' reunification outcomes. And the long-term, far-reaching effects of those outcomes, for better and for worse, cannot be overstated.

I examine the family-level consequences of family reunification success, failure, and uncertainty in chapters 4, 5, and 6. These chapters evaluate how family-level immigration status shapes individual- and family-level spatial, structural, and social integration for citizens and noncitizens alike. The logic driving the majority ruling in *Kerry v. Din* suggests that actions taken against a citizen's spouse only "indirectly" affect the citizen without meaningfully impeding her individual relationship to her country and the rights and responsibilities entailed therein. But mixed-citizenship couples' lived experiences tell a different story. In each dimension of integration, it is law—rather than culture, choice, worthiness, or anything else—that drives families' (dis)integration with society. For citizens whose spouses have been deported or denied legal status in the United States, that "third-party" rejection is not "incidental," as the justices suggest in *Kerry v. Din*—it is central to determining every opportunity those citizens can now access and will shape every decision those citizens make moving forward. Spousal rejection not only inflicts emotional harm and suffering on the citizen but also spatially, structurally, and socially distances the citizen herself from her country and its society. In these chapters, I also find that the family-level (dis)integrative effects of family reunification outcomes extend to "successful" families as well. For these families, the formal legal recognition of their family and the extension of legal status to all family members enhances spatial, structural, and social integration for every family member. Family-level (dis)integration is a dynamic process for all members of (un)successful mixed-citizenship families, moving each family member closer to or further from spatial, structural, and social inclusion.

The implications of these findings for individuals, families, society, and the state are vast. Policymakers have created the problems mixed-citizenship families face, and they also have the power to resolve these problems, even under the current citizenship regime and within the confines of present policy structures. There are a number of policy recommendations that would reduce the burdens borne by mixed-citizenship American couples and provide immediate relief from the threat of family separation, which are discussed in the conclusion. I end the book by recommending a shift in citizenship policy to treat mixed-citizenship families based on the rights and privileges of their *most*-entitled (rather than least-entitled) family member(s). If policymakers truly want to support US citizens and American families, they must adjust immigration and citizenship policy to explicitly acknowledge and account for the role of the family in mediating the citizen-state relationship.

The Same, but Different

Molly & Hector

When Hector went to a house on the outskirts of town to install carpet, he never imagined that he was about to meet his future wife. But there Molly was, the oldest daughter of her parents' ten children, serving Hector and his friend food and water while they worked. For Hector, it was love at first sight. Although the job only lasted two days, Hector was already smitten and looking for an excuse to come back and see Molly again. He left behind a sweatshirt and a pair of sunglasses, planning to return for them the following weekend. "Before he finished the job," Molly explained, "he left a sweatshirt in my closet to come back for it. And he had also left some sunglasses, right? And my brother was snooping around and said, 'Hey Mom, here are some sunglasses,' so my brother took them back to the carpeting company's office and left them for Hector. When Hector got there, the secretary told him, 'They brought you some sunglasses,' and Hector asked, 'Just the sunglasses?' 'Yes. Why? Was there something else?' 'No, no, no, . . .' The next Saturday he was knocking on our door"—Hector interrupted, "With the excuse of"—"the sweatshirt!"

It took them six months to convince Molly's parents to allow them to date, and even then they were only allowed to spend time together at Molly's house with her parents at home. If they ever went out, Molly had to take some of her younger siblings with her. "We couldn't even hold hands," Molly explained. "Nothing," Hector added. "It was hard." Molly agreed, "It was really hard." In time, though, they won over Molly's parents. And two years later, they married.

The prevailing notion of the ideal marriage as a "love match" between "equal" partners is a relatively modern invention, as Stephanie Coontz details in her history of marriage.[1] Despite its novelty, the fusion of "love" with "marriage" has stuck in the modern Western consciousness with such power that marriage is now seen as incomplete without love, and marriage for reasons other than love is often viewed as heresy. In the United States, as in many countries across the world, we judge relationships based on the quality of their "love stories," and reward couples who can convince us of their "true love." Mass media, literature, social norms, and even the law train us to believe that "love conquers all," in part by creating institutions and structures that prioritize and reward couples whose stories reinforce cultural narratives about the "power of love."[2]

Mixed-citizenship American couples seeking legal status in the United States through family reunification literally have to "prove" their love to government agents as part of their application. Couples who marry for reasons other than "love"—especially couples who marry explicitly for immigration benefits—do not qualify. Given the legal and cultural emphasis on love as the driver of marriage, I was not surprised to find that every couple I interviewed could relate their "love story" (the short, medium, and long versions) with ease. Without exception, their responses to questions about how they met and why they decided to marry were the most rehearsed and effortless, perhaps because it is a question they have been answering since their relationships began.

Chandra & Pancho

"We met officially, for the first time—like, shake hands—five years ago," Chandra told me. "I was working on a ranch, and my coworker's family lived about an hour-and-a-half away and they came to visit her. And Pancho was living with her family at the time. So that's how I met him." For the next few years after that initial introduction, they only crossed paths a few times and did not communicate much beyond a brief hello. Pancho (who is painfully shy) tried to find ways to get to know Chandra better and even asked her out, though Chandra turned

him down. "Two years ago is when, I guess, we became more friends—talked more, chatted more on Facebook, stuff like that." Shortly after they started to talk more, Pancho began working on a big project at the ranch where Chandra worked, and suddenly they were around each other all the time. "If you ask him," Chandra said, laughing, "he'll tell you that he waited for me to say yes to a date for two years—and I can agree with that. I just kept saying no. He tried to get me to date for a long time . . . I kept telling him no," she said, "and then, finally, I was like, why do I say no? He's not a bad guy. He's a nice guy. I don't have any real reason to tell him no. So I said yes, and here we are."

In many ways, Chandra and Pancho are very different. They grew up immersed in different cultures and speaking different languages. But they also both grew up on ranches and love the tranquility of rural life. They each described how their "rancho roots" and love of rural life presented the biggest hurdle in finding a partner. As Pancho put it, "I think, probably, me being from a ranch with a woman from the city, we probably would have broken up." Pancho did not like and did not want to be a part of busy city life. "I would rather see someone riding a horse with their cowboy hat and stuff like that" than be on "streets filled with people" in the city, he explained. Chandra agreed. "City boys don't like me. I didn't really fit with city boys. I intimidated them." Because a love for rural life so strongly informed each of their identities, something foreign to many other potential partners, Chandra concluded that, "Believe it or not, with all the cultural differences and language and everything else, this"—being with Pancho—"is easier than that"—being with a city boy. Their shared love of the rural lifestyle nurtured their love for each other. Now that they are married, they look forward to building a life they both always dreamed of: working the land together as a family.

At least one member in every mixed-citizenship couple has to cross a border in order for the couple to meet, suggesting that their relationships begin under extraordinary and unusual circumstances. But that is not what my couples' stories suggest. The fifty-six mixed-citizenship couples I interviewed for this project found each other in the same ways as other, "normal" couples.[3] They met at bars and birthday parties, at church and work, online and on vacation. Just over half of the couples I interviewed met through their social networks: connected by mutual friends, as neighbors, at church activities. Nearly one-third met through work or school. The remainder met through seemingly "chance" encounters in-person or online. A few of them met as children; others met well into adulthood. Some have moved multiple times across borders to live together; others have never left the city where they met. Many of these couples have maintained their relationships "long-distance" for an extended period of time. A few choose to "live apart together,"[4] but the majority live in the same physical space most or all of the time. In all of these ways, mixed-citizenship American couples' relationships follow the same trends as those of same-citizenship American couples.[5]

Mixed-citizenship couples are not only "normal" with regard to how they meet and marry; they also are increasingly "normal" in their frequency within the American populace. Data from the 2011 American Communities Survey suggest that one in every thirteen married couples in the US—representing approximately 4.1 million households—are "mixed-nativity" couples (one US-born spouse, one foreign-born spouse).[6] The actual number of mixed-citizenship American couples is likely much larger, as this estimate excludes cohabiting (unmarried) mixed-citizenship couples; families with a naturalized citizen partner and a foreign-born, nonnaturalized partner; and the millions of mixed-citizenship American couples living outside the US.

William & Berenice

William and Berenice were both relatively new to the city when their roommates introduced them at a neighborhood event. Eager to make new friends, they both took advantage of opportunities to spend time together along with other friends and roommates. Berenice was still recovering from a bad breakup and was not ready to seriously date anyone yet; she felt like "being single with nothing to worry about, it was perfect." They were "just friends" for a few months, "hanging out and all that, but not dating," Berenice explained. "I don't think I was interested in that." Berenice initially claimed that William was "not her type," but it did not take long for their friendship to evolve into some-thing more. As William describes it, they both "fell in love pretty quick, actually. Probably like a month after we started dating. So that was al-ways there from the beginning." But being in love did not insulate them from facing serious challenges in their relationship. During the course of their courtship, Berenice broke up with William twice, partly because she was afraid of having her heart broken again. But she was also con-cerned about how their visible ethnic differences and invisible citizen-ship status differences would affect their relationship. She was used to the stares and the judgments others directed her way, but would he be able to handle them? When I asked what made her change her mind, she said, "Little by little, I was getting to know him more. And he was very sweet and very kind to everybody. He was not just there to impress, you know?" Berenice struggled with the idea of moving from carefree, low-stakes dating to seeing William exclusively. Finally, unable to shake her attraction to William, she relented. "I think that was one of these things I had to tell myself: that it was okay" to date exclusively "and that he was a good person to do it with." In time, their love for each other grew large enough to overcome their fears, and they decided to get married.

For many of the couples I interviewed, real or perceived ethnic or ra-cial differences underlined the earliest challenges they faced from oth-ers. Racial biases in general, and those specifically directed at mixed-race marriage, shape partnering preferences among members of many different racial and ethnic groups in the US.[7] While the couples I inter-viewed did not identify race or ethnicity as something they were con-sciously thinking about when choosing their partner, they did note that it was something others regularly brought to their attention. Thirty-two of the couples I interviewed were interethnic (mixed White-Latinx) and twenty-four of the couples had partners who were both Latinx. Many couples described themselves as "mixed-race" or "mixed-ethnicity"; others felt ethnically and racially similar.

Regardless of their self-perceptions, many couples experience ex-ternal judgment from others based on their different phenotypes. As Rebekah recalled, "We would just go places and, every now and then—not all the time—we would get, kind of like, heads that would do a double-take." Rebekah's "first instinct" in recognizing these looks was to think, "They did that because I am White and you are Brown. Because we're obviously different. And sometimes, I was like, Whatever. And other times, it was a little offensive because I thought, 'We have the right to be with who we choose and who we love.' You know?" Rebekah and Miguel, along with many other couples I interviewed, have experienced the silent (and sometimes not-so-silent) bias against mixed-race couples that creates additional barriers toward mixed-race couples' relational success.[8]

Couples find different ways to process these encounters. Chandra flips "between irritation or just thinking it's hilarious that people [fall] into the trap of assumptions." Usually, she and Pancho just laugh when, once again, someone has assumed "that we are not together," but it also wears on her. "They don't know how many guys I dated before I finally found one that was good and had everything that I needed to be a better person. And just because he's from Mexico, I shouldn't be with him?!" Chandra groaned. "Those kinds of things frustrate me."

Grace & Lucas

Grace was three weeks into a seven-month trip conducting fieldwork for her doctoral dissertation in public health when she met Lucas, a local doctoral student in philosophy, at a dance. "And from that moment, we fell in love right away, and we were together all the time during those seven months" (Grace). At the end of the summer, Grace had to return home. Lucas traveled with her for a few weeks, meeting her family and seeing the places where Grace grew up. By the end of that trip, they both knew they wanted to marry as soon as possible. Before Lucas returned home, he explained, "We planned everything regarding when we could marry. Since I had to go back and she had to stay, we planned out everything to see when we could get married." Lucas went home in September and they were married before the year ended.

Although they had planned the outlines of the wedding before Lucas left, he did not officially propose until he was back home. "He sent my ring by FedEx and asked me to marry him over Skype!"

Couples' racial or phenotypical differences often expose them to outside judgment, and others' perceptions of their differences in skin color is often seen as the primary factor that makes their relationship "different," "unique," or "unconventional." Yet the couples I interviewed almost universally feel that their difference in citizenships creates much larger legal, social, and emotional conflicts in their relationships than their racial or ethnic differences. As an invisible status, (non)citizenship is not readily apparent to onlookers; it is a status couples can strategically disclose. While (non)citizenship's invisibility can insulate some couples from experiencing anti-immigrant hostility, it can also cause couples to confront significant challenges to their relationship due to their mixed-citizenship status without the support of family and friends.

Whether they like it or not, citizenship status will, in one way or another, come to define every mixed-citizenship couple and play a huge role in determining the success of their relationship and the family they form together. But, like most same-citizenship couples, when mixed-citizenship couples begin to write their "love story," their focus on love and compatibility almost always supersedes concern over potential conflicts posed by their differences, including their different citizenships. As Angelica put it, "We fell in love without knowing each other and our situations really well, and I thought, 'Oh, he doesn't have papers. He voluntarily deported. We can fix that.' It was all really easy." She paused and sighed before she continued. "We didn't think, 'It's going to take many years, it's going to be very expensive. We're going to have to—I'm going to have to live in Mexico as long as he can't cross.' We didn't think about any of that." Most couples who are falling in love do not think about any of those things, either. "There was simply a connection between us, and our problems have come little by little," Angelica explained. "The connection was about falling in love, regardless of whether or not it was convenient."

Brett & Mariana

Brett and Mariana met, of all places, at the Cancun airport. "I was learning Spanish and couldn't speak much," Brett began. "I was trying to—*we have a joke always that, when we met, she always flirted with me and"—"That's not right," Mariana interrupted—"to be honest, it was probably me seeking her down because we were in the airport line getting our tickets, and then there was that hour or two-hour wait before you get on the flight. Then I saw her at a coffee shop. I said, 'Why did you leave me in the airport line?' She was like, 'Who is this guy?!'"* They talked while they waited to board their flight and, once they boarded, Brett *"asked the person who she was supposed to be sitting with to go to my seat so I could sit with her more."* Before they parted ways in the Mexico City airport, they exchanged Skype information, unsure if they would ever see or talk to each other again.

Brett was persistent, though, and soon they started chatting over Skype and emailing regularly. A few months later, Mariana flew up to meet Brett, who was finishing his senior year of college in California. The following year, Brett enrolled in a graduate program in Mexico City and asked Mariana to move down there (from her hometown in northern Mexico) to live with him. They lived together in Mexico City for two years. Then Brett moved back to the US when his master's program ended. They tried keeping in touch, but began to drift apart. *"There was one moment where I said, 'Come here and marry me.' She didn't really believe me. She didn't think that my request was totally valid. She thought it was an act of desperation."* In her defense, Mariana interjected, the *"proposal"* was by Skype. Following her rejection, Brett *"tried meeting other people,"* but *"the connection was never really that good with other people."* Almost a year later, Mariana contacted him again and told him that she wanted to visit him. During that visit, they decided to become a couple again. After that, they dated long-distance again for two more years, talking multiple times a week and visiting each other every three or four months. Eight years after their fateful flight from Cancun to Mexico City, Brett and Mariana finally got married.

Like all of the couples I interviewed, the five couples profiled in this chapter have "love stories" that are simultaneously unique and unremarkable, as idiosyncratic and banal and dramatic and commonplace as other "normal" couples' "love stories." Yet the law interferes in the lives of these mixed-citizenship couples in a way that same-citizenship couples never experience. In this way, law becomes a third party to their relationship as they navigate through and around its seemingly endless regulations, requirements, and caveats. US immigration and family reunification laws create hurdles, walls, dead ends, and red tape for all mixed-citizenship couples. Many couples amass the time, resources, evidence, and, often, pure luck to overcome these barriers and access family-level legal status in the US; many other couples do not. So many of these couples' opportunities, successes, and failures flow from their (in)ability to secure family reunification, but securing family reunification depends greatly on dozens of factors, many of which are completely out of the couples' control.

As I show in the chapters that follow, arbitrary distinctions between different individuals and groups written into the law set some couples up for family reunification success and others for family reunification failure. Couples' actions (or inaction) also affect their family reunification opportunities to produce outcomes that could not be predicted from the written law alone. Couples' ability (or inability) to successfully reunify shapes opportunities for every member of the family in *both* of their countries of citizenship for everything ranging from freedom of movement to buying a house to feeling like they belong.

Successfully "reunified" couples follow a drastically different trajectory from those barred from family reunification in terms of their opportunities as a couple and the long-term viability of their relationship itself. Yet, to an unknowing onlooker, it would be nearly impossible to distinguish between them. Of the five couples profiled in this chapter:

- one couple acquired a fiancé(e) visa allowing them to marry and establish their family in the US;
- one couple adjusted from a temporary legal status to permanent residency and splits their time between the US and Mexico;
- one couple did not earn sufficient income to qualify for family reunification;

- one couple's "unauthorized" immigration status disqualifies them from family reunification, so they live together in the US under the constant threat of deportation; and
- one couple experienced deportation and a decade-long ban from legal reentry to the US.

Can you match each couple to their fate? Rather than being based on the quality of their "love story" or their commitment to each other, these couples' outcomes stem primarily from their standing with regard to US laws. As you read the chapters that follow, I encourage you to try to identify a defensible justification for why these families' outcomes and, subsequently, their lives differ so significantly because of US immigration law. If you can do so, perhaps our immigration laws are working as they should. But if not, something must change.

The Right Kind of Love(r)

JULIA AND SANTIAGO LEARNED the hard way that marriage to an American citizen does not automatically qualify a noncitizen for legal immigration status in the US. They met in the summer of 2005, just after Julia had graduated from high school, while working together at a fast-food restaurant in Julia's hometown in Idaho. When they fell in love and decided to marry two years later, during her second year of college, Julia spent her time worrying about wedding details and term papers, not Santiago's legal status. Julia knew that Santiago did not have "papers," but she trusted that her citizenship would be enough for the both of them. Acting on this assumption, Julia sent in a family reunification application to sponsor Santiago for permanent residency shortly after their wedding; they did not have enough money to hire a lawyer, so Julia filled out the application herself. A few weeks later, Julia received correspondence from the US Citizenship and Immigration Service (USCIS) in the mail. Its contents shocked her: the letter stated that Santiago had thirty days to leave the country or he would be forcibly removed. It explained almost nothing, other than stating that because Santiago had entered the US without authorization, he was ineligible for legal status in the US. She frantically called USCIS, begging for an explanation through her tears, hoping it was a mistake. The woman on the other end of the call told her "just to read the letter" and do what it said. So she did, and they left for Mexico a few days before their thirty-day self-removal window expired. Thus began a rocky cross-national saga during which Julia experienced separation and loss from both her husband and her immediate family.

When Julia and Santiago first arrived in Mexico, they traveled to Mexico City to visit Santiago's family, whom he had not seen since he migrated to the US years earlier and whom Julia had never met. Santiago's family was very poor and their living circumstances were extremely humble; Santiago had explained to Julia years before that he migrated to the US to help his family rise out of poverty, a goal that had been cut short by his forced "voluntary" removal. While they enjoyed being close to family, it was clear that Santiago's old neighborhood did not offer them the work opportunities necessary to begin rebuilding their life together in Mexico. They spent a few weeks with Santiago's family and then journeyed north to Monterrey, a large and prosperous city in the border state of Nuevo León. After researching their options, they had determined that Monterrey offered them the best economic opportunities *and* accessibility to the US. They found an apartment to rent and Santiago began searching for work. Julia headed back to Idaho to begin her junior year of college. During their first two years of marriage, while Julia finished her bachelor's degree, she saw Santiago only during school holidays. After graduation, she moved down to Monterrey permanently and began teaching at an international school.

When I met Julia and Santiago in 2013, they had been struggling with the effects of Santiago's expulsion from the US for the previous five years. They had consulted with multiple immigration lawyers, written letters to Julia's congressional representatives, and explored every potential remedy possible to facilitate their relocation back to the US. But they found no relief. Santiago was barred from legal entry to the US for at least five more years. Despite the fact that they could finally live together, Santiago and Julia both suffered from their inability to develop and nurture relationships with Julia's family in the US. At the time of our interview, the strain of their situation—of the cross-national life of separation and struggle that USCIS had forced them to live—had pushed them to the point of separation; shortly after our interview, they divorced. Rather than helping Julia's marriage thrive, the US government had seemingly done all it could do to ensure her new family's demise.

After Julia and Santiago divorced, Julia decided to stay in Mexico for another year or two. She had a great job, and she felt that she needed some more time to heal the wounds the United States had inflicted upon her. As luck would have it, history repeated itself. Julia fell in love with a Mexican coworker, Sergio, who ran the tech department at her international school. But, with regard to US immigration and family reunification laws, Julia's experience this time differed vastly from before. Sergio is from an upper-middle-class family in Monterrey and has possessed a tourist visa to the US since he was a child. His more privileged socioeconomic and educational background, combined with his lack of immigration history to the US, meant he encountered none of the barriers to family reunification that Santiago had faced. Furthermore, Julia's change in status from a young college student working part-time at a fast-food restaurant to a college-educated professional also made her a more "worthy" candidate to sponsor a spouse for permanent residency. Julia's application sponsoring Sergio for permanent residency in the US moved quickly through the system, and his green card application received prompt approval. Even before Sergio became a permanent resident, he was able to travel with Julia multiple times to the US to visit her family, developing stronger relationships with her parents and siblings than Santiago had ever been able to do.

While Julia felt that, when married to Santiago, she had been forced to live "two separate lives that just [could not] come together," she has been able to nourish and share both of those lives with Sergio. This extreme contrast in Julia's attempts as a US citizen spouse to seek family reunification raises a troubling question: how could the same person have experienced these two drastically different outcomes in the US immigration system? It happens because immigration applicants and their sponsors are not treated equally under the law. US immigration laws regulate family reunification based on the composition of the family, the quality or "legitimacy" of the mixed-citizenship marriage, *and* achieved and ascribed characteristics of both the citizen and noncitizen spouses. USCIS grants family reunification only to families satisfying requirements on *all* of these dimensions of worthiness.

Key policy changes adopted through the 1952 Immigration and Nationality Act (INA), the 1986 Immigration Marriage Fraud Amendments (IMFA), and the 1996 Illegal Immigration Reform and Immigrant Responsibility Act (IIRIRA) have changed the legal landscape of US-based family reunification for mixed-citizenship couples. These three laws collectively transformed the type, content, and quality of mixed-citizenship intimate relationships that qualify for family reunification under the law. The INA introduced a strict definition of family based on the nuclear family model, acknowledging only four immediate family relationships as relationships worthy of reunification—parents, legal spouse, siblings, children; it also codified the requirement that couples seeking reunification legally marry. The IMFA narrowed the definition of marriage for mixed-citizenship couples seeking reunification, forcing them to demonstrate that their relationships are "authentic" and "legitimate" according to traditional, Western notions of the appearance and content of marriage. And the IIRIRA redefined the American family by prioritizing the reunification of certain kinds of citizens (wealthier, Whiter, more highly educated, male) with certain kinds of immigrants (higher-class, better-educated, non-Latino, female).

Mixed-citizenship couples seeking family reunification do not bear the negative impacts of these three policies evenly. Rather, these policies only restrict specific subgroups of mixed-citizenship couples from accessing family reunification: those who are not married or are unable to marry; those whose marital relationships do not meet a particular definition of "legitimate" marriage; those whose noncitizen spouses crossed the border without inspection at a port of entry,[1] and those whose citizen spouses have low economic capital.[2] In 2007, Julia and Santiago were hindered both by Santiago's unauthorized entry to the US and Julia's low economic capital, problems that no longer existed when Julia and Sergio applied for family reunification in 2017. This unequal access to family reunification has disproportionately affected nontraditional, non-White (especially Latino), low-income, and less-educated American mixed-citizenship families. The changes enacted through these policies reach beyond the lives of mixed-citizenship couples to American society as a whole, reshaping the composition of society and altering broader notions of national identity and "belonging" in the US.[3]

Defining (Un)American Families

The Immigration and Nationality Act (INA), which has been the foundational policy organizing legal immigration to the United States since

1952, completely restructured immigrant selection in the US. In the process, it also introduced a new, narrower definition of family for the purposes of family reunification. Until the passage of the INA, legal immigration to the US was primarily organized around national origin and race, with "White" immigration almost completely unrestricted.[4] In response to international political pressure to drop overt racial restrictions on US immigration and in the face of Communism's rise, Congress overhauled the immigrant selection process by establishing new immigration priorities based on family relationships, employment needs and special skills, and refugee resettlement.[5] The INA did impose yearly caps on immigration (both based on country of origin and for immigration to the US as a whole), but certain categories of immigrants, including all "immediate" family members of US citizens, are exempted from those caps. This single provision of the INA has transformed immigration patterns in the US.[6] With the passage of the INA, family reunification—or the extension of legal residency and a path to citizenship to the family members of US citizens—became the primary organizing principle of US immigration policy. Today, nearly 75 percent of all permanent residency recipients in any given year qualify due to their direct family tie to a US citizen.

This new focus on family as the primary engine of immigration also brought with it a new definition of family. As outlined in the INA, four citizen/noncitizen familial relationships qualify for reunification: spouses (who must be legally married to the US citizen); children; parents; and siblings. Within the four family relationships contemplated in the INA, only some of them have been designated "immediate" family relationships, which qualify for quota-free entry. US citizens' spouses, parents, and unmarried children under age 21 qualify as "immediate" family members and thus are not subject to immigration quotas.[7] Other family members who qualify for reunification but are subject to the country of origin quotas—such as adult children, married children, and siblings of US citizens—can wait over twenty years for their applications to be processed with no right to live or work in the US while they wait.[8]

The INA interprets family based on the strict and relationally limited nuclear family model (parents and minor children), as well as the
notion that family relationships are biologically (blood) based.[9] The
INA narrowed the legal definition of "family" for family reunification
purposes in two key ways. First, it recognizes legal marriages as the
only intimate partner relationships worthy of family reunification. US
citizens in unmarried, cohabitating partnerships and common law marriages cannot sponsor their partners for legal permanent residency in
the United States.[10] With this definitional change, marriage became an
essential "ingredient" to qualify for family reunification.[11] A number of
the couples I interviewed had never planned to marry, although they often had lived together for many years and some also had children together. Sabrina and Joaquin did not marry until nearly a decade after
they began living together and almost five years after the birth of their
son. It was only after they learned that marriage provided the sole path
for Joaquin to (potentially) qualify for family reunification and legal immigration status in the US that they decided to marry. Other couples,
like Karen and Jo, expressed frustration at being forced to implicitly
sustain the institution of marriage—including both its social and legal
implications and obligations—in order to access family reunification.
But given the constraints written into the INA, marriage is the only option for couples seeking family reunification.

Second, the INA definition of family only acknowledges a nuclear
family model, ignoring many other preexisting family models common
in the US at the time the law was adopted and in the decades since.[12]
The INA's Western-specific, nuclear family model leaves no room to accommodate parents-in-law, grandparents, aunts, uncles, and other family members who often act as primary and secondary caregivers and/or
central members of multigenerational households.[13] It also presumes a
drastic shift in the parent-child relationship when a child either turns 21
or marries—as those children no longer qualify for nonquota reunification—despite the strength and persistence of the parent-child relationship
long into adulthood.[14] This limited understanding of "family" also complicates family reunification opportunities for adopted children, limiting

family reunification to families with children adopted under age 16 and denying any reunification opportunities for adopted children with their birth parents, siblings, and other biological family members.[15]

The INA's narrow definition of family put Diana and Leo in a difficult position shortly after they married, when Leo's father unexpectedly died. Diana had successfully sponsored Leo for permanent residency, but she had no similar ability to sponsor her mother-in-law, who was unable to support herself in Mexico on her own. Based on the law, only Leo—once he becomes a citizen—can sponsor his mother as a family member. But when his father died, Leo was still at least three years away from qualifying for US citizenship. Since they had no immediate access to a legal path to sponsor Leo's mom, they decided to have her overstay her tourist visa and live with them without authorization until she could qualify for family reunification through Leo. In the meantime, Leo's mom provides essential support to Diana and Leo's young family, including acting as a regular caregiver to their small children. As long as she is unauthorized, Leo's mother also lives with the risk of deportation; being deported would disqualify her from obtaining legal immigration status in the US for at least ten years.

The INA's definition of family overlooks the fact that many American households, including 25 percent of those with parents raising their own children under the age of 18, do not reflect the nuclear family model upon which INA family reunification policy is based.[16] It continues to hold families seeking family reunification to a narrower definition of family, limiting their ability to develop and maintain strong relationships with grandparents, aunts, uncles, cousins, and other "natural" and adopted family members. The "INA family" adheres to the fundamental American value of individualism that prioritizes autonomy and self-sufficiency over community and social interdependence, a notion that runs counter to cultural and social norms in countries across the globe.[17] In practice, it contributes to the long-term separation of millions of American families, with multigenerational repercussions.[18] Even as the INA shifted the US immigration system toward family reunification as the primary driver of legal immigration, it redefined "family" in ways that prioritized relationship categories over the substance of those relationships, declaring only some families and some family relationships worthy of reunification.[19]

Defining (Im)Moral Marriage

In 1986, Congress passed the Immigration Reform and Control Act (IRCA), a policy of sweeping immigration reform that included restrictive measures to increase the enforcement of immigration laws *and* redemptive measures providing more than a million unauthorized immigrants with a path to citizenship in the US. Just three days later, Congress passed the Immigration Marriage Fraud Amendments (IMFA). This law targets immigrants seeking to breach an "unprotected *bureaucratic* border," the crossing of which results in serious legal and, more importantly, "moral" violations.[20] The IMFA sought to address marriage fraud, or the act of fraudulently entering into marriage solely for the purposes of obtaining legal immigration status in the US. But rather than reducing marriage fraud (which has historically and consistently remained quite low), the IMFA created additional barriers to family reunification for committed mixed-citizenship couples by forcing them to prove the quality, or worthiness, of their relationship.

The Act of May 14, 1937, more commonly known as the "Gigolo Act," was the first immigration law to suggest the existence or potential existence of marriage fraud. This act allowed a (male) immigrant "alien" to be deported *at any time after entry* when found to have "contract[ed] a marriage which, subsequent to entry into the United States, has been judicially annulled retroactively to date of marriage."[21] The act defined fraud as an immigrant's failure or refusal "to fulfill his promises for a marital agreement made to procure his entry as an immigrant."[22] The motives behind the Gigolo Act—of preventing the abuse of family reunification laws by individuals claiming a false intention to marry— were incorporated into the INA when it was passed in 1952.[23] While the INA did not include sections specifically addressing marriage fraud, it did assert the power of immigration officers to subject "aliens" to inspection and require them to produce documents supporting their claim to a legal right to entry, including individuals who entered as fiancés and spouses of US citizens.[24]

Given the generally undefined nature of marriage fraud in the INA, it ultimately fell upon the Supreme Court to define what made a marriage fraudulent. In *Lutwak v. United States* (1953), the Court focused on the intent of the parties at the time of marriage, rather than defining a legitimate marriage by its content or duration.[25] Asserting that individuals who entered into marriage voluntarily and in "good faith" (i.e., not for immigration purposes) had formed a legitimate marriage—even if it dissolved for different reasons shortly thereafter—the Court denied INS the ability to revoke the legal status of immigrant ex-spouses whose marriages had failed.[26] The Court's time-specific interpretation of "legitimate" marriage—focused exclusively on the moment the marriage took place—and the subjective nature of the "good faith" standard severely limited the government's power to legally challenge couples suspected of marriage fraud.

Testimony from the IMFA congressional hearings suggest that a primary goal of the 1986 legislation was to more clearly define a "legitimate" or "viable" marriage beyond the "good faith" standard. While lawmakers were ultimately unable to create an explicit definition for "viability," they did include new clauses and regulations that outlined key qualities of a "legitimate" or "viable" marriage. The changes to marriage-related visa law imposed by the IMFA define nonfraudulent marriages according to the following standards:

First, a "legitimate" marriage lasts at least two years. The IMFA changed the law so that immigrant spouses receive only "conditional" permanent residency status during their first two years of marriage. That conditional status expires after two years, at which point both spouses must apply jointly for the conditional status to be lifted. Immigrant spouses failing to meet these requirements are subject to visa cancellation and deportation.[27]

Second, a "legitimate" marriage is entered into legally and in "good faith." This standard put into immigration law what the courts had previously interpreted to be the measure of a nonfraudulent marriage, which is that, at the time of the marriage, both individuals sought to marry for nonimmigration purposes (i.e., love?).[28]

Third, couples in a "legitimate" marriage will live together. According to testimony from the IMFA congressional hearing, both the INS and the State Department view cohabitation as the clearest evidence of a "legitimate" marriage. These agencies conduct more extensive investigations of all couples suspected of or proven to be living in different homes. Prior to the IMFA, little could be done to investigate or punish couples who did not cohabitate following a successful visa application. The IMFA extended the time period during which cohabitation could be investigated and used as evidence of legitimacy (or, in its absence, fraud) for up to two years following a successful family reunification application.[29]

Fourth, immigrants in "legitimate" marriages would not marry a foreigner (but could marry a different citizen) shortly after receiving legal permanent residency (LPR) status. During the IMFA hearings, a number of witnesses asserted that many would-be immigrants in fraudulent marriages immediately divorce their American spouse upon receiving LPR status and then sponsor a foreign spouse for LPR status, often a spouse to whom they were married prior to the fraudulent marriage scheme. To address this threat, lawmakers included a clause in the IMFA preventing immigrants from sponsoring a foreign-born spouse for LPR status within five years of acquiring their own LPR status through an American spouse.[30]

Fifth, engaged couples who seek to enter into a "legitimate" marriage will have met in person at least once during the two years prior to applying for reunification. As discussed in congressional testimony, the rise of "mail-order brides" and even arranged marriages challenged contemporary American cultural understandings of marriage as the product of "love," and "love" as the product of the coming together of hearts, minds, and bodies. While applicants can seek an exception, the rule requiring couples to have met at least once within the previous two years serves to reinforce the notion that a "legitimate" marriage is unlikely to result from a union in which parties meet for the first time on their wedding day. It also makes fraudulent fiancé(e) visa applications more expensive by forcing the petitioner to travel to meet their future spouse in the immigrant partner's home country at least once before applying for a visa.[31]

Sixth, "legitimate" marriages are not entered into under legal duress (i.e., provoked by the threat of imminent deportation). With this clause, lawmakers declared marriage between a US citizen and an immigrant in deportation proceedings to be automatic and undeniable evidence of fraud. Although one could imagine many different reasons why a "legitimate" couple could find themselves in this situation, the law only recognizes such a relationship as "legitimate" after the immigrant spouse has resided *outside* the US for at least two years following the marriage.[32]

The new definition of marriage in the IMFA pushes the boundaries of previous legal decisions and the state actors' interpretations of the meaning of marriage to consider "legitimacy" and "viability" and "good faith" and "bona fide" intentions not only at the moment of marriage but for years after the marriage officially begins. This new notion of marriage reinforces the importance of cohabitation and family life, love and fidelity, marrying for "the right reasons," monogamy, and long-term commitment as evidence of a "legitimate" marriage. But only mixed-citizenship couples must meet these standards; other American couples can marry with no proof of an existing relationship and no expectations of longevity, "viability," or "legitimacy," as long as each partner can demonstrate that they are legally single at the time of marriage. Couples who do not live together full-time, like Jessica and Julio or Jared and Aylin; those with brief courtships seeking family reunification early in their marriage, like Julia and Santiago or Daniel and Pachita; and those under deportation orders or recently deported, like Sonia and Sebastian or Angelica and Ramses—all face additional hurdles to proving the "legitimacy" of their relationships. Although the "traditional" expectations of marriage imposed by the IMFA do not apply to all American couples, they serve to reinforce and reify a specific understanding of marriage and family that excludes many American couples today, including many mixed-citizenship couples.

Beyond creating a new, morally driven definition of "legitimate" marriage, the IMFA also reinforced and expanded the standard that a "legitimate" marriage is a documented marriage. The IMFA requires couples to demonstrate satisfactorily that their marriage meets all of the standards listed above. Yet proving the subjective elements of a relationship—including "love" and "good faith" intentions—as well as objective elements, such as cohabitation and one or more previous in-person rendezvous, can be a difficult task. When applying on behalf of a spouse or fiancé(e), US citizen petitioners must submit hundreds of pages of documentary and photographic evidence supporting their claims of a "bona fide" marital relationship (or a "bona fide" intent to enter into a marital relationship). Acceptable evidence of a shared life together can include proof that the citizen and immigrant spouses' names appear on shared rental agreements, bank accounts, tax returns, and other formal administrative documents. Additional evidence confirming the legitimacy of the wedding and the relationship in general, including proof of cohabitation and joint biological children, can also be submitted to "prove" the validity of a couple's family reunification claim.[33] Couples are also encouraged to submit sworn affidavits from friends, employers, and other nonfamily acquaintances testifying to the validity of the relationship, as well as evidence demonstrating "mutual family involvement."[34] Having children prior to the application or reproducing during the two-year conditional-status period (when paternity can be confirmed) is the ultimate evidence of a "legitimate" and "viable" marriage.[35]

For Julia and Santiago, deciding to apply for Santiago's residency so soon after their marriage meant they had less documentary evidence proving the "legitimacy" and "viability" of their marriage. While they had a joint rental agreement, they had not yet accumulated the body of paperwork confirming a shared life together, nor had they had time to produce additional evidence of "legitimacy" (such as a child). When Julia and Sergio applied for family reunification, they took a different approach. They waited two years after their wedding before submitting their paperwork, proving that their relationship was "viable" based on the IMFA's minimum two-year legal expectation for marriage duration. They also had accrued ample bureaucratic and photographic evidence of their shared life together before and after their marriage. And, perhaps most importantly, Julia was pregnant and due to give birth to their first child around the time of Sergio's consular interview. While Santiago's forced "voluntary" removal from the US had not been attributed to a lack of "legitimacy" on the part of their marriage, Julia had learned from that experience that the failure to meet any legal expectation associated with family reunification law could lead to a rejection. With Sergio, she took no chances.

In cases of suspected marriage fraud, the "anti-fraud" section of the INS or USCIS consular office may also "review local church or civil registry records to determine if a previous marriage exists or . . . send an employee to perform a neighborhood check," producing their own documentary record of "(il)legitimacy."[36] But couples who submit too much documentary evidence—whose records are deemed too complete—also fall under suspicion of fraud, so applicants must balance the need to compile a comprehensive documentary record of their relationship with the need for the relationship to appear organic and unintentionally documented, rather than fully chronicled.[37] The documents deemed satisfactory for proving "legitimate" relationships generally require couples to engage with various branches of government and submit themselves to multiple forms of government regulation, suggesting that couples in "legitimate" marital relationships interact as a family unit with the government and society at large beyond the occasion of the marriage itself. US family reunification law requires that proof of a "legitimate" marriage be "based on objective, articulable facts," a standard that renders official documentation of the relationship not only necessary but indispensable.[38] In sum, a "legitimate" marriage is a regulated, surveilled, and—above all—an appropriately (yet organically) documented marriage.

Although witnesses at the IMFA congressional hearing testified that "two people who are really in love with each other will not be hurt" by the changes proposed and ultimately adopted through the IMFA,[39] legal scholars and mixed-citizenship couples forced to meet these new standards of "legitimacy" have argued otherwise. A number of legal scholars writing immediately prior to and following the passage of IMFA noted that the procedures necessary to ensure couples' satisfaction of the law—including heightened scrutiny, questioning, and surveillance during the application and interview process, as well as up to two years following approval of their application—violate couples' rights to privacy and marital intimacy by both establishing a specific norm for marital life and forcing couples to reveal details of their most intimate thoughts and habits.[40] This potential of the law as written and as interpreted to dictate the substance of "legitimate" marital life raises serious concerns in two regards. First, it can put pressure on couples to adhere to legally prescribed marital norms in both mundane and profound circumstances, from the amount of time they spend together on a daily or weekly basis to deciding whether and when to have a child.[41] Couples who are unable or unwilling to adhere to these "norms" risk suspicion of fraud and rejection of their family reunification claim, despite the authenticity of their relationship. Thus, instead of preventing visa benefits for fraudulent marriages, the law risks preventing genuine couples from reunification due to a narrowly defined understanding of what a "legitimate" marriage looks like in both content and quality.

Second, it confers a significant level of discretionary power upon the individual USCIS agents processing these applications who—in the absence of objective standards—tend to interpret the legal standard of "legitimate" marriage through their own subjective lens as they evaluate individual applications.[42] When Cesar attended his consular interview in Ciudad Juarez, the agent evaluating his application grew suspicious of a number of conditions related to Cesar and Anne's relationship, including their brief courtship, their lack of a shared language, and Cesar's unauthorized status. While the agent decided to conditionally approve Cesar's application, he also advised Cesar that US immigration authorities "wanted Anne to get pregnant" before the two-year conditional period ended to "show that it was a real marriage and not just for the papers." Anne and Cesar could not legally be held to such a specific standard, but this warning from an agent fully empowered to unilaterally accept or deny their application pushed Anne and Cesar toward ensuring that their two-year follow-up application contained overwhelming evidence of their marriage's "legitimacy."

Instead of addressing the marriage fraud epidemic that purportedly inspired the IMFA (which, ironically, was later shown to be a fraudulent claim),[43] the requirements instituted through the IMFA have primarily served to create additional barriers to family reunification for authentic mixed-citizenship couples and have forced such couples to live a much narrower definition of marriage than the general American public. The IMFA reinforced the heteropatriarchal order of the US political system.[44] It provided Congress—a legislative body generally prohibited from interfering in questions of marriage—with the opportunity to redefine marriage, privileging certain cultural norms and standards regarding the content, quality, and duration of "legitimate" marriages and empowering the government to impose that new marriage standard on all mixed-citizenship couples seeking to live together legally in the United States. Under the guise of reducing marriage fraud, Congress established a new norm for "legitimate" marriage that reinforces the postwar, suburban, White nuclear family model championed by conservatives at the time, ensuring that at least some American couples have to embody that ideal in order to be legally recognized as a "legitimate" family.[45] Even as "nontraditional" marriages and families have proliferated in the thirty-plus years since the passage of the IMFA, mixed-citizenship couples seeking family reunification must continue to adhere to this strict and increasingly outdated notion of "viability" in order to receive legal authorization to live together as a family.

Defining the (Im)Moral (Non)Citizen

Ten years after the passage of both IRCA and the IMFA, anti-immigrant sentiment dominated national politics once again. In response to both the failure of IRCA's enforcement measures and a backlash against the "amnesty" that IRCA had offered unauthorized immigrants, Congress passed a series of anti-immigration policies including the Illegal Immigration Reform and Immigrant Responsibility Act (IIRIRA), an overwhelmingly punitive policy targeting noncitizens with a range of immigration statuses. The IIRIRA introduced a number of devastating penalties against immigrants, two of which have specific impacts for mixed-citizenship couples: the bars to reentry and the minimum-income thresholds.

As established in the IIRIRA, any individual who has lived without legal authorization in the United States for more than six months but less than one year faces a three-year bar from applying for legal permission to enter the US; any individual who has lived without legal authorization in the US for one year or more faces a ten-year bar from applying. The bar is automatically imposed when the individual leaves the physical territory of the United States.[46] While this harsh penalty of the IIRIRA seemingly punishes visa overstayers and those who entered the United States without inspection equally—subjecting all to the automatic bars—one subgroup of unauthorized immigrants receives disparate treatment under the law: the unauthorized spouses of US citizens.[47] Immigration law enacted prior to the IIRIRA allows visa-overstaying spouses of US citizens—unauthorized immigrants who had previously been admitted to the United States with a valid visa through an official port of entry—to adjust to a legal immigration status from within the US. The ability to adjust status from within the US allows the unauthorized (visa-overstaying) spouses in these marriages to obtain legal permanent residency without triggering the automatic bars to reentry. Unauthorized spouses of US citizens who were not admitted through a US port of entry must return to their countries of origin to complete their adjustment to legal status. Upon leaving the United States to attend the consular interview, the unauthorized spouse triggers the automatic bar to reentry and thus becomes ineligible for a visa for the duration of the three- or ten-year period, whether or not she would otherwise qualify for legal entry.[48]

The automatic bars imposed through the IIRIRA have significantly altered the trajectories of these different unauthorized mixed-citizenship families.[49] Some families, like Jiancarlo and Sondra (who overstayed her tourist visa at age 16), continue to easily adjust to legal status, permanently establish their homes in the United States, and enjoy the rights and privileges of formal membership in US society. Others, like Trish and Alberto (who crossed the US border undetected), must choose either to maintain their precarious position as unauthorized families within the United States or leave the country and face a three- or ten-year (or, in some cases, permanent[50]) bar to legal reentry to the US.

The profile of unauthorized immigrants who have overstayed a visa differs significantly from that of unauthorized immigrants who have crossed the border without inspection. Noncitizens seeking tourist, student, or other temporary, nonimmigrant visas to the US are required to prove "sufficient funds to cover expenses in the United States," permanent residence in the home country, "and other *binding ties* that will ensure their departure from the United States at the end of the visit."[51] Although the definition of "binding ties" is unclear, evidence of binding ties appears to include home ownership, marriage to a resident of one's home country and/or children living in the home country, business ownership requiring regular oversight, enrollment as a student at a university in the home country, and proof of substantial income and/or savings.[52] The high economic and educational thresholds visa applicants must meet in order to qualify for a visa mean that visa recipients (and, therefore, visa overstayers) generally belong to their countries' middle and upper classes and demonstrate higher education and better English skills than unauthorized immigrants who have entered the United States without inspection.[53] Visa overstayers are also more likely to be nationals of European, Asian, African, and South American countries.[54] In contrast, due to geographic proximity and physical access to the US border, unauthorized immigrants who enter the country without inspection almost exclusively hail from Mexico and Central America and, at the time of migration, generally do not have the financial and social "binding ties" necessary to qualify for a visa.[55] These unauthorized migrants have also historically been disproportionately male.[56]

The uneven application of the three- and ten-year bars to reentry among unauthorized mixed-citizenship couples creates a structure in which certain kinds of families are harshly penalized while others are given a life-changing pass. This discrepancy in the law rewards some citizens for marrying the "right" kind of unauthorized immigrant (higher-class, better-educated, non-Latino, female) and punishes others for loving the "wrong" kind of unauthorized immigrant (lower-class, less-educated, Latino, male).[57]

The IIRIRA also introduced minimum income requirements for US citizens seeking to sponsor a spouse for legal permanent residency. These thresholds have placed new limitations on mixed-citizenship families, disproportionately affecting lower-educated, female, and disabled citizens—as well as citizens with children—seeking to sponsor a noncitizen spouse for legal immigrant status.[58] Before the IIRIRA, citizen spouses were not required to prove a certain level of income in order to successfully sponsor a noncitizen spouse for permanent residency in the United States. The minimum income threshold imposed by the IIRIRA—proven income of at least 125 percent of the poverty level[59]—prevents otherwise qualified citizens with insufficient income from sponsoring a spouse for permanent residency in the United States.[60,61,62]

This inequity stems primarily from the fact that only the US citizen spouse's income may be considered in meeting the minimum income threshold. Despite the fact that the noncitizen spouse would have permission to work once granted lawful permanent residency, the sponsoring spouse must satisfy the minimum income requirement without considering the ability of her spouse, once inside the United States, to contribute to the family's income. A single minimum-wage earner working full-time in the US could not meet the minimum income requirement, but a family income composed of two minimum-wage salaries could.[63] According to the 2021 Health and Human Services Federal Poverty Guidelines, a person with no dependents seeking to sponsor their spouse would have to earn more than $21,775 a year, the equivalent of at least $10.47/hour (working 40 hours a week, 52 weeks a year), to meet this minimum income threshold; a sponsor with two additional dependents would have to earn at least $33,125 annually—no less than $15.93/hour, 40 hours a week, 52 weeks a year—to meet their minimum income requirement.[64] And given that the real median personal income in 2018 (the year for which the most recent data is available) was $33,706, nearly one-half of all US citizens with at least three dependents (including their spouse) could not qualify as a sponsor for their spouse's permanent residency application.[65] The proportion of Americans disqualified as sponsors increases as their number of dependents increases. Several of my interviewees, including Felix, a US citizen who works on kitchen and bathroom remodels, could not yet sponsor their spouses for residency because their income does not exceed the 125 percent threshold.

These wage requirements disproportionately disqualify members of certain groups who are already structurally disadvantaged through nationwide income inequality. Women are more likely to fall below the required income threshold than men, given that they earn, on average, only 80 cents for every dollar a man earns.[66] Black and Latinx workers are also at a disadvantage, as their median household income falls $20,000 and $11,000, respectively, below the national median household income ($56,516), decreasing their likelihood of meeting the minimum income threshold.[67] The minimum income requirement also penalizes citizens with disabilities or other health issues that prevent them from working full-time. Finally, the minimum income threshold is determined based on family size; citizen sponsors with children from their current or previous relationships must meet a higher income threshold than those without children. US citizens with one or more of these traits who seek to sponsor a spouse for lawful permanent residency face additional barriers to accessing family reunification beyond proving the "legitimacy" of their relationship and the "worthiness" of their partner; they must also demonstrate their "worthiness" as self-sufficient, independent earners who do not need government assistance to meet their needs.[68] Angelica, a stay-at-home mom with an infant and toddler at home, felt pressure to return to work full-time to prove her earning potential and explained to me, "When the time comes to sponsor Ramses, they are going to ask me, 'How do you intend to bring him here if you cannot even support yourself?'"

Disallowing consideration of the noncitizen spouse's earning potential in satisfying the minimum income threshold further exaggerates these inequalities. Even though Tenoch earned enough through his construction job to support his family of five, Juliette could not use his income as evidence to demonstrate their financial viability as a family; because Juliette stayed home full-time with their three children, she was also unable to demonstrate her own earning power. Without finding a third party willing to sponsor their application, Juliette and Tenoch could not qualify for family reunification, despite meeting all other legal requirements.

Although this policy may seem like a logical safeguard to ensure that permanent residents will not become "public charges," it ultimately punishes citizens for having limited financial resources and potentially prevents those citizens from rising out of poverty through the financial support of their noncitizen spouses.[69] This policy may not only *not* "keep out" potential "public charges," but it could actually cause US citizens to become "public charges" themselves (through the use of social welfare benefits) by preventing them from increasing their combined family income through family reunification. The IIRIRA declared poor Americans undeserving of family reunification in that it declared female, non-White, and less-educated Americans—those most likely to earn below 125 percent of the poverty level—unworthy of forming an official American family with a noncitizen. Policymakers uphold family reunification as a system designed to support and strengthen American families, but the penalties imposed upon mixed-citizenship families through the IIRIRA reveal that family reunification is actually another policy that punishes poor Americans for their poverty and creates an additional barrier inhibiting their socioeconomic advancement.

Redefining the American Family

Collectively, the INA, IMFA, and IIRIRA have put some couples into a position of easier reunification than others, as shown in Figure 1.

These laws have gone beyond shaping family reunification outcomes to redefine the meaning of the "American" "family" altogether. The INA and IMFA both restrict "legitimate" "families" to definitions that exclude family structures and expressions of family life common in everyday America. Through the bars to reentry, the IIRIRA has redefined the "American" family by effectively prohibiting mixed-citizenship families in which one partner entered the United States without inspection from realizing the benefits of married family life with legal immigration status in the US.

This new, narrower definition of the American family—nuclear, "traditional," wealthier, Whiter, better-educated, non-Latino, and headed by a US citizen male—has not only precipitated the "othering" of some

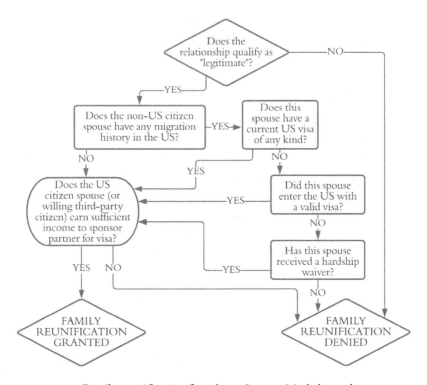

FIGURE I. Family reunification flowchart. Source: Made by author.

immigrants but also their citizen family members.[70] The INA, IMFA, and IIRIRA have marked all members of "unworthy" mixed-citizenship couples as less-than and unqualified to enjoy the benefits of American citizenship as a family. This more exclusive definition of the "American" family also shapes broader notions of who "belongs" in the United States.[71] When laws systematically exclude particular groups of people, they directly create and feed discriminatory national narratives dictating who is truly "American." The effects of these laws reach far beyond those explicitly excluded to include their spouses, children, grandchildren, and communities, leading to the mass legal and rhetorical othering of important members of our society, as can be seen in the criminalization and illegalization of Latino men throughout American society, regardless of their citizenship status.[72]

Preventing some families from accessing family reunification has ripple effects. Initially, it redefines which families are "American enough" to qualify for family reunification. Then, by extension, it also prevents the immigrant spouses who were denied family reunification from sharing those same benefits with their noncitizen parents, children, and siblings.[73] This burden is not spread proportionally across nations of origin, socioeconomic classes, and racial and ethnic backgrounds. Rather, because of biases written into family reunification law, the composition of American citizenry is, over time, skewed toward a richer, Whiter, better-educated membership. Collectively, these policies have resulted in a narrowed definition of both who "deserves" to be American and which Americans "deserve" to enjoy the full rights of their citizenship.

Although mixed-citizenship couples had generally been exempt from the racist quotas and other prejudiced policies implemented in US immigration law during the first half of the twentieth century, the class-based preferences (or, more accurately, punishments) imposed in the INA, IMFA, and IIRIRA specifically target mixed-citizenship families seeking family reunification through the US immigration system.[74] Collectively, these three laws have redefined family, marriage, and the American family, at least as they apply to mixed-citizenship American couples. Couples must be legally married and build their family and its support network on a strict interpretation of the "nuclear" family model. Couples whose relationships do not reflect conservative, middle-class notions of what marital relationships should look like (and how they should be documented) cannot meet evidentiary thresholds to prove that their relationship qualifies for family reunification. Working-class US citizens who do not earn enough money to qualify as a sponsor—and who do not have the social capital to find someone who does meet the income requirements and is willing to take on the legal responsibility of sponsoring an immigrant—are denied the opportunity to access family reunification, despite the social, emotional, and economic benefits such reunification would likely bring. Finally, noncitizen spouses (living within or outside the US) with an immigration history to the US that includes having entered the country without inspection—a status highly correlated with low socioeconomic

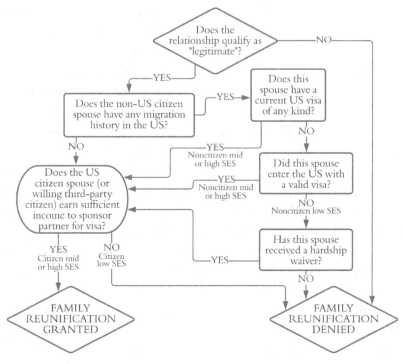

Note: SES = socioeconomic status

FIGURE 2. Family reunification flowchart (including socioeconomic status).
Source: Made by author.

status, the inability to qualify for a visa, and Mexican or Central American origin—must also face harsh penalties before they can qualify for family reunification. As a whole, these policies disproportionately exclude citizens, immigrants, and families with lower socioeconomic statuses from accessing family reunification, as shown in Figure 2.[75]

Many scholars and advocates have attacked current calls for an immigration overhaul that proposes a points-based, skills-focused system as an abandonment of the family values that have been the focus of American immigration policy since its outset, but I find that existing immigration laws already enforce a preference for higher-class, more highly educated, and better-resourced immigrant applicants and citizen sponsors.

If these laws were truly designed to help Americans reunify with their noncitizen partners, the vast majority of families meeting the definition of a mixed-citizenship couple should, in theory, have access to family reunification. While it is difficult to ascertain the true number of mixed-citizenship American families unable to access family reunification, recent estimates suggest that between 1.1 and 1.8 million mixed-citizenship American couples could not.[76] Thousands more mixed-citizenship American families living outside the United States also find that family reunification in the US is beyond their reach. Thus, rather than being a system of family reunification for all Americans and their noncitizen family members, the current immigration system uses specific immediate family relationships as a way to facilitate the legal immigration (or adjustment to legal immigrant status) of (a) middle- and upper-class noncitizens and/or (b) the partners of middle- and upper-class US citizens. As discussed above, this prejudice built into the law not only punishes specific families deemed "unworthy" but also serves, over time, to shape the American public in ways that disproportionately exclude certain kinds of immigrants, rendering members of some groups and their citizen family members "un-American."

Together, the INA, IMFA, and IIRIRA have changed the nature of mixed-citizenship families and altered American society both substantively and definitionally. Only certain kinds of mixed-citizenship families qualify for family reunification under these laws, and families denied this benefit are both figuratively and literally erased from official membership in America. Some families are pushed into the shadows of unauthorized status, other families relocate outside of US territory, and still other families dissolve altogether. Rejected mixed-citizenship families bear the brunt of these punishments—as I detail in the chapters that follow—but the policies' effects spill over into local and national communities and the broader American narrative. These policies disproportionately exclude certain kinds of families—especially mixed-race, non-White, low-income, Latino, and nontraditional families—rendering such families less visible to the general population and excluded from our collective understanding of who qualifies as "American."

Although the exclusions written into US family reunification law specifically (dis)advantage certain types of applicants and families, these legally enshrined preferences and exclusions alone do not reliably predict which couples ultimately qualify for reunification and which do not. In chapter 3, I examine how couples' (un)strategic approach to family reunification law can produce legal outcomes that could not be explained by the law-as-written alone.

Navigating the High Stakes of
US Family Reunification Law

BIASES AGAINST SOME RELATIONSHIPS and applicants written directly into family reunification law prevent certain types of citizens and noncitizens from qualifying for family reunification, as described in chapter 2. But these biases written into the law do not fully explain families' reunification outcomes; many couples' family reunification strategies produce legal outcomes that the law alone would not predict. Among the couples I interviewed, I met a number of families who had successfully applied for family reunification, despite the fact that they possessed one or more traits that, according to the law-as-written, disqualified them for family reunification. Similarly, I met families whose applications had been denied, despite the fact that they checked off all of the written legal requirements for reunification.

This inconsistency between the law-as-written and the law-in-practice raises a key question: why are immigration laws alone insufficient to explain families' reunification outcomes? Mixed-citizenship couples' experiences show that it is because citizens and their spouses can exercise agency in deciding *when* to apply, *what* information to disclose, and *how* to present themselves and their marital relationships to authorities of the US federal government. Since family reunification is a citizen-initiated process, meaning that mixed-citizenship families are not required to apply for family reunification as soon as they become eligible through engagement, marriage, adoption, etc., citizens and their families have control in deciding when to apply. And because most families are given only one opportunity to apply for family reunification, a strategic approach to deciding when and how to apply can significantly improve couples' chances of a successful application.

Family Reunification Poker

Family reunification laws require families and individual family members to demonstrate certain characteristics proving their individual and collective "worthiness" for reunification.[1] Many of these characteristics—including personal income, family structure, education levels, and physical and mental health—can change over time. The addition of biological children to a family can improve a couple's "legitimacy" profile; a new, better-paying job can help a citizen meet the minimum income threshold necessary to sponsor their spouse; even the onset of physical and mental health issues among citizen family members can increase eligibility for the Extreme Hardship Waiver and lead to an unauthorized spouse's successful adjustment of status. Because these different "qualifications" are constantly in flux, the same couple could be denied family reunification at one point in their relationship, yet qualify for family reunification at a different point in time. Knowing when and how to apply can drastically alter families' reunification outcomes and the subsequent opportunities and privileges available to them.

Couples are also able to exercise discretion in the amount and type of information they share in their reunification applications.[2] They can strategically withhold information from government agents, such as having made multiple clandestine border crossings or a false claim to citizenship, that would otherwise automatically disqualify their applications for reunification. While this approach can be risky—being caught lying on any visa or citizenship application permanently disqualifies families from reunification—telling the truth often guarantees rejection.[3] Couples can also present their backgrounds and relationships in ways that emphasize their "worthiness," as legally defined, for reunification. Curated photo albums, collections of sworn affidavits from friends and community leaders affirming both the legitimate quality of the relationship and the good moral character of the applicants, and documentation of shared lives and lifestyles can all improve couples' chances for reunification, even if many elements of their relationship (significant age gap, no shared language, no cohabitation, etc.) suggest fraud.[4] Collectively, mixed-citizenship couples' decisions concerning when to apply, what to disclose, and how to present themselves can contribute toward family reunification outcomes that could not be predicted based on the law-as-written.

These conditions make the family reunification process like a very high-stakes, all-in game of poker, with the following conditions:

- Couples can only play one hand, but they can choose to play or forfeit any round.
- Couples can see their cards before deciding whether or not to play.
- With time, couples can potentially trade in at least some of their cards to improve their odds of a winning hand. But the new cards couples receive could be worse than those they traded in. Some cards cannot be traded or upgraded.
- While couples can "fold" or wait for a future round of play (and a better hand), choosing to wait can have negative consequences, too. The rules of the game could change. The stakes of the outcome could increase. The game could be canceled altogether.
- Couples can "bluff" or "hide an ace up their sleeve" in an attempt to game the system, but these approaches add significantly more risk because anyone caught cheating is permanently disqualified from family reunification.
- There is never a guarantee that even the strongest hand is a winning hand. The dealer could be holding an unbeatable hand or decide the rules have changed as they apply to that specific case. A winning hand for one couple might not be a winning hand for another couple.
- As couples can only play once, should they realize they have a losing hand after deciding to play the round and go all-in, they must play through the end of the round and, after losing, cannot play again for many years (or ever, in some cases).

Given the nature of this "game," couples who shrewdly approach their one chance at play can secure a positive reunification outcome even if the law on the books would predict their failure. Couples' timing, strategy, and familiarity with the rules (and, potentially, a willingness to bend those rules) all shape their odds of playing a winning hand.

In the high-stakes context of "family reunification poker," a couple's approach to the law can make the difference between family reunification and family rejection and/or separation. The gap between the law on the books and the law in action leaves room for individual actors to shape legal processes and outcomes through (in)action.[5] Scholars have defined this interaction between legal structure and individual agency as "legal consciousness."[6] For mixed-citizenship couples navigating the US immigration system, legal consciousness explains notable differences in outcomes among otherwise similar families.

Existing academic studies of legal consciousness suggest that both individual and familial identities influence legal consciousness, shaping perceptions of the law as it functions and one's position within the legal and social landscape. Social class, gender, race and/or minority status, legal language, immigrant status, and political climate can all shape legal consciousness and the actions one takes in response to the law.[7] Access to resources, such as money, time, and legal advice, can also affect legal consciousness and one's ability to respond to the law.[8]

In the context of family reunification, couples' legal consciousness generally manifests through their active or passive approach to family reunification law. Couples who take this branch of law at face value tend to passively move through reunification without being able to shape their case or its outcome. But couples who exercise their agency in deciding when and how to tackle family reunification can anticipate and react to situations in the application process to increase their odds of a successful legal outcome.

Deploying an active approach to family reunification law matters more for some couples. For those couples whose profiles or histories include disqualifying characteristics, an unstrategic approach to family reunification carries more negative consequences than for couples whose qualities align with those prioritized in US immigration law. Mixed-citizenship couples I interviewed generally employed what Ewick and Silbey describe as either a passive, "before the law" approach or an active, "with the law" approach to family reunification.[9] In family reunification poker, these passive and active approaches employed by couples could be described as playing the first hand they were dealt (passive) or playing their best hand (active). Couples utilizing strategic approaches to family reunification poker often directly and positively influence their family reunification outcomes, even under circumstances when the law alone would predict their failure.

Playing the Hand They Were Dealt

Roughly half of the couples I interviewed approached family reunification uncritically, assuming that the authentic nature of their relationship and one partner's claim to US citizenship entitled them to long-term legal status in the United States. They often applied for reunification shortly after marrying, without consulting a lawyer, and without evaluating the extent to which their relationship in its current state met the requirements set forth in family reunification law. In the game of family reunification poker, these families were both novice and uncoached; many were also unaware of the high stakes they would be required to accept upon using their one shot to play the game. These couples tended to assume their odds of winning would be the same no matter when they played, or they were unaware that they could delay playing the game. And, most importantly, they assumed that both players in family reunification poker—the government and the couple—would play, and had to play, by the rules. In essence, they took the legal system at face value, even if they did not completely understand what the written rules actually entailed.

This approach to family reunification produced winners and losers whose profiles generally correspond with the qualifications defined by the laws on the books. Couples whose backgrounds and relationships fell in line with the expectations outlined in family reunification law walked into the game with winning hands and walked away from the game with their expectations about the family reunification process largely confirmed: that the US supports "legitimate" families and provides those families with the means to successfully establish themselves in the US for the long term. While these couples often complained about the time and expense involved in playing the family reunification game, they generally saw these temporary hardships as necessary and easily surmountable bureaucratic hurdles. Diana, a good-humored, optimistic young woman in her mid-twenties, applied for family reunification with her husband, Leo (an equally affable young man her same age), shortly after they married. Leo still had a valid tourist visa when they married and applied for an adjustment of status, setting them up for a straightforward application process. Diana recalled, "It wasn't a big deal for us," adding that she "was surprised at how painless it was." Before their interview ended, the agent interviewing them told them, "Okay, I'm going to approve you," and reassured them that their green card would arrive soon.

Other couples with profiles that set them up for "easy" reunification complained about the bureaucratic hurdle of applying, but they agreed that these hurdles were not a significant impediment to their short- or long-term plans. Will, a soft-spoken dentist who left most of the talking to his wife—Mayela—during our interview, spoke up to complain that the process to adjust his wife's Temporary Protected Status (TPS) to permanent residency "took forever because [US immigration officials] were incompetent" but later added that, because Mayela already had permission to work through TPS, "it didn't really impede our lifestyle." Even though they waited longer than expected for Mayela's residency application to process, her ongoing ability to work with TPS ensured that she could continue to support their family while Will finished dental school, making the transition from TPS to permanent residency feel more like a technicality than a trajectory-altering event.

Families with an "easy" path to reunification applying from outside the US expressed comparable sentiments that the process was generally straightforward. Molly's husband had never traveled to the US, even though he had lived for years just a couple of miles south of the US-Mexico border. Molly, a proud American who grew up on both sides of the border, felt confident that, as a US citizen, she had a right to live together with her family in the US, and the fact that family reunification exists at all reinforced that feeling for her. Because of this, Molly "wasn't nervous. I knew that they would give him the visa, we just had to wait for it." Judy and Franklin, who also met and married in Mexico prior to applying for family reunification, explained that their "easy" reunification experience was evidence that people can and should do things "the right way" with regard to immigration. For these families, applying for family reunification was burdensome and expensive but relatively painless, especially since each of their applications received approval.

But for families whose profiles did not align with the requirements outlined in the law—due to prior unauthorized entry to the US or relationship characteristics that suggest fraud—blind faith in the legal system and the belief that marriage to a US citizen automatically qualified a noncitizen spouse for legal status produced shocking and devastating outcomes. As discussed in chapter 2, Julia, a sophomore in college, filled out the family reunification application materials herself shortly after marrying Santiago. Rather than receiving information with a date for Santiago's interview in the Mexican consulate, though, she received a letter from USCIS stating that Santiago had thirty days to leave the country before he would be forcibly removed. Julia and Santiago obeyed the order and left the US before the thirty days had passed. Santiago was barred from returning to the US for ten years.

Yuliana and Mateo, junior high and high school sweethearts in Tijuana, also had their lives turned upside-down by their family reunification denial. Yuliana was born in the US, grew up mostly in Tijuana, and moved back to the US—just across the border in San Ysidro, California—when she was 16. She and Mateo continued dating long-distance, but Mateo soon decided that he couldn't live apart from her any longer. Mateo did not qualify for a tourist visa, so he entered the US without authorization. (He first tried, unsuccessfully, to cross through a port of entry using someone else's visa. He later entered the US successfully by walking across the unmonitored border just east of Tijuana.) "We were so young," Mateo noted. Yuliana added, "We did not understand the consequences at all." Mateo explained that living next to the border his whole life made crossing "seem so easy." He said, "You are on the border all the time and you think, 'Well, I'm going to cross to see. Just once.' Like, if you live in Central America or in the south [of Mexico], you think, 'No!' and you really think about it. But when you're here, every day you go by the border and you see it. It seems so easy. You believe that it will be easy." Crossing to the US, Mateo discovered, actually *was* relatively easy; but acquiring permanent legal status in the US was not, especially after having entered the US without permission. They did not know any of this at the time, though, and married shortly after Mateo moved to the US.

When they could finally afford to apply for permanent residency five years and two children later, Yuliana and Mateo submitted their application without consulting a lawyer. Mateo went to his interview in Ciudad Juarez expecting to be back at work in San Diego the following week. Instead, he was told he would not be allowed to enter the US for at least the next ten years. During our interview in their home in Tijuana, Yuliana and Mateo expressed that one of the most difficult aspects of being rejected by the state is the finality of that rejection. It is very difficult to appeal a decision, and most rejections include a minimum ten-year wait before couples are eligible to reapply; some denials include lifetime bans. Overnight, Yuliana and Mateo were forced to relocate their family to Tijuana and start building their lives again from scratch. As we sat around their kitchen table, Mateo, usually quite enthusiastic in his optimism, grew quiet as tears welled in Yuliana's eyes. In both of their faces, I could see them silently contemplating all of the ways their lives—their hopes, plans, dreams, memories—had changed forever as a result of their catastrophic loss in family reunification poker.

Vicente and Herlinda's lives also dramatically changed for the worse when they attempted to adjust Herlinda's immigration status. Years before Herlinda's deportation, Vicente and Herlinda met at a party in Mexico. Vicente, a reserved middle-school math teacher, was in town visiting family and Herlinda, a gregarious extrovert who is the life of every party, was a friend of the family. They both leaned into the spark of attraction they felt, connecting and reconnecting throughout the evening and then keeping in close contact, even after Vicente returned to the US. On his second visit to Mexico after they met, Vicente proposed, and Herlinda, who had a tourist visa at the time, traveled back to the US with him, where they were later married. When her visa expired during a trip home to Mexico for Christmas and they realized how long the family reunification application process would take, they decided Herlinda would cross the border clandestinely and then adjust her status from within the US. In retrospect, Vicente can see how his approach to the situation was perhaps "not naïve," but that he just was "not really aware of what the laws were." In his experience, "when something expires, you just renew it," so he thought, "well, we'll just renew her visa." But Herlinda no longer satisfied all of the requirements for a tourist visa, and her renewal application was denied. Vicente continued, "At that point, we were married. And I said, 'Wait a minute. I can't leave her there.' So, I've got to admit, we brought her across illegally." Vicente and Herlinda did not want her to stay in the US without status, so within six months of her unauthorized reentry to the US, they "went ahead and filled out her paperwork, stating that she was here in the US illegally," and sought to begin the process of adjusting her status.

After submitting the application, Vicente would check on its progress from time to time. But nearly three years after voluntarily informing the US government of Herlinda's unauthorized status, and after the birth of two children in the US, Herlinda's case had not progressed. So, when Vicente took the day off for his fiftieth birthday, they decided to go to the local immigration office and check on the progress of their application. "We were going and we were discussing, 'Wow! It's almost been three years. Wouldn't it be something? We're here just to check and see what's going on and all of the sudden, Oh, yeah! Guess what? Here's your green card.'" But, as Vicente recalled, "It turned out to be the complete opposite, kind of like the worst that could have happened."

Shortly after the immigration agent began helping them, "all of the sudden they ask her to step behind, kind of like a glass thing. The next thing I know they've got her handcuffed. They told her to take off her earrings and her ring and everything else, I mean, right then and there." Beyond the shock of the turn of events, what seemed so unreasonable to Vicente was that their case had been in the system for years. "It's not like we'd been hiding," he noted emphatically. If Vicente and Herlinda had not made the trip to USCIS that day, she might never have been deported at all, even though agents could have "gone to that address" on their application "and picked her up any time." But despite his pleas to give them a few days to arrange to take Herlinda to her family in Chihuahua, she was driven that same day from central California to the border with Tijuana, told to run as fast as she could across the long pedestrian bridge that crossed the border into Mexico (the agents gave the women in the van a five-minute head start before they released the men), and then left to fend for herself once she was officially outside of US territory. While US agents transported Herlinda to the border, Vicente found a family friend in Tijuana who could meet her at the border and help her get back to her family in Chihuahua, hundreds of miles away. Their three children—nine years, two years, and eight months old—remained with Vicente for the first few weeks, until it became clear that there was nothing he could do to get Herlinda back into the United States. With no other option, Vicente began making arrangements to live as a family in Mexico during Herlinda's ten-year ban.

Ironically, Vicente and Herlinda actually began their marriage with "easy" access to family reunification. Had they applied for family reunification as soon as Herlinda moved with Vicente to the US, they likely would have been able to adjust Herlinda's status with little fanfare. After she left the US and her visa had expired, they still would have qualified for family reunification had they understood the process and been willing to live apart while USCIS processed Herlinda's application. Even after Herlinda reentered the US without authorization, they could have opted not to apply to adjust her status and hope Herlinda's unauthorized status remained a secret. (And, as Vicente noted, had they not actively pursued answers to their case once they applied, she may never have been targeted for deportation, even though the government knew of her unauthorized status and where to find her.) But Vicente did not know at the beginning of their relationship that there was a family reunification game they should be playing, and once he discovered there was a game and that they should play, he went all-in right away without learning the rules or consulting an expert to know if and when they should engage the system. Like many other mixed-citizenship couples, Vicente and Herlinda's uncoached, underinformed, uncritical approach to family reunification led them to blindly go all-in with a losing hand in family reunification poker, a move that brought with it forced removal from the US and myriad long-lasting consequences resulting from that removal. For some families, playing the first hand they were dealt led to the win they had expected and a smooth transition into legal membership as a family in the US. But for others, playing the game without an understanding of the rules and with no game plan brought only cataclysmic loss.

Playing Their Best Hand

Couples who try to play their best hand recognize they have only one chance to win and are more critical of the hands they have been dealt and how their cards will play. These couples are calculated in their approach to timing—that is, in determining when, in their relationship and in the broader social and political context, their hand will be strongest. They develop game plans, considering which cards (individual and familial conditions) they should strive to improve and the order in which to play their cards. They are also often coached (advised by legal experts and/or friends who have navigated the system) and learn tips and tricks to increase their odds of winning. Applying for family reunification for most mixed-citizenship couples is a once-a-decade (and, sometimes, once-in-a-lifetime) opportunity. Most family reunification denials carry with them harsh penalties that disqualify rejected families from future reunification for years, even if family circumstances during that time change in a way that would otherwise make them eligible for reunification.[10] In most cases, family reunification application decisions are final and cannot be appealed.[11] Thus, strategizing when to play their hand, including waiting for better cards or a favorable change in the rules, can improve a couple's chances of securing a positive reunification outcome.

For many of the families I interviewed with low odds of a positive outcome based on the law-as-written, the decision to wait for a better set of cards or for the rules of the game to change made a significant difference in their family reunification outcome. Had any of these families played the first hand they were dealt, they would have lost. But waiting for a better hand helped some couples overcome the odds and win the game. June and Stefan found a way to start and stop playing multiple times while they waited for a better hand. Stefan came to the US without authorization after receiving direct threats from drug gangs in his hometown in Veracruz, Mexico. He and June, both still in their late teens, met at work in a T-shirt design and print shop shortly after Stefan arrived in the US. Once they both overcame their initial bashfulness and found ways to communicate in spite of their language barrier, they became inseparable.

A year later, when June got pregnant, they decided to marry and, shortly after that, they began investigating what they could do to adjust Stefan's status. As June explained, "Stefan came here illegally," which meant that they had to apply for an Extreme Hardship Waiver (EHW) if they wanted Stefan to be able to live with legal status in the US.[12] When I met them on a sunny December day outside their home just a few miles north of the border, June told me that they "had been working on the waiver on and off" for the past nine years, "since I was pregnant with my first baby." When they had first consulted with a lawyer nine years earlier, as newlyweds with a baby on the way, their lawyer told them to "wait until you have your baby. You're very young. We will wait to build up a better case because the pardon is hard to get." So they waited.

A few years later, after the births of their first two children, June and Stefan decided to apply for the waiver. At that time, though, they could not find out whether or not the waiver would be approved until before Stefan had to leave the US for his consular interview. They applied a few times, but knowing that Stefan faced a ten-year bar to reentry if his petition for the waiver was denied, June never let Stefan go to any of the interviews he was assigned to attend at the consulate in Ciudad Juarez. She knew that, without the EHW in hand, Stefan's risk of rejection and being barred from readmission was too high to justify making the trip.[13] Following the 2012 executive action by the Obama administration, which allows couples to receive approval for the hardship waiver *before* leaving the country for their consular interview, June and Stefan applied for the EHW again. Stefan "eventually got rejected two times" for the waiver; "the third time, we found a better lawyer and they helped us out, and we got accepted." With the waiver approved and in hand, Stefan finally returned to Mexico just three months before our interview, where an agent in Ciudad Juarez approved their family reunification petition and Stefan, June, and their family finally felt "free."

In total, June and Stefan waited nearly a decade for a better hand to play.[14] Thanks to changes in the rules of the game (the 2012 executive order) and in the cards they held (they had four more children, increasing their dependence on Stefan as a provider), they managed to put together a winning hand. While June and Stefan both acknowledge that those nine years were filled with stress, anxiety, and guilt, playing the long game with the law—including abandoning multiple applications mid-process—ultimately gave them access to their desired legal result without having to face the ten-year bar, family separation, and/or relocation to Mexico.

Juliette and Tenoch also knew they held a weak hand due to Tenoch's unauthorized status. In 2013, after three years of marriage and the births of two children, they hoped their case would be strong enough for the EHW. Their lawyer encouraged them to apply, charging them thousands of dollars to prepare the necessary paperwork. After a series of delays and more fees, the lawyer submitted their EHW application, which was summarily denied. (They later learned that the "lawyer" who had "helped" them was a fraud who had stolen thousands from them and other families seeking assistance with immigration cases.) Following their failed EHW application, Juliette developed a case of severe anxiety and depression as her fears of Tenoch's vulnerability to deportation grew. It reached a critical juncture shortly after the birth of their third child, when Juliette began having suicidal thoughts. Ironically, Juliette's mental health crisis—which grew directly from the constant stress of living in an unauthorized family—actually improved her family's eligibility for relief from the threat of deportation and the opportunity for Tenoch to adjust to a legal immigration status.[15] Armed with extensive documentation of Juliette's condition, along with letters from doctors, psychiatrists, and others, they applied again for the waiver, and in the summer of 2017 they received word that their EHW application had been approved.

Waiting for a better hand had not been easy for Juliette, as demonstrated by her mental health crisis. In fact, we had spoken on multiple occasions about work and education opportunities for Juliette, Tenoch, and their children in Mexico (where I was living with my family at the time) and the logistics of making that move. Had their second EHW application been denied, Juliette and Tenoch were ready to leave the US, potentially for good. The stress of waiting for a better hand—which included remaining in an unauthorized, vulnerable state—had grown so great that it began to outweigh the potential benefits some future adjustment of status could bring. Luckily, their cards fell into place just in time. For couples with difficult access to family reunification, like Juliette and Tenoch, waiting for a better hand was often the only option they had to increase their chances of securing legal status in the US and avoiding deportation. Although this approach comes with no promise of success, the alternative (playing the hand they were dealt) guarantees failure. And for some couples, waiting for a better hand ultimately leads to a successful bid for family reunification.

Couples whose profiles set them up for easy access to family reunification also utilized timing to maximize the benefits and minimize the costs of applying for family reunification. While securing permanent residency and a path to citizenship is a huge benefit of a successful family reunification application, it comes with strings attached. All lawful permanent residents of the United States must live in the US at least 180 days of every calendar year. Failing to meet this requirement can result in cancellation of permanent residency status and ineligibility for citizenship.[16] For some couples, this requirement interferes with their plans to live full-time outside the US or to split their time between the two countries. Other couples feel satisfied with their status quo—long-term tourist visas that allow regular entry to and from the US without the extra baggage of residency; work or student visas that give them the freedom to live and work in the US without having to make a long-term commitment to their partner (through marriage) or to the US—and have not yet felt the need to go "all-in." For these couples, waiting to play the game is not as much about cultivating a better hand to play but just waiting for the need to play at all.

Carolina and Enrique had been married for years before they decided to move to the US and apply for Carolina's residency. Although

Enrique inherited US citizenship from his American-born mother, both were born and raised in upper-class political families in Baja California and had enjoyed free movement throughout the US and Mexico (and beyond) since they were children. After they married, they settled in Tijuana and both began working for large, international corporations. As long as they both wanted to live and work in Mexico, there was no incentive for them to apply for Carolina's residency in the US, despite the fact that they could easily qualify. For them, the decision to apply for family reunification came about when, shortly after Carolina quit her job to care full-time for their two small children, Enrique started a job that required significant travel throughout the US and Mexico.

These changes in their family life led them to reconsider their housing situation. They knew that, no matter where they lived, they would continue to move regularly between Tijuana, Mexicali, and San Diego, as they had since they married. But with an uptick in violence in Tijuana, Enrique felt that if "I'm going to keep traveling this way, I prefer you guys to be in a more secure place." They called a family meeting and weighed their options: stay in Tijuana or move to San Diego or Mexicali. Enrique asked Carolina, "Which one do you like best?" After Carolina contemplated Enrique's question, she confidently replied, "San Diego." It helped that her mother and multiple siblings already lived in San Diego, but it had more to do with her sense of security and ability to run her household alone while Enrique traveled for extended periods of time. In San Diego, Carolina feels "like I can be in charge of my household and protect the kids and whatnot." Enrique agrees: "I feel more secure leaving them here."

As they began to make their plans, Carolina realized that she could also apply for family reunification and transition from her tourist visa to permanent residency: "I hadn't done anything about my status regarding my marriage. I said, 'You know what? If we live in San Diego, I can take advantage of doing this green card thing and getting naturalized.'" This realization further solidified their plans to move. It just "made sense" to do it. For Carolina and Enrique, securing Carolina's permanent legal status in the US never felt like a necessity, let alone an urgent one. But when the timing seemed right for them to live in the

US for a while, applying for family reunification became a natural next step. Because they held a winning hand, they easily acquired approval for Carolina's residency (and, later, citizenship) applications as soon as they decided the time was right to apply.

Aylin and Jared, who also felt no rush to play their winning hand, are two fiery intellectuals who delight in discussing, debating, and critiquing political and social issues. They had dated off and on long-distance for almost four years, ever since a friend introduced them over tacos shortly after Aylin moved to Chicago to attend graduate school. Jared, a high school teacher, was living in New York and had only come to town for a brief visit, but after that initial meeting, they kept in contact and soon began dating long-distance. After two years, Jared took a job in Chicago and they moved in together, but they broke up about nine months later. After a seven-month break, they got back together, but then Jared moved back to New York and they started their long-distance life all over again.

Given the ambiguity surrounding their long-term relationship prospects and the likelihood of needing to live in different cities for the near future, neither Aylin nor Jared felt the need to add the legal complications of marriage to their already complex relationship. But all of that changed four years into their relationship, after the presidential election on November 8, 2016. Aylin had gone to bed early on the night of the election in preparation for an important meeting the next day. She awoke the following morning to a stream of increasingly worried texts from Jared, culminating in the news that Donald Trump had won the election. Jared's final text to Aylin "literally was, 'I don't know what you're thinking about. I don't know what you're thinking re: anything. But I think we should get married.'" Even though both had been thinking (if not necessarily talking) about marriage, they had hesitated to make that legal commitment for a lot of reasons, both practical and philosophical. But the election changed all of their calculations and fears, and Aylin accepted Jared's text-based proposal. "It was definitely a response to the elections," she admits. It might sound "so corny," Aylin continued, but given the depressed and despondent state of seemingly everyone around her in the days following the election, "it felt like such a good, truly political act to say, 'This sucks, but at least we love each other,'" and no matter what action the president-elect took against immigrants once in office, "we're going to be married under his government" and he would have no say over whether or not they could be a family. Aylin described how "it felt a little bit weird and a little bit protest-y" as they went to the courthouse in Brooklyn a few weeks later, with Jared's sister, their witness, in tow. Jared made clear that there was no fanfare or big party: "We went home, took a nap, and then later went out for dinner with my sister," to which Aylin sarcastically responded, "That's the super-romantic story" of how they got married. Jared, to reinforce the political and calculated nature of their decision to marry, immediately countered: "There's nothing romantic about the election. There's nothing romantic about the story. It doesn't need more romance. This is real life."

Trump's threat of significant change to the immigration system—a cornerstone of his presidential campaign platform—and his specific attacks on Mexican immigrants like Aylin shifted the terms of the family reunification game in a way that made Jared and Aylin perceive their need to play to be much more urgent. Aylin had a current visa as a graduate student, so their path to family reunification was straightforward once they married. As Jared put it, "We wanted to be able to be in the country of our choosing together at the same time." Reflecting on their shift to a defensive stance following the election, Jared added that they "got married as a preventative measure, and prevention is better than reaction." Jared and Aylin realized that the strong hand they held in family reunification poker might not be a winning hand once Trump assumed office, so they took the steps necessary to apply for family reunification right away. Families like Jared and Aylin, who timed their reunification applications to the ideal moment in which their qualifications as a couple simultaneously peaked with broader political and legal conditions surrounding immigration law, experienced more successful reunification outcomes along both objective and subjective measures than families who did not.

In addition to strategically timing their applications, families seeking to play their best hand also altered their profiles in calculated ways to better match the requirements outlined in family reunification law. Implementing these game plans helped couples satisfy basic qualifications for reunification: getting married, naturalizing as a US citizen (from LPR status), getting a better-paying job. Others improved the "worthiness profile" of individual applicants and/or the couple as a whole—filing joint tax returns, having a child, and even preempting deportation through voluntary removal. These couples' efforts confirm the concerns many legal scholars raised when Congress considered the IMFA in 1986: the procedures and evidentiary record necessary to ensure couples' satisfaction of the law impose specific norms of married life that couples feel compelled to meet, including expectations of cohabitation, procreation, and culturally specific lifestyle choices.[17]

Unsurprisingly, couples who designed and implemented a "game plan" in their approach to family reunification used the templates for "legitimate" and "worthy" marriages (and applicants) outlined in the law as the framework for their family reunification strategy. High school sweethearts Juanita and Heri launched a multipronged plan to better qualify themselves for reunification. First, Juanita applied for citizenship. She came to the US as a teenager after ten years of separation from her father while he regularized his status through IRCA, became a legal permanent resident, and applied to sponsor his wife and children to come to the US as permanent residents. Juanita knew firsthand that immigration laws subjected permanent residents' spouses and minor children to admission quotas, which significantly lengthened the application process, whereas those quotas did not apply to citizens' spouses and minor children. From this experience, Juanita understood that applying as a citizen would strengthen both her "worthiness" profile as a sponsor and speed up the process for adjusting Heri's status. As she put it, "The reason for me to become a citizen was Heriberto, because I wanted him to be safe."

Second, Juanita and Heri timed their application to maximize Heri's worthiness as an applicant, despite his unauthorized status. Heri and his older brother journeyed to the US as unaccompanied minors in an effort to reunite with their mother, who had immigrated to the US without authorization years earlier. Heri was just nine years old when he and his brother joined their mother in the farming community in northern California where she lived. Heri enrolled in school and learned English quickly, enabling him to demonstrate his strong academic aptitude. But after graduating at the top of his high school class, he confronted the challenges of pursuing higher education as an unauthorized immigrant. He first attended community college and then transferred to a four-year university, where he tried his best to stretch out his academic career as long as possible, in part because he loved to learn and in part because he was waiting, hoping, that some kind of legal relief (for "dreamers" or for all unauthorized immigrants) would finally arrive. "I was trying to buy time, you know. I did—I'm like, okay, I'm going to work on a history major, I'm going to do this, I'm going to do that, I'm going to do a philosophy major and then I kept waiting, you know, what's going to happen? Is the immigration [reform] going to go through? Or it may never happen." As the years dragged on, his optimism for some kind of immigration reform dwindled.

When Juanita and Heri decided to marry, Heri was nearing the end of his undergraduate career and knew that, even with his degree, he would have no opportunities to legally work unless they could adjust his status. Sensing that his identity as a strong student would make a better impression than an unemployed (or unlawfully employed) college graduate, they decided to apply for family reunification immediately so that Heri could still be a full-time student when they submitted their EHW application. At the interview in Ciudad Juarez, the immigration agent asked Heri, "Why should we admit you into the US?" Heri's response was simple, but true: "I just want to learn. I want to keep going to school. I love the university. In fact, I love books." He told them he wanted to "do research" and become an academic.

Worried that Heri's clean record and educational aspirations might not be sufficient to secure the EHW, legal advisors also counseled Heri to accrue debt in the US to give immigration officers another reason to let him back into the US. This made Heri a bit uncomfortable because, as he explained, "I never had any debts. I never had money problems, so I never got anything on credit and I always paid in cash." Heri's lawyers "told me to go get loans and go buy things at Best Buy on credit, so they have an excuse to bring you back, so you can pay off your bills," so he did. Ultimately, Juanita and Heri's multifaceted game plan worked—after a four-month separation while Heri waited in Mexico, USCIS approved their family reunification application and Extreme Hardship Waiver petition. The many benefits that have come with Heri's legal status have enabled Juanita, Heri, and their son to pursue their dreams as a family together in the US.

Other families, like Sandra and Esteban, felt they could better prove their "worthiness" by leaving the US and applying from Mexico for "forgiveness" for prior unauthorized status in the US. For Sandra and Esteban, this strategy best suited their needs because the majority of their extended family members still lived in Mexico. Sandra did not think she could live apart from her family, who live just a few hundred feet south of the US-Mexico border, for all of the years that it might take to adjust Esteban's status, and they both worried that living in California near the border would also make Esteban more vulnerable to immigration enforcement than when he lived in Tennessee prior to their marriage.

When I asked Sandra why they decided to live in Mexico rather than in the US, she said that, after moving from Tennessee to the California border region, they realized that "the immigration laws and consequences are stricter" near the border. "In Tennessee, you didn't see immigration officers around as much as you do" in California. "So that was the concern that we were living with. We said, 'If they pick you up, there is going to be a penalty and everything will be more difficult.'" So they packed up their things and moved to Mexico, right next door to Sandra's parents, and began saving money to be able to submit a residency and waiver application for Esteban. Their strategy still involved living outside the US for years—6.5, to be exact—before Esteban could legally enter the US, and during this time Esteban missed out on many meaningful moments with Sandra and her family that took place in the US. But they lived together in the same home and secured legal status for Esteban in less time than the ten-year bar would have required, in part (at least as far as Sandra believes) because they voluntarily left the US, sought official "forgiveness," and chose to do things "the right way" before deportation forced them into that position.

Some families built effective game plans around unique family circumstances that qualified them for relief from deportation or family reunification following deportation. For these and many other families, consulting with legal experts familiar with the fine print in US immigration law played a key role in developing a successful family reunification strategy. Cathy, a generous and energetic fifth grade teacher, was set up with Samuel by one of her students; the fifth grader invited her to one of his soccer games without telling her that he planned to introduce her to his soccer coach, Samuel. Not too long after they began dating, Cathy and Samuel found themselves in dire straits when Cathy found out in the same week both that she was pregnant *and* that she had a brain tumor that would require surgery as soon as she gave birth. Unmarried and unsure of how to proceed, Cathy and Samuel sought advice from their local priest, as Cathy explained: "So we went to the priest, and the priest said, 'Don't do it. Don't get married because this is kind of a bad time. You're under duress. Don't make a decision like this under duress.' And so we didn't." They kept dating, but Samuel "didn't move in or anything. We just still saw each other, and I just kept getting bigger and bigger." Everything seemed to be going as well as could be expected, until immigration agents raided Samuel's job in north Texas and deported him to Mexico that same day. Cathy was six-and-a-half months pregnant.

From Mexico, Samuel applied for a temporary thirty-day emergency visa to be able to accompany Cathy during her brain surgery and be on hand to care for their baby in case she experienced complications. Once Samuel was back in the US, they sought legal help. Their lawyer counseled them to get married immediately and apply for an adjustment of status. Their attorney knew that they could not qualify for any family reunification options unless they were married. He also knew that Cathy's precarious health situation combined with the birth of their child made a strong case for their dependence on Samuel. In Cathy and Samuel's case, consulting with a legal authority (and not just a moral authority) saved their relationship and generated the possibility for them to secure family reunification and the legal permission to live together as a family in the US. While developing and implementing a game plan did not guarantee these couples' successful and immediate family reunification, it did give couples—especially those with unauthorized status and a "difficult" path to reunification, like Cathy and Samuel—a better chance at qualifying for access to legal status.

I also interviewed couples who bent the rules in order to appear to meet the expectations of family reunification law without actually doing so. These couples used misrepresentation as a direct strategy under two very different scenarios. In the first scenario, couples who generally meet the qualifications outlined in family reunification law have lifestyle preferences or needs that clash with legal requirements associated with marriage, such as cohabitation, and permanent residency, such as needing to live in the US at least 180 days of every year. Rather than waiting for those conditions to change, these families misrepresent their circumstances to present an image of abiding by the law while maintaining their preferred lifestyle discreetly. Because they otherwise do not raise flags as potentially fraudulent couples, most of these couples do not receive additional scrutiny from immigration enforcement agents beyond the standard interview.

In the second scenario, couples have in their background one or more violations in their history that would automatically disqualify them for family reunification. This can include having violated the terms of a previous visa status (such as working in the US on a tourist visa), multiple clandestine entries into the US without authorization, or having falsely claimed US citizenship.[18] But for many families, these violations remain unknown to US governmental authorities. When such is the case, families can opt *not* to disclose this information in their applications; as long as they are not caught in their failure to disclose, these families do not face the consequences of those prior violations.

Couples with profiles lending them "easy" access to family reunification may not always want to live within the constraints that family reunification and legal permanent residency impose, or they may need the benefits of legal status before they are actually ready to begin their journey as a family. Such was the case for Jiancarlo and Sondra, who met in college in a Spanish literature class. Both were born and raised in towns on the US-Mexico border—Jiancarlo in the US and Sondra in Mexico.

Sondra grew up with a tourist visa and traveled regularly back and forth across the border. When she was 16, she and her mother moved to the US in search of better work opportunities. Shortly after they arrived in the US, their visas expired.

When Sondra and Jiancarlo met, she had been unauthorized for several years. As a result of her unauthorized status, Sondra had to pay out-of-state tuition at the state university they attended, an extraordinary expense that forced her to work full-time while in school. Sondra and Jiancarlo dated and began planning a future life together, but both felt that they needed to accomplish certain personal goals—graduate from college, begin a career—before they would be ready for marriage. They were both driven to accomplish their professional dreams: Jiancarlo was going to be an engineer and Sondra hoped to pursue a future in journalism, a dream she was on her way to realizing through an internship with the local newspaper. At the time, they both felt that these individual dreams were more urgent and important than getting married.

But as Sondra neared her graduation, she realized that, because of her unauthorized status, her bachelor's degree would not improve her access to most jobs, access she felt would be necessary in order to be personally prepared for marriage. She thought to herself, "Okay, so now I'm going to have a bachelor's degree. I have all this experience, and I have this internship, but I have no way of getting a job." Unsure of what she could do, she "talked it over" with Jiancarlo, "and then I remember him asking me, 'So, what can we do?'" Together, they "came up with the solution" that, since they were "probably going to end up getting married" eventually, they might as well just do it now. Because they both hoped and planned that their courtship would eventually lead toward marriage, they decided to get married "by the court" immediately, long before they actually planned to begin their life together as a married couple.

Soon after their courthouse marriage, they applied for Sondra's permanent residency (based on her status as Jiancarlo's wife), which she received. For the first two years of their marriage, though, they continued to live in separate houses and date as they had before, in direct violation of the "legitimate" marriage expectations outlined in the IMFA.

They only began living together as a couple and started what they considered to be their true married life after marrying "in the church" two years later. During this two-year period, no one knew that they had already legally married—not even their parents. While Jiancarlo and Sondra planned to marry eventually, they pursued "marriage by the court" with the sole intent of adjusting Sondra's immigration status, meaning that the marriage had not been entered into "in good faith."[19] According to the law-as-written, Jiancarlo and Sondra's marriage—at least for the two years following their courthouse wedding—was a fraud.

While Jiancarlo suggested that some people who hear their story could think it was just a "marriage of convenience," he claimed that, in the moment, "there was no question whether this was right or wrong. It was just, this is how we need to move forward, and we wanted a future together. There was no question about what we have to do." Jiancarlo and Sondra planned to marry eventually, and Sondra needed to adjust her status in order to continue to progress in her education and career and prepare for their life together. So they applied for family reunification even before they became a family—at least as far as they were concerned—because they needed the benefits of family reunification first in order to become the family they wanted to be. But, had US immigration officials become aware of this arrangement, Sondra's residency status would have been nullified and their plans for a shared future together in the US denied.

Melodia and Chuck also easily satisfied the requirements for family reunification, despite the fact that the lifestyle they wanted to live did not correspond with the requirements that accompany permanent residency in the US. They met working in management at the same factory in Mexico, just south of the border with California. Melodia grew up in a well-resourced Mexican political family and had previously studied in the US, France, and the Dominican Republic. She had a long-term tourist visa to the US, and neither Melodia nor Chuck had profiles that raised red flags with regard to their worthiness or the legitimacy of their relationship.[20] But they did not intend to live in the US and, under the rules governing permanent residency, green card holders must live in the US at least 180 days of every year.

After they married, Chuck and Melodia immediately applied for family reunification and lived in the US for a few months while waiting for Melodia's green card interview. Chuck commuted back and forth, but Melodia was unable to leave the country while she waited. As soon as their application was approved, they moved back to Mexico. Assuming (correctly) that Melodia's lack of actual residency in the US would not raise the suspicion of border agents or other immigration officials, they continued on with life as usual, crossing the border to the US when they wanted to (including for the births of both of their children), but with both Chuck and Melodia working and residing in Mexico. Three years later, Melodia is now a US citizen, despite the fact that she has never lived in the US during her adult life except for the few months while she waited for her green card interview—a direct violation of LPR policy and something that should automatically disqualify her from citizenship. Given their employment constraints and personal preferences that persuaded them to continue living outside the US, Chuck and Melodia technically should not have qualified for family reunification. But they were able to play the legal game in a way that gave Melodia access to permanent residency and citizenship without sacrificing their work and way of life in Mexico.[21]

For families with a disqualifying condition in their past, bending the rules centered more on withholding information regarding past actions rather than misrepresenting current or future plans. With the help of a lawyer, Georgina and Moises adapted their familial "truth" to fit the requirements necessary to qualify for an EHW, despite the fact that Moises technically did not qualify. Georgina's ongoing health issues and her need for Moises's physical and emotional support seemed to clearly qualify them for relief from the ten-year bar. But unauthorized immigrants who have entered the US more than once without authorization do not qualify for an EHW. Moises had crossed the Rio Grande on two separate occasions years apart, but Border Patrol agents did not catch him either time. Because there was no legal record showing that Moises had violated this rule, their lawyer recommended that he report his earliest date of entry to the US and simply never reveal that, sometime during the six years that followed (between his original entry and his application date), he had left the US and reentered without inspection. Georgina and Moises only mentioned this to me when I asked Moises to tell me about his experience coming across the border, which Georgina noted he did twice, but then immediately added, "but nobody knows that." Moises went on to explain that their lawyer told him to only admit to having entered the US without permission once, because "if you leave and then come back undocumented [again], you can't get a green card."

Despite tailoring their story as closely as possible to the requirements as written in the law (and as their lawyer interpreted them), Georgina and Moises had to endure more than a year of separation following his visa interview when USCIS denied his original hardship waiver application. After collecting more evidence of the extreme hardship this separation was already causing Georgina, and while working very closely with their lawyer, Georgina successfully reapplied for the EHW and Moises was granted legal entry into the US. Ultimately, Georgina concluded that success in the family reunification process was "all about money and persistence. If you've got that, then you could get it done." Through hard work and, at times, pure determination, Georgina and Moises worked with the law to position their family in a way that qualified them for family reunification. Knowing the rules and how to bend them made all the difference in helping Georgina and Moises secure a positive family reunification outcome.

Leticia and Mario, who met in a Mexican border town where they both have lived for most of their lives and where they planned to continue living, had to overcome two challenges in order to qualify for family reunification. First, Mario had been working as a long-haul trucker in the US on his tourist visa for a number of years, a serious violation of the terms of that visa. Should the US government learn of this violation, Mario's visa would be cancelled and he could be barred from acquiring any legal (non)immigrant status in the US for a decade or more. Luckily, the government was not aware of Mario's unauthorized work record and likely would not know of it as long as Mario and Leticia kept it a secret. Second, Mario and Leticia planned to continue to live in Mexico even after USCIS approved his residency application. In this case, the nature of Mario's job, which requires him to travel within the US for multiple days at a time, has made it easier for them to hide the fact that they do not live in the US full-time. With a standard shift job, Mario would be entering and exiting the US on a daily basis—a well-documented red flag that could jeopardize his status as a permanent resident and any future attempt to naturalize. Bending the rules by withholding information of Mario's past visa violations and not disclosing their continued residence in Mexico (a violation of his current residency status) has helped Mario and Leticia secure positive immigration outcomes despite violating visa policies in both the past and the present. All of these "rule-bending" families—those hiding past rule violations, like Georgina and Moises; those hiding current and future violations, like Sondra and Jiancarlo; and those hiding both, like Leticia and Mario—actively engaged the law, adapting both their interactions with the law and the narratives they provided to government actors to best position themselves for a positive legal outcome in the family reunification process.

The Risk of (Not) Playing Family Reunification Poker

The stakes associated with deciding to play—or not to play—family reunification poker are much higher for some couples than for others. Some couples—like Enrique and Carolina, Jared and Aylin, and Melodia and Chuck—could play, and likely win, at any time.[22] For them, choosing to play or not at any given time generally carries few risks; rather than needing a better hand, these couples typically wait for a need to play at all. Similarly, Jessica and Julio, two accomplished professionals with established careers in their respective countries, split their time and their lives equally between the US and Mexico. They want to maintain their status quo in which they both can travel freely between countries without having work authorization and legal authorization to live full-time in their country of noncitizenship. Not playing the family reunification game serves their needs better than permanent legal status through family reunification would—primarily due to the additional residency, taxation, and other obligations associated with that change in status. Many couples like Jessica and Julio do not need the definitive outcome that engaging with family reunification law would produce, even if that outcome is positive.

But waiting to play family reunification poker does carry risks for all families, whether they hold a winning or a losing hand. Salvador and Dina thought they could have the "best of both worlds" with Salvador just holding a tourist visa to the US. Salvador has a well-paid government job in a Mexican border city, and he recently helped Dina get a job in a different department in the same city government offices where he works. But they both feel strongly that their three daughters, all elementary school–aged, should take advantage of one of the benefits of their US citizenship: high-quality public education and English-language training (something Dina, a US citizen by birth but who grew up in Mexico, never received). For about a year, they lived together on the US side of the border, and Salvador and Dina crossed back into Mexico each morning for work and returned home just as their daughters finished their school day. One day, the Customs and Border Patrol agent processing Salvador's reentry to the US decided that he did not believe Salvador's story—suspecting instead that Salvador illegally worked an evening shift at a US job—and revoked Salvador's visa. USCIS denied Salvador's appeal for his visa to be restored. Now Salvador lives alone in Mexico, and his wife and daughters, who still sleep in the US so they can go to school, cross the border multiple times a day for work and to spend time with Salvador. Because Salvador's tourist visa was revoked, his chances of successfully applying for family reunification and permanent residency in the US have dropped significantly. In the course of waiting for a need to go all-in, Salvador and Dina ended up trading a winning hand for a losing one.

For couples with losing hands who wait to play the family reunification game, deportation remains a constant threat. Waiting for a better hand delays the finality of a rejection, but unauthorized mixed-citizenship families can be rejected through immigration enforcement without ever applying for family reunification. Such was the case for Chuy, who was deported after living unauthorized in the US since age seven and after more than fifteen years of marriage to Esther, a US citizen. Uprooting their whole family to join Chuy in Mexico ultimately tore their family apart, leading to Esther and Chuy's separation and divorce four years later.

The rules of the game can also change while couples wait for a better hand or a reason to go all-in. Despite what appears to be an inability on the part of Congress to pass any meaningful immigration legislation, immigration laws can still be modified through administrative or executive action. Executive orders implemented by the Obama administration created opportunities for families, such as the ability to apply for the EHW before leaving the country for the consular interview, that improved families' chances of holding a winning hand. But a number of administrative and executive orders proposed and implemented under the Trump administration changed the game in ways that set up many more families for failure. Rule changes imposed while couples wait to play can leave mixed-citizenship families in a more vulnerable position, effectively forcing them to trade in their cards for a weaker hand.

An error in play can also turn a winning hand into a losing hand. For Vicente and Herlinda, fifteen years of exile followed their misplay when they failed to play their winning hand and then went all-in without realizing that Herlinda's change in status had also set them up for failure. Similarly, Christian and Sharon's error in playing the family reunification game permanently ended their chances of living together with legal status in the US. Everything went well for them when they applied for the EHW and Sharon's adjustment of status, despite working with what they described as less-than-stellar legal advisors. When it came time to apply for Sharon's citizenship, they decided not to work with a lawyer at all; the application seemed straightforward enough. As they answered the different questions on the citizenship application, they felt the need to answer each one as honestly as possible. When they encountered the question, "Have you ever claimed to be a US citizen?," Sharon thought she probably had when she was an unauthorized youth applying for a job, so she checked the "yes" box next to that question. What Sharon and Christian did not know is that USCIS revokes the legal status of anyone who admits to having fraudulently claimed to be a US citizen and permanently bars that person from ever obtaining legal status in the US, a consequence that cannot be appealed. Sharon and Christian's error in play automatically and permanently disqualified them from family reunification.

Finally, it is important to note that some couples will always hold a losing hand. Couples in which the noncitizen partner has been permanently barred from legal status—either through the rule described above or due to a deportation following conviction for a qualifying "aggravated felony" as defined in the Illegal Immigration Reform and Immigrant Responsibility Act—can never qualify for family reunification (barring an act of Congress). No matter how long these couples wait or how hard they strategize, their hands will always lose under the current rules of the game.

"Family reunification poker" helps to explain why inequalities written into US immigration law cannot completely account for which families are ultimately approved for family reunification by US Citizenship and Immigration Services authorities. Each couple's response to the constraints delineated in family reunification law significantly affects their likelihood of receiving a positive outcome in the application process. The decision of when, how, and under what circumstances to apply for family reunification can affect families' legal status outcomes as much or more than the distinctions written into law itself. Thus, legal consciousness can directly contribute to family reunification outcomes to help some families achieve success where the law would predict failure. The law-as-written, the law-in-practice, *and* couples' orientation toward these laws and their enforcement all contribute toward families' reunification outcomes.

In the chapters that follow, I examine the consequences of family reunification outcomes—both positive and negative—and the life-changing, family-altering effects of family reunification policy, practice, and "poker." The gravity of these consequences cannot be overstated. The official acceptance of a couple through a successful family reunification application expands the opportunities, networks, experiences, and sense of belonging of both spouses. Formal rejection by the US government closes doors for both spouses and symbolically (and, often, literally) pushes them to the margins of American society. Families who choose to wait to play the game can potentially avoid the most devastating repercussions of a family reunification denial but also cannot access many of the benefits and opportunities that would be available to them if they secured a positive family reunification outcome. As we will see in the following chapters, these consequences touch every aspect of mixed-citizenship families' lives, determining the physical spaces they can inhabit, dictating the institutions and services they can access, shaping their social worlds, and molding their psychological and emotional well-being and sense of belonging to their families, communities, and countries.

(Dis)Integrated Families, (Dis)Integrated Lives

VICENTE SERRANO WAKES UP at 4 a.m. every weekday. He is always the first one awake. Before he takes his shower, he wakes up his wife, Herlinda, and their daughter, Stephanie, who then help wake up the two older boys, Jonathan and Luke. While Vicente showers, Herlinda irons his dress shirt and slacks and packs lunches for Vicente and the two younger children, Luke and Stephanie, who are both in high school. By the time I arrive at their house at 4:30, everyone in the house is awake and rushing to make sure they are ready for our impending departure. Vicente's voice grows progressively louder as he reminds the children that it is time to go. By 4:45, Vicente, Stephanie, Luke, and I are in the car and on our way to the border. (Jonathan leaves for the border about fifteen minutes after we do in his own car.) The oldies station plays in the background and the air conditioner blasts, overpowering the summer heat that has lingered overnight. Although the Serranos' house is only three blocks from the border fence, we have to drive a few miles east to the border crossing, where we take our place in the single-file line about a mile back from the border checkpoint, with cars as far ahead as we can see and more arriving behind us each minute. Vicente turns off the car, but he keeps the radio going. Luke and Stephanie are already asleep in the back seat.

The border crossing here opens at 5 a.m., but it takes a while for the momentum to reach us. At 5:20, taillights ahead of us light up and engines start to turn. The line moves quickly today, and we're through the border checkpoint and on our way by 5:40. Forty-five minutes later, we drop Luke and Stephanie off at their otherwise empty high school, where they will wait another hour and a half for school to start. After

Vicente drops the kids off, we drive fifteen minutes further to the middle school where he teaches seventh-grade math.

Vicente is almost always the first teacher to arrive at school. We have over an hour to set up his classroom and chat before the students arrive at 8:15. It's only the third week of school, but Vicente already has his students trained to stand up anytime a visitor enters the room and to shout "Go Bulls!" at the end of the morning announcements. Although we have traveled thirty miles northwest from Vicente's house to get to his school, we are still only a few miles north of the border. Many of his students speak Spanish as their first language; some of them make the daily commute from Mexico, too.

On our lunch break, we sit outside at a picnic table in the school garden with some of Vicente's coworkers and talk about our victories of the week, which range from helping kids get excited about reading for fun to simply surviving a long workweek. As I observe Vicente, his classroom, his interactions with students and coworkers, I am keenly aware that, despite the fact that this is his twelfth year in the same classroom, Herlinda has never seen what I am seeing. She has not read the school rules posted on the back wall of the classroom or made small talk with other teachers. Since Herlinda's deportation (discussed in chapter 3) forced the family to relocate from the central California coast to the Mexican side of the border, she has been forcibly disconnected from every aspect of her family's life that takes place in the US.

Vicente uses the last half hour of his workday to do some grading, and then we start the commute home. The Serranos' oldest son, Jonathan, who works at a fast-food restaurant near Vicente's school, has already picked up the kids from high school, so we run errands without them and then head back home. We're back at the Serranos' house at 4:45— twelve hours after we left this morning—which Herlinda says is a record (though she also notes that we forgot to do some of the errands on Vicente's list, an oversight that might account for our "early" arrival). This is Vicente's routine every day, and has been for the last twelve years, ever since Herlinda was deported on his fiftieth birthday. His life is a constant battle between separation from his wife and home and separation from his country and the rights, opportunities, and privileges it offers him. Vicente's days are nonstop, from border wait to commute to school to errands to home, with few opportunities to rest his body or his brain.

Herlinda's days, on the other hand, are mostly empty, and she struggles to fill her time while the rest of her family go about their lives in a place that is completely inaccessible to her. Although she wakes up at four with everyone else, she stays behind in a too-quiet house after the cars pull away. During the week, Herlinda teaches an hour-long religion class to high school students from her church between 5:30 and 6:30 a.m., which keeps her moving after Vicente and the kids head to school. After her students leave, she waters the fruit trees and other plants in their front garden and plays with their big Alaskan husky for a while. And then? Sometimes she naps for a bit before making breakfast and doing the laundry or other household chores. Other days she visits with friends who live nearby.

On the day I spend with Herlinda, we drive a few blocks to refill water jugs with filtered drinking water and spend the rest of the morning chatting, watching TV, passing the time. Stephanie is home sick from school. She was sent to the nurse's office the day before with a fever, but no one could pick her up from school early since Herlinda cannot cross the border and Vicente was at work. Moments like these—in which Herlinda is available to fulfill her familial duties and yet unable to do so—serve as reminders of her forced disintegration from her husband's and children's lives, the product of harsh penalties linked to her deportation following previous unauthorized residence within the US. Herlinda feels that, in many ways, her banishment from the US has left her powerless in her ability to fulfill her responsibilities as a stay-at-home mom. When her children were younger, they attended elementary school in Mexico, and Herlinda's days were filled with school runs, volunteering in the classroom, making costumes for cultural celebrations, and a variety of opportunities to actively involve herself in her children's lives. But now, as much as she would love to be involved, Herlinda is both spatially and socially removed from her children's daily lives, despite the fact that they live in the same home and eat dinner as a family every night. Herlinda has never met her kids' friends at school, their teachers, nor the parents involved with school activities. She could not attend Jonathan's high school graduation. She cannot even pick up a sick child early from school. Additionally, because of concerns over availability, quality, and cost, Vicente does most of the grocery shopping and buys the kids' clothes in the US. Apart from packing lunches and making dinner, Herlinda's ability to contribute to the family's daily routine and ongoing needs remains limited because of her status as a deportee.

At about 3:30 in the afternoon, we make a quick trip to the corner market to pick up a few ingredients for the evening's meal. Back at home, Herlinda prepares dinner, which she likes to have ready by five, though she is never quite sure when everyone will get home. Vicente and the boys arrive home at 6:15 and head straight to the dinner table, where we enjoy a typical family meal in which Vicente and Herlinda try, unsuccessfully, to coax the kids into talking about what they did that day. An observer walking in on the Serranos during dinner or observing the rest of their evening routine would confuse this family for any other "normal" family. And yet the juxtaposition of Vicente and Herlinda's daily routines—coupled with the fact that I, a relative stranger, had easy access to their lives in a way that Herlinda did not—underlines the disconnection, isolation, and injustice of their family's forced spatial disintegration from the US.

Because mixed-citizenship families are composed of members with at least two distinct citizenships, they have (in theory) at least two different countries in which they *could* reside and, potentially, belong. But this same membership to a foreign country is offered as a justification in US government deportations and family reunification denials, resulting in the legal exclusion or deportation of US citizens' intimate partners, like Herlinda Serrano.[1] Thus, for many mixed-citizenship couples, having legally established ties to more than one country becomes a liability rather than an asset.[2] And even for those couples living in their preferred country, unauthorized status can limit their ability to live, work, and travel safely within the communities in which they reside.[3]

Limitations on the movement of spouses within and across borders affects spatial integration for all members of the family unit.[4] Classic assimilation scholars have studied spatial assimilation as the residential integration of different racial and ethnic groups, usually measured as the movement of cohorts of non-White immigrants into neighborhoods with high concentrations of White residents, which movement is also often associated with increased socioeconomic attainment.[5] Setting aside the problematic racial assumptions underpinning much of this research,[6] these macro-level studies of residential mobility and (de)segregation have provided useful data on the spatial integration of immigrant groups in the US over time and the particular conditions that may facilitate group integration beyond "ethnic enclaves" into more diverse geographies.

But this macro-level—whole group, whole neighborhood, whole generation—definition of spatial integration does not capture the lived experience of individual immigrants and immigrant families as they undergo spatial (dis)integration. Experientially, spatial integration is about physical presence within a community *and* the legal, social, and economic conditions in that community that regulate daily life within those physical spaces. Laws and social practices targeting unauthorized individuals may not prevent those individuals from being physically present in a specific geography, but they can significantly inhibit those individuals' spatial, structural, and social integration inside that geography.[7]

For mixed-citizenship families, spatial integration has two separate dimensions: first, living in their country of preference, and second, freedom of movement within the community and country in which they live. Authorized couples have broad access to both of these dimensions of spatial integration; they have freedom under the law to live wherever they want in either country of citizenship.[8,9] Unauthorized couples often face restrictions along one or both dimensions, unable to live where they would like to live and/or limited in their movement within the physical spaces they do inhabit. My interviews reveal that spatial (dis)integration affects individual and family movement, opportunities, and relationships. Authorized couples, who have the freedom to move within and between countries and communities, maintain strong relationships in both countries and pursue the best opportunities available to them, which often means moving across borders at least once after they marry. Unauthorized couples experience strained relationships with friends and family in both countries (even within their immediate family) and find that most doors to opportunity are closed to them. These consequences apply to all family members, regardless of their citizenship status.

Families without legal status in the US all experience physical separation of one kind or another—separation from deported family members; separation from extended family members outside the US (if living in the US) or inside the US (if living outside the US); separation from their country of citizenship; separation from economic, educational, and social opportunities. While the details of their experiences differ based on their immigration histories, all mixed-citizenship American families without legal status face restrictions on their ability to physically live together and to move within and between their geographic and social spheres. These restrictions affect unauthorized mixed-citizenship families in two ways, through spatial disintegration and spatial isolation. *Spatial disintegration* occurs when individuals and families previously spatially incorporated into community and country are physically excluded through the collateral effects of legal restrictions on the presence and movement of unauthorized family members. *Spatial isolation* transpires when individuals and families are dislocated and detached from the social and relational spheres of the geographies they physically inhabit and those they legally cannot.

Spatial Disintegration

Sonia and Sebastian lived for years in the US, despite Sebastian's unauthorized immigration status and the fact that he had been deported multiple times in the past. Each time he was deported, he found a way to get back into the US and reunite with Sonia. But while he was being processed during his most recent deportation, immigration authorities detained Sebastian for months and told him that if he was caught inside the US or at the border again, he would be incarcerated for years before they would release him for deportation. This threat of extended family separation persuaded Sonia and Sebastian to move their family to Mexico, with Sonia commuting across the border each day for work. Sonia feels like Sebastian's deportation forced her to choose between staying spatially integrated in the US or staying together as a family: "I would mind less living in Mexico if it was a choice that I made, not that I was obligated to make this choice. Because we did try the whole weekend thing where [my daughter and I] would come and stay with him on the weekends, but it did not feel like we were a family when we were doing that."

As we sat together in the living room of their newly rented apartment in Mexico, Sonia showed me the binder full of certificates of achievement, letters of support, and other evidence they compiled for Sebastian's most recent deportation proceedings. She tearfully recounted that, at Sebastian's final hearing preceding his deportation, the judge said that he would have let Sebastian stay if it were up to him but, unfortunately, he had to follow the law. As a consolation, though, the judge told Sonia: "You all can go visit him." Sonia feels that this comment ignores all of the pain and hardship that the deportation brought to their family: "That's something that really stayed with me because if [the judge] had—I don't know if he had a family or not—but I don't think he would have liked someone to tell his kids or his wife, 'They can visit you.' Families are not to be visited, they are to be lived with." While Sonia tried to maintain her spatially integrated position in the US and a strong relationship with her deported husband, she ultimately felt that current laws required her to choose between the two. Choosing to prioritize the family she had created with Sebastian literally forced her and Dulce, their daughter, outside of the physical bounds of American society, as they have to live outside of the US in order to live together as a family.

As Julia recounted her family's five years of separation and exile, she described a similar disconnect between her personal freedom of movement and the limited movement she and her husband, Santiago, could enjoy together following his forced "voluntary removal" from the US just months after their wedding. For the first two years after Santiago's forced relocation to Mexico, when Julia was still finishing college in the US and she could only visit him during school vacations and summer break, Julia described her marital state as a premature widowhood. "We were husband and wife, but I felt like a widow because I was devoted to someone and I wore a ring. So I didn't—I definitely never felt single. I didn't feel divorced. I just felt like I loved someone who I never ever see." As hard as they tried to maintain close communication during their long months of separation—"we Skyped, we sent letters to each other"—the separation in and of itself "takes a toll on your relationship," Julia lamented. "You're not connected with the other person."

After Julia graduated, she moved full-time to Mexico to live with Santiago. But while she was finally able to share a home and her daily life with her husband, she was cut off from the close family relationships that she had always found so meaningful and central to her identity when living in the US. Because of Santiago's ten-year bar from legal reentry to the US, Julia could never be with Santiago and her parents and siblings at the same time—unless her family traveled to Mexico to visit, something only her parents had been able to do. Now, rather than feeling like a young widow, she felt more like an orphan. As Julia acknowledged, her freedom of travel between countries remains unrestricted—"I can come and go as I please"—but that freedom comes at a cost because she must always travel alone. "When I do go home every year, it's just, I'm alone. Everyone's there with their husbands or everything. And everyone knows I'll be coming alone." Santiago's government-mandated departure from the US resulted in a series of ongoing family separations for Julia—first from Santiago, then from her own family—that drove a deep wedge of loneliness into Julia's life that she simply could not overcome.

This loneliness, and the guilt Santiago felt at having "caused" this separation as a result of his "voluntary" removal from the US, directly contributed to Julia and Santiago's decision to divorce. I met them both for the first time and interviewed them together before they had finalized their decision to divorce, but after they had separated. While they both acknowledged that Santiago's banishment from the US was not the only contributing factor in weighing this decision, Julia felt that it was the most consequential one because of the relational void Santiago's deportation order and his subsequent departure from the US had created. As Julia choked back tears, she described a recent realization she had on another solo trip to visit her family, when she finally understood that "a lot of the emptiness that we've had in our relationship—or the hole that I have that cannot be filled—is just having, like, I have two separate lives that cannot come together. And it really does come down to that." Their inability to enjoy full "family unity" clouded every other aspect of their lives. Julia wondered aloud how things would be different if they had a marriage that "allowed" Santiago to be with her family and her family to be with his, something "normal marriages have," something they both expected to have when they married. Julia felt confident that, if they could have that kind of marriage, "we would both feel more complete. Santiago hurts and he carries a constant guilt because I'm here in Mexico, whether I like Mexico or not, that's just something I can't change for him. He made an action, and it has long effects and consequences for what happened. So he carries guilt, which causes a wedge in our relationship."

Although Julia acknowledged they had faced other issues in their relationship beyond Santiago's banishment from the US, she still felt that "if none of it was ever this way, if we never went through immigration or he would be legal and it was able to be ratified or whatever, I think we would be—have a happier marriage today. And that we—my needs would be more fulfilled because we'd be a lot closer on the same page than we are now." Santiago's expulsion from the US dealt a blow to their young relationship, leaving deep wounds that never healed. Julia concluded, "I think we've just been kicked when we were down a lot. And it's been hard to recover. And now we're at a crossroads where we don't know if we can keep trying, and it would have made all the difference, I think, if Santiago was able to stay inside the United States." Through their five-year family-separation saga, Julia and Santiago discovered firsthand that being able to live together *somewhere* was not the same as being able to live together in their country of choice. Santiago's forced spatial disintegration from the US meant separation for both Santiago *and* Julia from the life they had planned to build and the people with whom they wanted to build it.

This spatial disintegration not only interrupts daily life in the present, it also shapes the lives and futures of unauthorized families unable to live together within the US in ways that diminish key family relationships. For Mateo, who lives in Tijuana with his wife and children while waiting out a ten-year bar before he is eligible to apply for permanent residency, his inability to travel to the US physically and emotionally prevents him from being fully present in the lives and memories of his children who, from time to time, must travel to the US without him. "Like it or not," he said, "we live from our memories. All of our children, my children, are growing up, but there's a part of their lives in which I am not present. I am not a part of those memories, which is half of their life—their life in the United States. I am not there." When his wife and children are in the US without him, Mateo feels their absence viscerally, as he recognizes his erasure from their real-time experiences and from the memories those experiences create: "It is half of their lives, and I am present in their memories here, but there? Erased." We often talk about punitive immigration policies in macro-level terms—the ten-year bar, the millions deported every year—but for Mateo, it is the everyday, micro-level separation from his children that he experiences that has hurt the most. "You want to be with your children and you want to do so many things with your children, and the fact that you cannot be part of something in their lives hurts," Mateo concluded. "It hurts a lot."

In Mateo's view, his spatial disintegration from the US separates him from his family in the present and, to an extent, in the future, as he will be absent from the memories his children make without him. Similarly, his US citizen wife and children must constantly negotiate their spatial disintegration from either their country of citizenship or their husband and father. They adjust their movements accordingly, restricting their trips to the US in order to limit the amount of time Mateo is absent in their lives. But necessity—doctor's appointments, grocery shopping, work—often requires their separation and his regular "erasure" from their lives. And, of course, all of the time they do spend together as a family is time in which, by necessity, they must be spatially disintegrated from the US.

The banishment of one family member from the US also often leads to disruptions in the roles and responsibilities different family members can assume. Like Herlinda Serrano, whose inability to travel to the US kept her from fulfilling most of her duties as a stay-at-home mom, Chuy has found that deportation has rendered him incapable of doing many of the things he has always done as a husband and father, despite the fact that he continues to live with his family in Mexico. Being with his family, doing things with and for them, was a huge part of Chuy's identity. As a high-school dropout without any specific job training, his income was minimal and, at times, inconsistent. Chuy never had much money to buy things for his children, but he could always give them his time. Now the ability to give his family time has been taken from him, creating an identity crisis for Chuy, even as Esther has been forced to take on all of the tasks and trips that Chuy always managed before:

> ESTHER: He gets really, "Why you always in San Diego?!" but he doesn't understand I have to be in San Diego for the kids. I have to go my doctor's appointments and can't leave them alone a lot. In Oregon, we were always together. If I had something, he would take me. We were always more united over there than we are here, because here I have to cross over. I have to leave him here alone.
>
> CHUY: I would take the kids to school. I would take them to the doctor. I would take care of anything that had to do with the kids.
>
> ESTHER: And now it's me, me, me, and he feels like we have taken him out of that part, but it's like, I wish I could take you with me. I wish I could tell you, "Go with me here." But we can't.

While Chuy will sometimes ride in the car with his family as they wait to cross the border, they all know that he will not be able to travel with them to their destination and take care of them like he used to. His deportation stripped him of the duties he most proudly fulfilled as a husband and father. And this forced spatial separation has introduced disunity in Esther and Chuy's relationship, despite the fact that Esther and their children relocated outside the US in order to continue to live with Chuy. The inequality of movement among family members has introduced new tensions in their relationship that exacerbate the effects of Chuy's deportation and his spatial disintegration from the US,[10] contributing to his recent relapse in drug use, which has further alienated him from his wife and children.

Even though Salvador and Dina work together every day and live in homes only miles apart from each other, Salvador's visa cancellation (discussed in chapter 3) transformed their life from an "eternal picnic," spending evenings grilling in their backyard, into a stressful dance for Dina back and forth across borders as she takes her daughters to school in the US, goes to work in Mexico, travels back to the US to retrieve her daughters from school, takes them to Mexico to see their dad, and then drives them back across the border to the US to sleep. The time they used to spend together as a family has been replaced by this constant separation and reunification of their family straddled across the border. As I interviewed them in the small apartment they rent in Mexico, their children played and giggled outside while Salvador and Dina—seated closely to each other, holding hands, their shoulders leaning on one another—told me their story. I met them in a moment of happy, "normal," and seemingly natural family togetherness. But I will never forget the stark image Salvador drew for me as he explained his routine every night once Dina and the girls make their trip back across the border. As his home transforms abruptly each evening from one filled with movement, laughter, and energy to one that is empty and dark, the loneliness and depression hit Salvador each day like a ton of bricks. At first, he struggled to sleep, to find a way to end his day as the silence engulfed him. But he has since found a solution that has helped fill some of the emptiness. "I have a TV routine now," he explained. "There's a channel that plays *The Simpsons* all day long, so I just watch that." He turns the television on when they leave—a way to help drown out the deafening silence all around him—and sets it to turn off on its own at midnight, after he's asleep, "and that's how the day ends."

One spouse's rejection from the US pushes the other partner into a complicated situation in which they must either spatially dislocate from their country of citizenship or from their spouse. Families that decide to relocate outside the US have to abandon their friends, family, and communities with whom and in which they had built their lives. They forfeit jobs and other opportunities for economic and social advancement. And the sting of this rejection often pollutes their lives outside the US, weakening their relationships as a family and inhibiting the development of strong relationships to their new cities and countries of residence even as their ties to family "back home" grow increasingly strained.

Couples living outside the US who have never had status or lived together within the US also experience spatial disintegration, from place and from each other. Antonio commutes across the border every day to work at the naval shipyard in San Diego. His wife, Lizeth, has only been to the US once on a school trip to the zoo in fifth grade (students without visas were given a one-day pass to attend). Both admit to being painfully shy, something that might have helped their relationship to blossom, having met over the internet, spending much of their early courtship "chatting" via text message. Even now that they live together in the same home, they spend most of the day communicating through text messages while Antonio is at work across the border. They have not yet been able to save enough money to apply for Lizeth's residency, and they also need approval from Lizeth's former partner in order to sponsor her son for residency, too.

As we sat around their kitchen table discussing their situation, I could sense both partners' frustration at their inability to truly share in each other's lives. While Antonio hopes to begin their application process in the next year or two, he struggles in the meantime to spend so much of his daily life in a place that is unknown to his wife. This loneliness manifests in his inability to show his wife where he works, take her to the company holiday party, or travel with her around the US. He talks about how Lizeth is constantly puzzled by what he does at work and how he could be on the clock at work and using his phone to send messages to her at the same time. He would like to show her where he works and explain the answer to her question but, since he has not been able to afford to sponsor her for a visa, this huge part of his life and his identity remains inaccessible to her. Antonio explained, "I would like to take her and show her what I do, my work, my friends, my coworkers and all of that." Antonio's inability to fulfill this basic desire to share his work life with Lizeth, something his coworkers can do but he cannot, has introduced cleavages in their relationship that add emotional distance to the physical separation they daily endure. Determined not to experience this separation any longer than necessary, Antonio declared, "That's why I decided that now, no matter what, we are going to get her papers in order this year." Assuming Antonio can meet the minimum income thresholds for sponsorship and save up enough money to afford the green card application for Lizeth, this spatial incongruence in their lives can be resolved. But, in the meantime, they both spend their days negotiating the incomplete nature of their relationship that stems from Antonio's spatial disintegration from the US and Lizeth's inability to travel there.

Karen and Jo are also hopeful they will eventually be able to live together in the US, even while currently enduring a very difficult process of daily separation. Karen is a mellow, "old soul" who has a keen ability to help you feel at ease, even in moments of high stress; Jo lives her art—sporting a half-shaved head / half-shoulder-length hair with bangs hairstyle on the day we met—and oozes a self-assured confidence that immediately drew Karen to her. They met in Oaxaca while Karen was doing research for her PhD and Jo was working as an artist and activist with a local collective. They moved in together in Oaxaca, sharing nearly every facet of their lives together for more than a year, but since they recently moved to Tijuana so that Karen could participate in a research fellowship in San Diego, they now experience daily spatial disintegration. Jo has never applied for a tourist visa or any travel permit to the US, and they were advised that Jo would have a stronger chance of legal admission through a fiancée visa rather than a tourist visa. Unfortunately, the fiancé(e) visa process lasts much longer and therefore Jo has been unable to travel with Karen to meet her family and coworkers living just miles from their Tijuana apartment. When I interviewed them in their apartment in mid-December, these tensions had increased with the impending visit of Karen's family to her brother's house in San Diego, where most of the family events over the holidays would occur and where Jo would not be able to attend. Karen wants to spend time with her family, but she "also really had planned to spend the holidays with Jo—like our first Christmas together. And neither of us are super religious, but it's just about passing that time together, having a break, and whatever." Karen's family never asked her what her holiday plans entailed before they decided they would visit, "so it's been stressful for the two of us to just try to figure out the best way to manage a very un-ideal situation given that Jo won't be able to cross over to visit my family there, that they may be able to come here once but to ask them to do more than that would be hard."

After four months of experiencing daily dislocation and disintegration while Karen commuted to her fellowship in San Diego, the holiday break seemed like the first real opportunity they would have when they could spend every day together, just like they used to. Karen's family's plans ruined all of that. Karen continued, "It just breaks my heart that we're dealing with this and that Jo is unable to share in that part of my life and that part of her world and being so close but not be able to go over. The fact that I can take our dog to work and I can't bring her. It's just heartbreaking." As Karen explained the situation to me, she reached out to hold Jo's hand and offer her some comfort. For Karen, this complication means she will be making family memories alone; but for Jo, her inability to travel to the US means she will not be making family memories at all. While Karen and Jo will likely be able to live together in the US and both move freely between the US and Mexico eventually, this cross-border living situation—in which the life they share is in a city unfamiliar to both and much of Karen's daily work and interactions happen in spaces inaccessible to Jo—has hindered their ability to develop and strengthen relationships with key individuals (parents, friends) and with each other.

For couples waiting for a visa application to be processed or unable to afford a visa application but also unable to live together, this forced spatial disintegration also often means missing out on key events in family life. Carlos and Estrella moved into a small house next to my in-laws in Mexico when they were newlyweds. Carlos, a quiet, determined young man in his early twenties who lights up every time Estrella enters the room, commuted across the border every day for work, which was quite time-consuming. But as soon as he was home, he and Estrella—who seems reserved when you first meet her, but can talk your ear off once her initial reservation wears off—were inseparable. Less than a year into their marriage, they got pregnant and realized that, on Carlos's minimum-wage salary, there was no way they would be able to afford Estrella's permanent residency application and a new baby. So Carlos moved back to the US to take a job with a high-enough income to qualify to sponsor Estrella for permanent residency, and Estrella moved back in with her parents in Michoacán, thousands of miles away.

When I interviewed Carlos at his parents' home in the States, where he had been living while he worked to save up for their family reunification application, we talked about what it felt like to be separated from Estrella and to miss the birth of his daughter and the first nine months of her life. During the time that Carlos and Estrella were separated, Carlos's brother and his wife—who live in the same town as Carlos and his parents—had their first child, which became a constant and painful reminder for Carlos of all that he was missing with his own family. "I try to avoid those moments with his family," Carlos told me, explaining that his parents and siblings "get upset pretty bad" when he fails to attend a family gathering, "but I don't think they understand what I feel, you know?" It wasn't about not liking his sister-in-law or the baby, he said. In fact, "I like the baby, you know, it's my nephew. I like to hold him and I have fun with him and stuff. But you still have that thought in the back of your mind, '*Man, I can hold my nephew, but I can't hold my own daughter.*' It's hard." Seeing his brother enjoy the family togetherness Carlos could not yet experience caused him a deep pain he could not explain and that his family seemingly could not grasp, adding an extra layer of family separation and disintegration beyond his physical separation from Estrella and their baby girl.

As Carlos and Estrella know all too well, US family reunification processes often produce extended and painful family separations, even for families ultimately approved for reunification.[11] While citizens never lose their right to live in and move freely within the US, their spouses' inability to do so results in spatial disintegration for all family members. Until that (generally) years-long process is complete, these families, like the families who have been formally barred from the US, also experience territorial exclusion, lost opportunity, and strained relationships, both within and beyond their immediate family.

Spatial Isolation

Mixed-citizenship families living together without status within the United States may be living in their preferred country, but they often face significant restrictions on the cities or even neighborhoods in which they can safely reside. Research on the spatial integration of immigrant and ethnic minority groups suggests that US residential neighborhoods remain segregated by race, immigration status, and, to some extent, income.[12] For mixed-race and mixed-nativity couples, spatial (dis)integration can both be a cause and a consequence of marriage across racial, ethnic, and citizenship lines.[13] In general, scholars have found greater spatial integration—which generally comes with more residential diversity, reduced neighborhood poverty, and greater neighborhood resources and amenities—among both mixed-race and mixed-nativity couples compared to same-race (non-White) and foreign-born couples.[14] These data suggest that mixed-citizenship couples living within the US may have some control over the neighborhoods in which they reside, but some research suggests that, for mixed-race and mixed-citizenship couples, where couples end up living is affected by structural forces, not just preference.[15] Unauthorized couples face additional barriers to residential mobility due to their vulnerability to immigration enforcement and the extent to which settlement in a less diverse neighborhood could increase their visibility to immigration agents.[16]

The legal and social contexts of neighborhoods, cities, counties, and states also shape spatial (dis)integration experiences for mixed-citizenship couples.[17] Many local and state governing bodies have passed policies targeting unauthorized immigrants, and these laws create significant barriers for unauthorized families' spatial integration within such restrictive communities.[18] Unauthorized immigrants have developed a number of strategies to minimize risk of detection by immigration authorities, including adapting clothing and behavior to mimic the local nonimmigrant population, using social networks to learn about and avoid police checkpoints, and avoiding unnecessary travel outside the home.[19] While some of these strategies may ultimately contribute to immigrant integration along other dimensions,[20] most strategies spatially isolate unauthorized immigrants and their family members from their local and national communities because they lack the necessary freedom of movement to meaningfully integrate.

Unauthorized families in my sample who are living in the US feel spatially isolated, limited in their day-to-day movement and fearful of traveling (or moving) outside of their familiar local context. Families discuss limiting travel outside of their regular routes and feeling geographically bound to neighborhoods close to the unauthorized spouse's place of work in order to reduce the risk of detection. Most families also avoid travel outside of their state (and even city) of residence, as they feel such travel involves too many risks of exposure. And, of course, they can never leave US territory together, unless they plan to stay outside the US for at least ten years.[21]

When I first interviewed Juliette and Tenoch in 2012, their young daughter, who was just learning to walk, toddled around us as we chatted in their living room. At the time, Juliette identified Tenoch's inability to travel and live outside of the US as one of the biggest impediments they faced as an unauthorized family. Juliette expressed hope that, once Tenoch could "leave and return easily," they could live an "easier, more peaceful" life together outside the US. "Because here, it is always about money, money, money; pay the bills and debts that you have. This consumes life, and you can't enjoy life." Juliette desperately wanted to see the world with Tenoch, especially to see the world he left behind when he migrated to the US years before. She pined for a day when they could be free to go where they wanted and free from the financial burdens of life in the US as an unauthorized family. They had dreams of traveling the world, but the truth is that, as long as Tenoch remained unauthorized, they rarely traveled beyond a forty-mile radius as a family because they felt Tenoch's risk of detection and deportation increased whenever he ventured beyond the neighborhoods and routes they knew best. Now that Tenoch has finally acquired LPR status (seven years after they married and first began applying to adjust his status), they have more freedom of movement. But the debt they incurred from years of immigration applications and legal fees, having to take lower-paying jobs, and paying rent instead of a mortgage has left them tethered to their life in the US and continuing to struggle to spatially and economically integrate in ways they had not anticipated. This debt also prolonged their spatial and social isolation from family, friends, and opportunities in Mexico, despite the fact that they all can now, in theory, finally travel there together.

Unauthorized status also complicates families' ability to pursue opportunities for socioeconomic advancement. In many cases, couples must choose between pursuing opportunity and nourishing intimate relationships. Carmela and Rodrigo live in California just miles from the US-Mexico border, but Rodrigo has not been back to his country of origin (Mexico) since he arrived in the US in 1999. Life in this border region includes additional limitations on Rodrigo's movement, as the Border Patrol roams freely within fifty miles of the border and runs checkpoints on most routes enabling travel beyond that range. To minimize the risk of detection, Rodrigo cannot travel beyond San Diego County and must be careful in selecting his routes of travel within the county.

When I met Carmela and Rodrigo in a cafe near their home, I immediately felt their chemistry—the way they finished each other's sentences and could anticipate each other's thoughts and punchlines—and tried my hardest to keep up. They both talk a mile a minute, sometimes bursting out in laughter mid-sentence as they remember an old story or an inside joke that they then try to explain to me, as I smile and nod and keep glancing back and forth between the two of them, trying to figure out who is going to take the conversation and run with it next. Carmela, who wants to pursue a PhD in engineering, has been debating how to deal with Rodrigo's unauthorized status. There are only three PhD programs in her specialty, and they are all multiple states away. Traveling to any of these schools would expose Rodrigo to a greater risk of deportation, both on the journey and, potentially, in the new, less diverse communities in which these universities are located.

As soon as Carmela decided to apply for the doctoral programs, she began the process of applying for an Extreme Hardship Waiver to facilitate Rodrigo's status adjustment to permanent residency. But there is no guarantee that his application will be approved, especially in time for the start of Carmela's doctoral program. Carmela explained that, after talking through "the different scenarios that could happen," they had decided that, at least initially, Rodrigo would stay behind. "I told him, 'If they accept me out of state, you stay here and I'll go by myself first to see what the atmosphere is like, because if I don't like it, I'm not going to stay there forever. Or if there is a lot of discrimination"—something she fears is likely given the rural, supermajority White communities in which her target doctoral programs were situated—"let me see what it feels like there, and then I'll tell you if it's yes or no. Or I'll come back, or you'll come to me." But Carmela coming back would be a lot easier than Rodrigo's coming to her. "If you come to me," she continued, "I don't know if you'll have your papers yet or not. And if you don't, you will have to find a way to figure out how to get there."

Carmela wants to return to California after she finishes her degree, so the deportation threats that they would face if Rodrigo moves with her feel especially risky. If they will only be away for a few years, is it worth leaving his job, a geography he knows and feels save traveling within, and his ethno-racial "invisibility" as one of many Latinx Southern Californians to go to a place that might be unwelcoming to Brown people—especially an unauthorized immigrant from Mexico? Even though the alternative is Carmela and their son's extended separation from Rodrigo, they both felt that the answer to that question, at least initially, was no. While Carmela is hopeful that Rodrigo's permanent residency application will ultimately be approved and he will be allowed to travel freely and work legally, she is also realistic about the implications of his current unauthorized status on their ability to move as a family for her doctoral program. In this instance, she has made the painful decision to sacrifice the closeness and quality of her relationship with Rodrigo in order to pursue an opportunity that could change her life and her family's future for the better.

For couples like Carmela and Rodrigo, even though they are able to live in the US together, their ability to live in the same home in the same city together is often limited to one particular geographic region rather than the country as a whole.[22] Christian and Sharon were thrown back into this "open-air prison" after Sharon's citizenship application was denied and her residency revoked based on an unintentional error on her application. Sharon came to the US from Mexico with her parents at age 13; by the time she met Christian while in college, she had adapted to life in the shadows. About two years into their marriage, they applied to adjust Sharon's status, which meant Sharon had to leave the US and wait months to find out if she qualified for the Extreme Hardship Waiver.[23] Seemingly miraculously, USCIS granted Sharon the waiver and she became a permanent resident. As soon as she could apply for citizenship, she did. Unfortunately, they completed the application without professional assistance and a simple error resulted in the denial of her citizenship request, the revocation of her residency, and a permanent bar from any legal status in the US.[24] According to Christian, being thrust back into unauthorized status has "changed our trajectory and our lives." They had planned to serve as missionaries overseas, but now they can no longer leave the country.

As the three of us chatted in a noisy restaurant taking turns holding our two wiggling babies, Christian explained, "we fully realize that any day we could get that letter in the mail that says, 'Appear in immigration court,'" though he expressed in our interview (pre–Trump administration) that he hopes "she's a little bit lower on the priority deportation list." They have not let the threat of deportation completely derail their lives—Christian still works, Sharon is in graduate school, and they just had their first child seven months ago—but they have been forced to make some significant adjustments to the way they move within US borders and obviously no longer travel outside of them. "At this point," Christian explained, "we don't travel internationally. We don't go to Mexico. We've been advised that she could very well be detained at the border and deported. It's changed a lot for us." In addition to not traveling internationally, they also avoid traveling on planes, as they feel Sharon would be at greater risk of apprehension. And, if at some point Sharon is deported, she could never legally reenter the United States, where all of her immediate family and much of her extended family (as well as Christian's entire family) still live. Right now, their unauthorized status has prevented them from pursuing some of their shared dreams. But this spatial isolation from the world beyond the US is preferable to the more extreme spatial and relational disintegration they would experience if forced to leave the US permanently.

"We felt trapped," June explained. Now that Stefan received the Extreme Hardship Waiver and is a permanent resident, their lives have completely changed. Stefan can work in a much better, higher-paying job in the wealthiest neighborhood in San Diego that, at forty-plus minutes away, was too risky to travel to when he was unauthorized. Stefan's new legal status has been physically and psychologically liberating for him. "It is the whole world for me," he said, "the whole thing." For years, Stefan has wanted to take his children camping (something June has no interest in doing with them), but he was always "afraid that if I go, something would happen." His fear that he would be pulled over or stopped at an immigration checkpoint and his children would be left alone without him held him back because he "always had in my mind, 'I can't do that. I can't do that.'" Now that he is a permanent resident, "I don't feel like that," Stefan says. Now he goes camping or takes his kids to the beach, "and I go and I feel free."

Unauthorized couples in the US feel trapped, within the confines of US territory but, for most couples, even more narrowly within their communities of residence. Fears of DUI and driver's license checkpoints or just being pulled over by police lead families to restrict their movement within their communities. And many couples have turned down better housing or work options because these opportunities would require them to move to a new city or expose themselves to more risk through a longer commute. Although they are technically able to live in their country (and, often, city) of preference, these couples sacrifice many opportunities and experience significant strain on their relationships with each other and with other loved ones due to their restricted movement and the spatial limitations associated with unauthorized status.

Spatial Integration
Mixed-citizenship families who have been able to choose where to live because of their family-level legal immigration status express extreme satisfaction with their living conditions and their access to both

countries. Enrique and Carolina both grew up in upper-class political families in Baja California. Carolina always had a visa enabling her to travel to the US as a tourist; Enrique attended prep school and college in the US and has always lived a binational life. He and Carolina planned to continue living in Mexico after their marriage, but two conditions pushed them to consider living on the northern side of the border instead. First, Enrique had recently changed jobs and his new position required him to travel regularly to different parts of Mexico and the US. Carolina felt that, with two young children, she would be more safe and secure caring for them alone in the US than in Mexico. Second, in order for Carolina to meet the requirements of permanent residency, she would need to live in the US for at least six months of every year of her residency, which would last at least three years before she could apply for citizenship. They saw a move to San Diego as an opportunity for Carolina to qualify for citizenship while living a more comfortable and secure life. As Enrique put it, "I say that living here in San Diego, we have the best of the two worlds. We go to Mexico a lot. I like to eat street food, and we get to enjoy Mexico. We go to Ensenada, and we go to Mexicali. Then we come here, and we come to the security. Sometimes we forget to close the front door. In Mexico, you would never do that." And now, years after Carolina naturalized as a US citizen, they continue to live in the US (despite the higher cost of living), because they feel it is the safest and best environment for them, offering their family the most opportunities for success over the long term.

Authorized couples see their multiple citizenships as an asset, doubling their access to opportunities and relationships while liberating them to choose where to live based on their current and future priorities. Mayela and Will also enjoy being able to visit El Salvador while living in the US, where they have chosen to build a life together. Mayela came to the US on a tourist visa and later acquired Temporary Protected Status (TPS) as a result of the ongoing civil war in El Salvador. She obtained permanent residency and, later, citizenship, through her marriage to Will. Mayela and Will have lived in a number of cities in the western US during their marriage as they finished college, Will attended dental school, and, later, he began a private practice. Even though Will speaks fluent Spanish and they have traveled throughout Central America together, Mayela is confident that they are living where they want to be, "especially now. We've traveled back to El Salvador a few times and just more recently with [our daughter]. I think that my husband and I could get used to a life down there if we had to move down there, like if we *had* to go back," but as long as they have a choice, Mayela says, "I wouldn't want to move back, for the safety of my children. So, I don't see myself ever wanting to leave here or anything like that."

Lola also feels a similar satisfaction with her home in the US. Lola's husband, Thomas, died unexpectedly three years ago due to a number of chronic health issues, including depression. Lola, who is both soft-spoken and quick-witted, was a permanent resident at the time that Thomas died, working at the Mexican restaurant her sister and brother-in-law own. Lola, a trained lawyer in Mexico, could have chosen to go back to Mexico and pursue a career there rather than starting to train as a paralegal in the US. But Lola realized that she had adapted to her American life in ways that made her feel more at home in the US than in Mexico. She also felt that, even after losing her husband, the US could offer her and her teenaged daughter more opportunities than a life in Mexico could. To honor Thomas's wish for her to become a US citizen, she recently underwent the naturalization process. As she explained to me, now, more than ever, "I feel like this is where I belong. When I recently went to Mexico, I remembered a lot of things from when I lived there, but I still felt like I needed to come back here, because my home is here. I am making my life here now." After living in the US for so long, and especially now that she is a US citizen, she feels that "while I'm here, I am more American—not that I'm American because of these papers, but in the way I'm getting used to so many things here in the United States." Despite the loss of her husband, Lola feels more at home in the US than in Mexico and sees her future life as one based on American soil, rooted in the home and life she has built in the US over the last decade.

Many of the authorized families I interviewed emphasized the importance of living in the right place in shaping their socioeconomic opportunities and their general familial happiness. Lucy and Javier waited over a year for Javier's fiancé visa because they knew that life in the US had more to offer both of them than life in El Salvador. Additionally, Lucy has type 1 diabetes and, even though she is a nurse and fully capable of monitoring her condition, she felt that it was also necessary for them to live in the US so she could maintain easier access to high-quality healthcare. When I first interviewed Lucy—a friend I had known long before she met Javier—I already knew her as a quintessential optimist with a contagious laugh, one I heard many times during our conversation that day. She remained optimistic, in spite of the year-long wait and separation they were experiencing as USCIS processed Javier's fiancé visa, but I could tell that the stress—and the uncertainty of when, if ever, the wait would end—had taken a toll on her. Luckily, Javier's visa finally came through shortly after our interview, and they were able to establish their family and their lives in their country of preference, just a few miles away from Lucy's parents and her childhood home.

Jessica and Julio met at a salsa dancing class in Puerto Vallarta when Jessica was vacationing there. While she had planned to move to Italy for an internship after her trip, she extended her time in Vallarta and moved in with Julio. As she began to contemplate staying in Vallarta long term, she realized that there were not many career opportunities for her there beyond working in the tourism industry or teaching English. So she worked in Mexico City for a couple of years and then moved back to the US to work and study. Julio, who owns a successful construction and supply business in Vallarta, was never interested in or willing to leave his family and his business. But, because they both enjoy freedom of movement in the US and Mexico, they have found a way to keep their relationship strong while pursuing work and educational opportunities as they arise. Jessica and Julio have been together now for fourteen years, but they have never lived together full-time. Rather, they each spend about one-third of the year visiting the other, cumulatively spending about eight months out of the year together. While they admit that this arrangement can be stressful at times—Jessica says that "obviously, it's unreasonable and it's not easy" to have a life that takes place in two different countries—they are pleased to have found a way to be a couple and pursue their careers. "I think for us," Jessica explained, "thinking that Julio would give up his family and all of his work—which is important to him—to be in the US, or that I would give up the opportunity that I have to have a career myself to be in Vallarta, which is a lovely place but basically it's a tourist kind of place, that would put a lot of strain on our relationship, too. I think that the opportunity to live back and forth between the two places creates a lot of richness in our lives as well." While it may seem to some like an "unreasonable" arrangement, for Jessica and Julio, this option of splitting life between their two worlds has worked best for them.

A number of other authorized and "pre-authorized" couples I interviewed enjoy the benefits of free movement within both of their countries of citizenship, even if they choose to spend most of their time living outside the US.[25] Joanna and Joel could easily qualify for family reunification, but because Joel is well established in his career as a banker in Mexico, they choose to continue to live full-time in Mexico knowing they can travel together to the US whenever they would like. Jaime and Rita have lived for extended periods of time in both the US and in Mexico; they prefer life in Mexico more and are happy that family reunification and naturalization have enabled them to live in Mexico and travel to the US as often as they choose, which frequently means crossing the border multiple times a day. Couples like these who have the legal permission to live freely in both of their countries of citizenship can pursue opportunity without having to sacrifice their relationships, all the while reaping extra benefits from regularly enjoying both countries and cultures.

Other authorized couples also see their status as an insurance policy against separation and spatial isolation and disintegration. Aylin and Jared, who describe themselves as an "international bourgeois" couple, decided to get married to ensure that they could "be in the country of our choosing together at the same time." Following the 2016 election, Aylin's student visa for her graduate studies suddenly felt very temporary and precarious, which prompted their decision to finally get married, as discussed in chapter 3. "We got married because of the scare that I would not be able to stay here," Aylin explained, something she had not ever worried about before Donald Trump's election to the presidency. Jared elaborated that their decision was not just about making sure Aylin could stay in the US, but also about securing their ability to live and travel together more broadly: "The description I always give is because we wanted to be able *to be in the country of our choosing together at the same time,* so if that country was Mexico, we wanted to be able to be there, but if we were in Mexico and wanted to come visit my family, we wanted to be able to do that without it being a problem." Recognizing her privileged status within Mexican society and as a student visa-holder in the US, Aylin confessed that the fear and uncertainty they felt was "a world that neither him nor myself had ever inhabited, or just that possibility never crossed my mind." Before the 2016 election, being together "was always something that was achievable. Of course," Aylin continued, "I come from a family that works a lot, that has property. Then, all of the sudden, I was like, 'Oh man, this is so terrifying!' Then again, getting married allows us now to be in that super-privileged world" of not facing the imminent threat of their potential separation again. Aylin and Jared had never worried about deportation or separation, their combined privilege sheltering them from the harsh realities unauthorized immigrants regularly face. Now Aylin's green card and access to citizenship will insulate them from those fears once again, despite the threats that the Trump administration made to temporary and unauthorized immigrants' ability to stay in the US.

In addition to having the security and flexibility of choosing the country in which they would like to live, Aylin and Jared—along with the other couples I interviewed with legal status living both within and outside the US—are living in the communities and cities where they want to live. None of these couples mentioned barriers to spatial integration or an inability to move to their community of choice within their current city, throughout the US, or outside the US. For each of these couples, being part of a mixed-citizenship marriage means *twice as many* options and opportunities with regard to their goals to live, work, and thrive together. And their relationships with friends and family living in both countries have grown stronger as they freely travel between countries and create connections between the different geographies of their lives, rather than being split between them or forced to choose one place or the other.

Overall, an examination of family-level spatial integration reveals the limits of the individual-level citizenship logic employed by the majority in *Kerry v. Din*.[26] Although the US Supreme Court claims that a citizen's rights are not jeopardized by the denial of those same rights to her spouse, mixed-citizenship couples' experiences demonstrate the shortsightedness and incomplete nature of that claim. Spatial integration occurs at the household level—the family level—and the inability of one family member to physically (and legally) reside and move within the country directly affects all family members' ability to do so. Family-level (non)citizenship status affects individual and family integration beyond space, place, and physical access to US society. It also shapes families' access to key social institutions—including higher education, the labor market, and the home mortgage market—which serves to facilitate integration across a broad swath of outcomes. In chapter 5, I examine the role of family-level status in mediating individual and familial structural integration and the consequences of limited access to basic social institutions for citizens and noncitizens alike.

Institutional (In)Visibility

I MET JUNE AND STEFAN at their home on a breezy, sunny Southern California day in early December. We talked outside in their front yard as their five children, ranging in ages from eighteen months to nine years old, climbed the trees, played tag, and jumped on their trampoline. June has lived her entire life in her grandfather's modest home in a small, lower-income city near San Diego. June's grandparents adopted and raised her and, while they were not financially well-off, they provided June with a stable and loving childhood. At the age of 19, June began seriously dating Stefan, a coworker at her new retail sales job. Initially, her grandfather was wary, fearing that Stefan "only wanted papers." But those fears dissipated as he got to know Stefan, and now June claims her grandfather "probably likes him more than me." Although he was initially skeptical of their serious relationship at such a young age, June's grandfather has grown to love Stefan and happily made room in his home for June and Stefan and their growing family.

As detailed in chapter 3, June and Stefan had been married nine years with five children when USCIS finally approved Stefan's permanent residency application. Before he gained legal status, Stefan worked seven days a week in three low-paying jobs to help cover their expenses while June stayed home with the kids. He made sure his jobs were all close to home to minimize his risk of being stopped by police or Border Patrol agents, who roam freely throughout San Diego County. They felt lucky to be able to live with June's grandfather, since they could not qualify to own their own home due to Stefan's low income and their joint lack of good credit and earning power. For a decade, their day-to-day lives were marked by the limitations they faced because of Stefan's lack of status and the droning fear of his potential deportation.

Even though Stefan had been granted permanent residency just three months before our interview, the effects of that change had been immediate and dramatic for both of them. "It's just crazy!" June exclaimed. "Now we feel that all the doors are open and we can do anything." Before Stefan's change in immigration status, "not being a resident to work here legally" impeded their ability to progress as a family, but "now he got a way better job" with "a lot of benefits, a lot of perks." This positive change in Stefan's work prospects and conditions—increased salary, new benefits, better hours, etc.—has been a huge relief for them both, as June acknowledged that "the main reason" they applied to adjust his status and kept working at it for so long was to help Stefan get a better job and improve his ability to provide for their family.

In only three months, Stefan's new legal status had already significantly improved their lives by qualifying him for work in the legal labor market. But the benefits of his new immigration status extended far beyond better employment opportunities, opening doors in every aspect of their lives. The stark difference in their opportunities and new access to seemingly basic institutions stood out most to them as they pondered the impact of Stefan's adjustment of status. "I value it more," June said, referring to Stefan's new status as a permanent resident. "It is a gift not everybody gets to have." Having lived without that status and the institutional access that comes with it for so long, June felt like they had just been given the key to a treasure chest. "To me, it is like gold: the Social Security number, the fact that he can get any job now, and do anything and travel and that kind of stuff is like gold." Stefan nodded in support as June continued, "Everything seems so much more open, the opportunities. Like he said, I feel really super rich, too. Like I am on top of the world." Not rich monetarily, she added, but rich in ways that, after all the years of limitations and closed doors they faced, felt even more important: "We are rich in opportunities." Stefan agreed, reiterating that they now enjoy a freedom they had never experienced together before. "You felt trapped, no?" June asked Stefan. "Yeah," Stefan affirmed, "I felt like, 'You can't do nothing.' The thing is that you have faith, but something is going to go wrong. And now I don't feel like that. I just go with my kids" wherever they want—camping, to the beach—"and I go, and I feel free." Picking up on Stefan's description of feeling free, June elaborated, "That is what it is. It's like a lot of weight lifted off. Freedom, that is what we feel right now. Free. Because we felt trapped. Now we are free."

With legal authorization for employment, Stefan has secured a job with better pay and regular hours, reducing financial stress in their relationship and giving him more time to spend with his family. They finally have good health insurance for themselves and their children. And they can go camping now without worrying about whether Stefan might be stopped by immigration agents. For the first time in their relationship, the future they see before them is full of opportunities rather than closed doors.

Structural integration can take on many forms, and it includes access to important social, cultural, economic, and governmental institutions that enable integration and inclusion in other dimensions of local and national social life. In this chapter, I define structural integration as access to the educational, economic, legal, and bureaucratic institutions that regulate nearly every aspect of daily life. Because most of these institutions manage access based on specific individual-level qualifications and documents, legal immigration status is a primary determinant in shaping individual and family-level structural integration. Lacking a Social Security number or state-issued ID, such as a driver's license, can make everything from opening a bank account to enrolling for college classes much more difficult. Basic but crucial processes, like building up strong credit, can be nearly impossible for individuals without the proper state-validated identification documents.

Limited access to one social institution affects access to other institutions and structures, too. For example, all kinds of institutions use credit scores to inform their decision to hire, lend to, rent to, or otherwise trust an individual. Having no or low credit leads to increased expenses—in the form of higher interest rates and security deposits—and decreased cash flow—in the form of lower-paying jobs and limited access to loans.[1] Unauthorized immigrants in particular, but also noncitizens with temporary legal nonimmigrant status (like students), face these barriers to access across multiple institutional and social settings.[2] In nearly all cases, lawful permanent residents and citizens do not.

As a result, families with legal immigration status in the US can access many of the most important structures for social, economic, and cultural integration, including higher education, banking systems, and the full labor market.[3] Due to their ease of access in both countries to quality K–12 and postsecondary education, the labor market, healthcare, and more, many authorized families I interviewed did not specifically recognize institutional inclusion as an important benefit of their mixed-citizenship status. Those who most clearly acknowledged and articulated this benefit were families who had previous unauthorized status in the US and had successfully adjusted to legal immigration status. As June described it, "Now we feel that all the doors are open and we can do anything." The change, she said, was immediate and completely liberating: "We felt trapped. Now we are free."

In this chapter, I focus on the experiences of currently and formerly unauthorized families to examine the extent to which legal status mediates structural integration for individuals and families. I contrast the experiences of newly authorized families with those of unauthorized families, who continue to face significant hurdles to structural integration and are often forced to make excruciatingly painful decisions—like enduring long-term family separation—in order for citizen family members to retain their structural and institutional access. In my analysis, I find that families' structural integration hinges on the ability of all family members to gain entry to economic, educational, and bureaucratic (e.g., legal, welfare) institutions.

Citizens with authorized spouses can accelerate their partners' structural integration by capitalizing on their own familiarity with and experience navigating these institutions. But not all mixed-citizenship couples experience this same direct trajectory toward social, economic, and political inclusion. As Milton Gordon, an early scholar of immigrant incorporation, noted, "A vastly important and largely neglected sociological point about mixed marriages . . . is in the social structures the intermarried couples and their children incorporate themselves."[4] Many families face continued barriers to structural incorporation into the

American mainstream and are forced to navigate around those barriers or face exclusion from that sector of society. Consequently, the relationship between the citizen and her state grows increasingly strained when she is married to an unauthorized immigrant. While her individual access to most, if not all, social institutions remains intact, her partner's limited access to—or even exclusion from—those same institutions complicates both spouses' ability to progress individually and as a family. And citizens tend to experience that change in access—finding doors closed to their family that had previously been opened to them as individuals—more bitterly than their unauthorized spouses, who had always known those doors were closed to them. This shift in experiences forces many US citizens in unauthorized families to reconsider their place in American society and the extent to which they truly belong.

Educational (Dis)Integration

Unauthorized immigrants face many barriers to accessing higher-education institutions in the United States, and these barriers to access create significant, long-term disadvantages for unauthorized immigrants and their family members.[5] Obstacles to higher education present considerable challenges to unauthorized immigrants, especially for 1.5-generation immigrants[6] who arrived in their youth and studied in American primary and secondary schools.[7] While the 1982 *Plyler v. Doe* Supreme Court decision mandated that unauthorized children have unhindered access to K–12 schools in the US, it did not eliminate barriers to accessing higher education or occupations in which immigrants could apply the skills and knowledge they acquire through their studies.[8] Regardless of whether they are able to pursue postsecondary education, most 1.5-generation unauthorized immigrants find that their immigration status works as a "master status" to limit their short- and long-term opportunities.[9]

Among the unauthorized and formerly unauthorized couples I interviewed, seven had a noncitizen spouse who had arrived in the US as a child or youth and attended American elementary and/or secondary schools. Every one of these couples cited limited access to higher education as having shaped their future in significant ways, whether they pursued schooling after high school.[10] Because education so closely tracks with socioeconomic status, unauthorized immigrants' inability to access postsecondary education directly affected their families' economic stability. For these unauthorized immigrant youth, termed "early exiters" by sociologist Roberto Gonzales, exclusion from educational opportunity had practical and psychological effects, as noncitizen spouses carried the long-term economic and cultural consequences of only having a high-school education. "College-goers" enjoyed the satisfaction and cultural capital of being college-educated, but they could not transform that education into professional opportunity without also acquiring legal status.

The "early exiters" in my sample did not pursue education past high school after recognizing that their unauthorized status would prevent them from utilizing additional education to access better job opportunities. Ramses and Chuy felt that their futures had been decided for them long before they ever got to choose how they would play out. Both were brought to the US as small children, and both ended up getting involved in gangs as young teens in search of protection and a sense of belonging. Neither Chuy nor Ramses ever received support and encouragement from teachers to pursue a different path. Before age 20, each had children to support and few educational or career prospects. They both sought employment, but found few opportunities outside of construction and entry-level service jobs. As they struggled to provide for their young families, they also found themselves increasingly under surveillance by the police and threatened with potential incarceration and/or deportation.[11] Ultimately, both Ramses ("voluntary removal") and Chuy (deportation) were forced to leave the US.

Unauthorized immigrants who choose to push against barriers to pursue higher education (Gonzales's "college-goers") find most doors closed to them during and following their collegiate studies, too. They face challenges in applying for, paying for, and completing college, bogged down by out-of-state tuition rates, ineligibility for federally funded grants and loans, disqualification from most public and private scholarships, restricted travel, an inability to secure privately funded tuition loans, and no access to the legal labor market to help them earn enough to pay for tuition, food, and housing.[12] Sebastian, who immigrated to the US at age 15 to reunite with his parents after years of separation, had a much more positive experience in high school than Chuy and Ramses, learning English rapidly and earning a number of honors and awards. But he quickly discovered that, despite his accomplishments, he could not access most postsecondary education opportunities. He faced higher tuition rates and did not qualify for most scholarships, grants, and loans. He also would not be hired for most jobs that require a college degree, even if he managed to obtain one. He enrolled in the local community college, but soon dropped out after recognizing the long-term limitation his status presented and began working in construction instead. Sebastian became a highly skilled carpenter, but he always felt bitterness at his exclusion from higher education and the white-collar jobs he could have pursued after having received additional academic training. "I feel impotent," he explained. "It makes me angry and ashamed" because the laws "don't give you a chance." His wife, Sonia, agreed. "He is a very smart man. He had a lot of potential to continue with his education. Unfortunately, because of how laws are set up, he could not continue with that education." Sebastian's stifled potential has affected them both, as his exclusion from opportunity contradicts his identity as an intellectual, taking a significant psychological toll. These issues have only compounded since Sebastian's deportation, as he has been unable to secure a job in Mexico that pays enough to support his family and feels increasingly powerless in his ability to fulfill his individual and familial aspirations.

Heri is extremely bright and graduated at the top of his high school class. But his unauthorized status limited his postsecondary education options. When Heri graduated from high school in the early 2000s, unauthorized students did not qualify for in-state tuition rates at California public universities, which meant he would have to pay tens of thousands of dollars a year to go to college. Without the ability to raise or borrow those funds, he enrolled in the local community college instead. Through his full-time work as the head of produce at a local supermarket and a change in California law that qualified him for in-state tuition, he finally saved enough to pay to attend a nearby four-year state university. But even after he transferred, he encountered additional barriers to success. "The problem was that when I was a perfect student—when I was a 4.0, when I was on the Dean's List—as an 'illegal,' I couldn't, you know, it was so sad to me that I was getting scholarships that I couldn't claim. I got a scholarship to go to London, and I couldn't take it. And it was very embarrassing because the dean called me to his office. He's like, 'Oh wow, what's happening? Why aren't you going to London?' And I had to say, 'Oh, I have other things going on.' Then I got another scholarship to Mexico to study Nahuatl," a language that would be key to the linguistic research he hoped to conduct in the future, "and I couldn't take it. You see, that's when I started really feeling how restricted I was," Heri explained, frustration rising in his voice. "*I could only go so far.* So my only thing was, like, maybe there's a scholarship for unauthorized people. Maybe there's a PhD program for that. But there wasn't."

Despite his academic success in college and his desire to continue studying and researching, Heri could not afford to pay for more degrees out-of-pocket, and his unauthorized status continued to disqualify him for most scholarships and other funding opportunities. When Juanita and Heri married during his senior year of college, his future academic and economic prospects were unclear. Fortunately, Juanita and Heri's Extreme Hardship Waiver application was approved, and Heri adjusted his status to lawful permanent residency. He is now a PhD candidate in literature at a top California university. He is finally pursuing his dreams uninhibited, something he could never have done without being able to adjust his status.

Sondra, who overstayed a tourist visa at 16, confronted similar challenges in college: expensive out-of-state tuition at her local state university, ineligibility for scholarships, and limited opportunities to exercise her degree once she graduated. As Sondra described it, she and her mother "were paying a fortune—out-of-state tuition, and out-of-pocket because I couldn't get any loans or anything" so that she could obtain a college degree. "The fact that I worked full-time, a lot of the money went to pay for that." Paying cash tuition in full every semester is a challenge for most families, let alone two women with unauthorized immigration status who face extra barriers to finding jobs that pay enough to cover the basic necessities. Finding thousands of extra dollars each semester to pay for Sondra's tuition was a huge challenge, requiring great sacrifice from them both. "At the time, it was really hard to come up with that kind of money, especially when I wanted to finish as soon as I possibly could, so paying a full load every semester was hard. I lost my job and then I tried to get another one, which I lost due to the immigration status. It was very painful because that had never happened to me." As discussed in chapter 3, it became clear to Sondra as she neared graduation that, even with a college degree in hand, she would still have no legal way of getting a job and would continue to face these kinds of setbacks. In spite of all of her hard work to pursue her degree, Sondra had reached a point at which it became clear that her future would still be filled with closed doors. She arrived at this realization just as her relationship with Jiancarlo was blossoming. She wanted to build a future with him, but her unauthorized status put everything in her life—including love—in jeopardy.

Up to that point in their relationship, Sondra had not revealed her unauthorized status to Jiancarlo, and she worried about how he would respond. Seeing no other option, she told Jiancarlo everything. This revelation served as a wake-up call for Jiancarlo who, as a citizen, had never had to face such challenges to accessing opportunity before. He described it as "our very first real life drama," a moment "where reality kind of hit us," breaking the spell of new love and the seemingly endless possibilities it suggests.

> Because for so long, we were so in love and our relationship was going well. We were so happy. We were studying, we were going out, we were having fun. Things were just going really well. Then we were realizing we were nearing graduation, and she's nearing graduation, and she's encountered these issues. I had never been in this situation before. I had never had to face these obstacles that she did, but it was a bit of a rude awakening to both of us realizing that we were coming into some difficult currents, or some difficult waters. Things were just getting to be a challenge.

Jiancarlo and Sondra saw marriage as the only option to remedy their situation because Sondra (who had overstayed a visa) could adjust to a legal status through marriage to a US citizen (see chapter 2). So Sondra and Jiancarlo pursued marriage sooner than either had anticipated, recognizing that securing legal status for Sondra was the only way their love could have a future. Acquiring legal status allowed Sondra to "continue my relationship with him, to have a job, to be able to actually utilize my degree." In the eyes of both Sondra and Jiancarlo, adjusting Sondra's immigration status was the turning point in her future and in their relationship, enabling her to freely pursue her intellectual and occupational goals and setting them up for a successful life together. For them, as for other mixed-citizenship families, the benefits of higher education can often only be enjoyed when combined with legal immigration status.

Notwithstanding the significant barriers to accessing higher education and even more roadblocks toward being able to utilize that education in a career, fighting to access higher education institutions appears to yield one significant benefit for college finishers over the other 1.5-generation immigrants I interviewed: proof of "worthiness" to acquire legal immigration status. Of all the couples I interviewed with one unauthorized spouse who had arrived in the US as a child, the successful pursuit of higher education was the most distinct difference between couples who were able to obtain legal immigration status in the US and those who were not. All of the college finishers I interviewed adjusted to legal immigration status,[13] while none of the "early exiters" (nor Sebastian, who dropped out of community college) did.[14] This trend in my data is consistent with changes in US immigration law that increasingly require noncitizen applicants and their citizen sponsors to "prove their worthiness" and demonstrate their efforts to "earn" a chance to become a citizen by satisfying specific cultural expectations of success (see chapter 2).[15] The few noncitizens able to persevere in the face of educational disintegration appear to have an advantage when seeking relief from the same system that excludes them from educational opportunity in the first place. Education can be part of a package of "worthiness" that helps unauthorized mixed-citizenship families qualify for legal status. But in many cases, unauthorized family members' educational disintegration acts as a precursor to further structural disintegration for the whole family.

For these reasons and others, a number of the families I interviewed chose to experience family separation in order for their citizen children to receive an education in the US. Sabrina and her son, Junior, live on the US side of the border Sunday night through Friday night so that Junior can attend school in the US. On the weekends, they travel south to Mexico to be with Joaquin. Before Junior started elementary school, Sabrina commuted across the border every day for work, and Junior stayed home with Joaquin. Now that Junior is six, though, both Sabrina and Joaquin feel it necessary for Junior to study in the US. Sabrina explained, "I feel that, if he studies in the US, his education will be respected no matter where he lives." Sabrina, who received all of her education in the US, said she has seen how this works firsthand. "If my son studies in the United States and has a master's degree, that degree will count here in Mexico. It will count in other countries." In her experience, though, that is not true of Mexican-based education, at least in the US. "I have known people with the same education here in Mexico"—with master's degrees or medical degrees—"and they are waiting tables in the US. Because in the United States, they don't count that education. But, as I say, the education in the US is respected wherever you go." Once Junior entered first grade, they tried to do the daily commute, but when Junior asked why he had to leave home in the dark and come home in the dark every day, Sabrina decided they had to live in the US during the week. Because Sabrina and Joaquin have observed that the cumulative value of an American education translates better than that of a Mexican education, they have decided to sacrifice precious time together as a family in order for Junior to access the most valuable education available to him.

Salvador and Dina have made a similar bargain, sleeping apart every weeknight so that Dina can take their three girls to school in the morning. Salvador says that, after ten years of marriage and living in the same home with his family, "sleeping alone makes me itch," but he believes that, "as citizens," his daughters should "take advantage" of their citizenship right to education. More than half of the couples I interviewed living outside the US with school-aged children made these and other significant sacrifices in order for their children to attend school in the US. In every case, they justified this decision and its consequences as one of the most important investments they could make in their children's futures. It is not a coincidence that all of these families had one parent who had experienced deportation or barred entry to the US. Punitive US immigration laws and enforcement required them to choose between the educational disintegration of their citizen children or the forced separation (whether temporary or prolonged) of their families.

Economic (Dis)Integration

Unauthorized immigrants' exclusion from most facets of the economy is perhaps the most familiar consequence of unauthorized status. And while many unauthorized immigrants resign themselves to these restrictions, often long before migrating, the reality of it all is quite punishing. It is unsurprising, then, that couples who transitioned from unauthorized to legal status uniformly identified their new unfettered access to the legal labor market as one of the most significant positive outcomes of legalization. As June and Stefan noted, acquiring legal status was the equivalent of gold for their family, providing them with a wealth of opportunity they had not known before. Erick was able to go from working two entry-level service jobs "morning, noon, and night" to a professional-track job gardening at a world-renowned museum in Washington, DC. His transition to a legal immigration status has not only enabled Erick to earn a much better salary on fewer hours of work but has also helped him develop what his wife, Reeves, described as the "cultural expectation" to be able to choose what he wants to do with his life. Acquiring legal status has given Erick economic agency that has brought both financial and psychological benefits to his marriage with Reeves, as they now have more compatible expectations for what they can accomplish individually and as a family.

Moises's adjustment to legal status helped him transition from "working twelve hours every day with a half hour break, one day off, and only earn $280 a week," to launching a binational organic farming business. And Tenoch went from working unreliable hours in construction to opening his own concrete business in which he could set his hours and maximize profits from his own skilled labor. Almost without exception, couples who transitioned from unauthorized to legal status—especially those couples whose primary breadwinner was the noncitizen spouse—describe the new economic opportunities that accompany their legal status as financially and metaphorically transformative.

Unauthorized couples, though, identify a combination of limited work opportunities, exploitation at work due to their lack of legal status, and restricted access to mortgages, car loans, and other long-term economic resources as direct impediments toward meeting their full economic potential. When I asked Rodrigo about his job, he detailed his work history in a number of service-sector jobs. While he is a hard worker and enjoys the opportunity to learn new jobs and prepare new meals, he complained that at most of the businesses where he has worked, the owners have taken advantage of his unauthorized status and cheated him out of his proper wages. "I currently work in a hamburger restaurant, where I have been working for the past eight years. And, like in everything, you start at the bottom. Before that, I worked other places." He lifted his hand from the table and began counting on his fingers: "My first job here was at a car wash. After that I went to a different car wash where we did car details and everything. And from there I went to a bar where they sold burgers, wings, onion rings, etc. That's where I learned how to cook hamburgers. But then I got bored with that job, too." Now holding up a fourth finger, he continued, "And I went back to the same car wash as before, but then I left that job again because the owner began to get high on his money and he stopped paying us what we had earned." He put his hand down. "Oh! I also worked in a taco shop," he suddenly remembered, "but it was the same thing. The boss told me that . . . when I learned more he would pay me more, but that day never came."

While Rodrigo has not felt exploited at his current job, he has not been rewarded for his eight years of consistent hard work, either. Despite the fact that "when the manager is gone, I am the one the restaurant owner trusts," Rodrigo continues to be treated similarly to brand-new hires at the restaurant. He has not received any promotions and is paid only slightly more than minimum wage in a state where two minimum wage salaries combined barely exceed regional poverty levels. Rodrigo's status has kept him from receiving fair pay, from promotions, and from job security. After nearly twenty years of working entry-level, service-industry jobs, opening his own business seems to be the only option for meaningful economic advancement. Rodrigo concluded, "I want to keep learning more things and hopefully someday I can open my own restaurant, be my own boss, and then things will be a little bit easier."

Kate and Juan also recognize that Juan's unauthorized status makes him vulnerable to exploitation at work. Juan is a highly skilled machinist whose expertise could attract much higher wages and benefits than he currently earns. But his fear of mistreatment has kept him at the same company for the past six years, despite a lower salary, bad hours, and a long commute. As our toddlers played in the living room of their tidy suburban home, Kate and Juan explained how unauthorized status limits their employment and economic opportunities. When I asked them if being an unauthorized family changes the way they do things, Kate identified Juan's work situation as one thing that is significantly limited by his inability to approach the labor market as a legally employable worker. "I think work," she said, turning to Juan to see if he agreed. "Being able to find any job that you want. He's been at this job, and we've talked about him moving closer or getting a job with different hours. It's so hard. He has a really good job right now, so do we want to risk that just for better hours or being closer to home? No, probably not." Juan agreed, reiterating that his status forced him to make calculated decisions about work based on the increased risks of unemployment and deportation that he faces. "The thing is that, again, it's about risk. I'm so qualified on what I do that I have the confidence that I know that I can find other jobs. But I don't want to risk that employer tricking me into it and, then, 'You know what? You don't have your papers, so I'm going to end it.' It's hard," he continued, because "you want to work." When his current employer hired him, "they told me that they could find ways to keep me employed. If there was a point that they couldn't employ me legally, they would pay me with cash. How much truth is there? I don't know, but they told me that. It's also because of" this promise that they would find a way to keep him employed "that I've been with them for the last six years." Like many unauthorized workers, Juan sacrificed higher wages and better working conditions for the security of working for an employer who did not overtly exploit his "illegal" labor.[16]

Unauthorized couples' economic barriers extend beyond limited work opportunities and vulnerability to labor exploitation. In fact, many of the unauthorized couples I interviewed, like Kate and Juan, earned middle-class wages, but they were unable to translate those incomes into financial investments that would help them get ahead in the long term. Most immigrants with unauthorized immigration status cannot build credit and therefore do not qualify for most kinds of loans.[17] Unless the US citizen spouse has sufficient salary and strong credit to qualify for a home or car loan as the sole borrower, unauthorized couples cannot access these crucial financial services, even if the noncitizen partner earns sufficient income.

Kat and Beto, a couple in their late twenties who were days away from welcoming their first child into their blended family, are each the kind of person who has a constant smile on their face and is always looking for a reason to enjoy a good laugh. Their optimism and willingness to laugh at life has helped them weather many of the challenges they have faced due to Beto's lack of status, but they acknowledge that some of those challenges cannot be laughed away. The issue of building credit and qualifying for financial loans is something they immediately identified when I asked them what would be different about their relationship if Beto had status in the US. Kat began, "We would have more things in his name because everything is in my name. It has to be because we can only get loans in my name. That would be the biggest difference. We would be able to qualify for things," for example, "like a house." Beto continued, "I earn a lot more than a middle-class American, but I can't do anything with it because I cannot apply for anything." "It's true," Kat agreed. "I'm the one with citizenship and a degree, and he makes twice as much as I do." But income without status means that Beto "can't do anything with it. Anything he wants has to go through my name, but now I have so many things in my name that I can't apply for anything more because everything is in my name." Kat and Beto's inability to access these crucial financial tools felt increasingly limiting as they planned for the birth of their first child. Kat identified these challenges brought on by laws explicitly excluding Beto from key legal and social institutions as the cause of "a lot of problems in our marriage," because those laws have prevented Kat and Beto from doing the "totally American things," like buying a house, that they are otherwise completely qualified to do.

During the seven years before Tenoch received legal status, Juliette could not qualify for a mortgage on her own, as she primarily stayed home with their small children while Tenoch worked in construction. Even though Tenoch earned enough for them to qualify for a loan, his lack of credit and Juliette's lack of income made owning a home impossible. Juliette even asked if she could list Tenoch's income as hers, as if he paid her directly, but she was told she could not. With no other options, they continued to pay much more for housing as renters than they would as homeowners.

Even when the US citizen spouse earns enough money to qualify for a mortgage on her income, she still faces challenges in securing a mortgage because of her spouse's unauthorized status. Kate, an elementary school teacher, noted challenges in trying to qualify for a mortgage to buy their home since Juan's income could not be taken into consideration. "He provided a lot of the funding, like the down payment and stuff, but all the mortgage stuff we just did through me. He doesn't really have credit, so I had to do it all." Luckily, since Kate works full-time and earns sufficient income as a teacher, she qualified for the home loan on her own.

Unauthorized families face not only restricted access to economic institutions but also additional, significant expenditures in the form of thousands of dollars in legal fees and government processing charges when they apply to adjust to a legal immigration status. For many families, like Juliette and Tenoch, these extra costs push them further into debt and away from the financial solvency they desperately seek. Juliette noted that by the time Tenoch became a lawful permanent resident (seven years after they married), they had spent more than $10,000 on application and legal fees and additional tens of thousands in higher rent payments. Even with Tenoch's new access to better, higher-paying jobs, she estimated that it would likely take them another seven years just to get back financially to where a "normal" couple would have started.

Vicente made a similar observation to me shortly after Herlinda's residency application was finally approved. Their fifteen-year exile from the US significantly affected their familial economic integration, despite the fact that Vicente was lucky enough to keep his seniority in both salary and retirement benefits as a California public school teacher. By the time they could move back to the US, Vicente had missed out on more affordable housing options—the typical purchase price for single-family homes in San Diego County increased 223 percent, or more than $350,000, between 2000 and 2020—and fifteen years' worth of mortgage payments.[18] Now, with Vicente only two years from his target retirement date, he has just begun thirty years of monthly house payments at more than double the price, rather than being halfway toward owning his home outright.

Unauthorized families' economic disintegration permeates every aspect of their lives, impeding their short- and long-term financial security. Not only are they subject to greater vulnerability to lower wages, exploitation, and sudden job loss, but they also face exclusion from the foundational economic institutions and tools that undergird financial stability over the long term. This blocked access to financial institutions is a symptom of broader legal and bureaucratic disintegration processes that render unauthorized immigrants and their families invisible to many essential social programs and protections.

Bureaucratic (Dis)Integration

In addition to educational and economic institutions, many legal and bureaucratic institutions also either explicitly bar or implicitly discourage access for immigrants and their family members. Laws like the 1996 Personal Responsibility and Work Opportunity Reconciliation Act prohibit the vast majority of legal permanent residents from utilizing federal social welfare benefits, including Medicaid, food stamps, and disability payments, during their first five years in the US.[19] Unauthorized immigrants are disqualified from all federal social support.[20] While not explicitly barred from other programs and protections—like the

Occupational Safety and Health Act (OSHA), Workers' Compensation, and antidiscrimination laws—many immigrants, especially unauthorized immigrants, do not make claims through these programs for fear of retaliation, job loss, or deportation.[21]

This legitimate fear of accessing social services and protections also affects immigrants' citizen family members, who often do not seek social support—like Medicaid and WIC (which provides food and health benefits for low-income pregnant women, infants, and children)—even though they qualify.[22] Citizen spouses in mixed-citizenship families often avoid accessing social welfare benefits for which they qualify for fear that their use of government support would be used against them in the future if they ever sponsor their spouse for permanent residency. Complicated rules and regulations, regular changes to eligibility requirements, and the demonization of welfare users have all contributed to mixed-citizenship families' confusion regarding when, whether, and how their citizen family members can access social welfare benefits. During my interviews, respondents living within and outside the US reflected that complexity and confusion, variously informing me that they did not qualify for benefits; that they did qualify but did not access them for fear it would hurt them in the future; that they were currently receiving benefits; that they would have to pay back the value of any benefits they used before they could sponsor their immigrant family member for a visa; and that their spouses' status directly affected their eligibility. My investigation of these laws suggests that citizens should have uninhibited access to social welfare support regardless of their immediate family members' immigration status, but misinformation—often provided by the case managers helping families access these programs—and the mis-execution of the law contribute to the underutilization of social welfare benefits by qualified citizens in mixed-status families.[23]

One of the ironies Juliette discovered is that, while Tenoch's income could not be considered when trying to qualify for a home loan or other financial investments, his income had to be reported when determining whether or not she and her children qualified for basic social benefits such as Medicaid. Like most unauthorized immigrants, Tenoch did not receive health insurance for himself or for his family through his construction job. Juliette's part-time work did not offer health insurance, either. Their combined family income fluctuated at the upper limit for Medicaid qualifiers, so some months Juliette and her children qualified and other months they did not. They could not afford insurance through the Affordable Care Act health insurance exchange, so they went without insurance when their combined incomes came in too high. At least once, Juliette had to apply for emergency Medicaid coverage shortly before she gave birth because their monthly income had dropped precipitously during the slow construction season, newly qualifying them for coverage. For all four of her pregnancies, Juliette paid the hospital in advance of the delivery because she was never sure if she would have health insurance at the moment she went into labor. When she did have insurance, the hospital did not reimburse any overpayment of services. US laws pertaining to unauthorized immigrants, it seems, work desperately to render unauthorized immigrants and their labor invisible, except when the state seeks to disqualify their citizen family members from accessing the benefits for which they have a valid claim.[24]

Citizens who leave the US to join deported family members find that their access to many welfare programs is strictly limited and that the rules governing the programs they could potentially access—especially those living near the border who can travel to the US when necessary—are hard to interpret (and misinformation about them abounds). Sandra and Esteban self-deported to Mexico's northern border shortly after marrying in hopes of reducing the penalty for Esteban's unauthorized presence in the US. Once in Mexico, Sandra became pregnant, and they decided that Esteban would work while Sandra stayed home with their son. During that time, Esteban "was the only one working," and his income barely covered their monthly expenses. Sandra told him they could do "what lots of people do" and "ask for help with food or health insurance" for Sandra and their infant son. But she was told that because she did not live in the US, "I couldn't ask for any help. Even though I'm a citizen, I need to be living there for them to help me. This," she emphasized, is how their lack of family-level legal status has affected her "because you *have* to be there. But how are you going to be there if your family—okay, your husband—is here? You cannot get help. I'm not even talking about money. I just mean help with health insurance and food. This is what made it so hard for us, because we simply could not" access the social welfare support to which the US citizen members of their family were entitled. Ultimately, they decided that Sandra would have to work if they ever wanted to be able to afford housing, food, and healthcare expenses, let alone pay for Esteban's immigration application. For the next six years, Sandra commuted across the border for work daily—a three-hour round trip—while Esteban stayed home with their son, until Esteban was finally granted legal status and they could live together as a family in the US.

Through her experience navigating her collateral deportation, Esther has also felt the US pressuring her time and again to choose between her husband and her citizenship rights, including her right to access the social safety net. Despite living in Mexico, Esther has continued to qualify for food stamps and disability due to an abnormality requiring multiple surgeries on her foot. But the exact same benefits Esther received before Chuy's deportation do not stretch as far for her family now that they are in Mexico. Her disability benefits do not even cover the fuel and travel expenses she accrues when crossing the border to travel to her regular medical appointments and those of their autistic son. She also has to do all of this without the support of her husband, who used to manage their healthcare appointments when they lived together in the US. Esther and her citizen children need these benefits, but they have found the efficacy and accessibility of these benefits—like many of their other citizenship rights—significantly diminished following their collateral deportation.

Other citizens feel pressure not to access social welfare programs like WIC and Food Stamps because they need to "prove" they can support themselves and their noncitizen spouse. As Angelica described it, not only did she need to avoid accepting social welfare resources, she also needed to find official work that used her Social Security number to create a record of income earned and taxes paid. When they first married, Angelica explained, Ramses "was working, and I did not work. I was pregnant, and then pregnant again; I had a little baby, and then I had two babies. But then they laid him off from his job, and in Mexico there are not very good job opportunities." With a one-year-old and an infant at home, they needed money to care for their family. But Angelica also realized that "I needed to use my Social Security number" to show immigration authorities that "when Ramses comes to live in the US, I can take care of him, and we will not ask the government for help. So, when he lost his job, I went to find a job" in the US. To make sure I understood the motivation for that change, I asked Angelica the main reason that prompted her to start working in the US. She immediately responded, "It was for his papers." Not "financially motivated," I asked, because of the wage differential and the buying power of the dollar in Mexico? "No," she replied, "because we lived for two-and-a-half years with him as the breadwinner." But relying on Ramses as the sole earner had created a problem, Angelica said, because "I would submit my tax return with a zero-dollar bottom line. I did not earn anything. So, I did not have to pay [taxes], but when the time comes to sponsor him, they are going to ask me, 'How do you intend to bring him here if you cannot even support yourself?' So, that's why. That is what motivated our decision because he lost his job, and he wanted to look for another job, but that's when I said, 'We have to get your papers in order first.'"

Angelica first worked in fast food and later obtained certification to work as a nursing home aide. But the pay for these positions was so low that she still qualified for many federal welfare programs, especially as the sole breadwinner in a home with two small children. She admitted to feeling tempted at times to apply for support, but she worried that any dependence on federal aid could sabotage Ramses's future chances of legalization. "There are many government programs that I could apply for—for food, for housing, for money, for everything—and I could apply for my two girls, because my husband is not in the US. But if I ask for that, when they review my immigration application with Ramses, they are not going to give me papers for him." She paused for a moment, then continued. "They only give papers when you can support yourself all on your own. So, sometimes I would like to do it because it sounds nice to have them give you things, but I can't. The disadvantage is that I can't apply for anything because I would be ruining his chances to get papers. So I'm not going to do it." Having gone through the immigration and naturalization process herself as a dependent of her parents, who immigrated to the US while she was a teenager, Angelica remembered the emphasis immigration agents placed on financial self-sufficiency. Based on her understanding from that experience, not only did she have to prove current earning capacity but she would also have to pay back any benefits she had received from the government before someone she sponsored could qualify for permanent residence.[25]

Unauthorized families in the US also find it difficult to access legal protections—even those to which they have a valid claim—and generally fear that making a claim will expose them to significant negative consequences. For example, many employers deny unauthorized immigrant employees workers' compensation benefits even if they qualify, threatening to fire them or turn them over to immigration authorities if they try to make a claim.[26] Unauthorized immigrants who do manage to make a successful claim often find themselves receiving fewer benefits for a shorter amount of time.[27] When Mateo fell from over two stories high while working in his construction job in the US, he broke both of his knees, leaving him incapacitated and unable to work for months, even as the bills kept coming in. He filed for workers' compensation, but the support he received woefully undercompensated for the loss he and his family experienced. Mateo's injuries required multiple surgeries, which the compensation program covered. He received a few checks to make up for lost pay, but was soon told that he would receive no more support because he was unauthorized. As Mateo explained, "[the Workers' Compensation] board said, 'That's it.' They said that I needed Social Security, but since I didn't have a Social Security number, well . . ." Mateo's voice trailed off. "They give you a disability rating, and it was my knees, but [the doctor] only put that I was 'four percent affected.' How are they going to put *four* percent when it's more like twenty percent?! It's both of my knees and the parts of my body that my knees move." Without a valid Social Security number, Mateo felt incapable of challenging the decision and resigned himself to the minimal remuneration he did receive. Unable to make rent, Yuliana and their newborn moved in with her parents while Mateo stayed with extended family and looked for work. They decided their only hope was to apply to adjust Mateo's status, but at his interview in Ciudad Juarez, Mateo learned he would have to wait at least ten years before he could reenter the US legally. Mateo had been scheduled for another knee surgery soon after his visa interview, but it has been postponed until he can legally enter the US again. Eight years later, he is still waiting for the surgery.

Bureaucratic rules and hurdles compound for mixed-citizenship families who live outside the US, especially those with a noncitizen spouse unable to travel—even as a tourist—to the United States. In Mexico, only drivers with valid US driver's licenses can drive cars with US license plates. This law, designed as a tool to curb the importation of stolen cars from the US into Mexico, has ultimately punished many mixed-citizenship couples living along Mexico's northern border, as non-US citizen spouses residing in Mexico do not qualify for US driver's licenses. When police identify a driver in violation of this law, they confiscate the vehicle and charge the driver with a fine equivalent to the estimated value of the car. Mexican federal police confiscated Mateo and Yuliana's only car when Mateo could not provide a US driver's license, and they fined him over $15,000. While lawyers managed to negotiate a lower fine, Yuliana and Mateo still paid more than $3,000 in fines and legal fees before the authorities returned their car to them months later. Like many other mixed-citizenship couples living in the border region, Yuliana and Mateo were completely oblivious to this law until Mateo was pulled over. They could not imagine that driving a car they owned, which had been legally purchased and was legally registered in the US, was a crime. Now, Mateo and Yuliana only drive cars with Mexican license plates, and every time Yuliana crosses the border into the US, the border guards interrogate her about why she—a US citizen—drives a car with Mexican plates. Policies like these complicate mixed-citizenship families' daily lives on both sides of the border and subject them to increased scrutiny by police and other bureaucratic agents in both countries.

Other seemingly simple tasks, like amending vital records, become insurmountable hurdles when one spouse is unable to physically present themselves at the appropriate government office in the US. Sabrina and Joaquin encountered this issue when they sought to obtain Mexican nationality for their son, Junior. When Junior was born, Sabrina and Joaquin had been living together for five years, but they had not yet married. At the hospital in the hours following Junior's birth, Sabrina listed only her information for inclusion on the birth certificate. Now that Junior is old enough to attend school, Sabrina wants to enroll him in public school in Mexico, but he needs to be a Mexican citizen to enroll in a Mexican public school. Since Joaquin's name is not on the birth certificate, the Mexican government will not acknowledge Junior as Joaquin's son, which makes Junior ineligible for Mexican citizenship. When they asked a Mexican civil servant how they could work around their problem, her response was simple: "The boy will not be able to become a Mexican citizen, unless someday the father's name appears on the birth certificate." Without Mexican citizenship, Junior cannot attend public school, own property, or gain lawful employment.

Sabrina investigated what she needed to do in order to add Joaquin's name to Junior's American birth certificate. While it is a relatively simple process, Joaquin must physically present himself in the County Recorder's office in order to prove his identity and sign the appropriate paperwork. Because Joaquin cannot travel to the US and has been permanently barred from obtaining legal entry to the US, his name cannot be added to the birth certificate. Although dual citizenship is less essential for Junior right now while he attends school in the US, Sabrina sees it as an increasingly necessary status for his long-term opportunities: "He is going to want [Mexican citizenship] when he's older because he really likes it here. And what happens if we want to buy a home or something? Who can we leave it to? My son will not be able to own property in Mexico. He needs Mexican nationality, but we simply cannot get it." Basic problems like these, even those with seemingly simple solutions, become insurmountable barriers for many unauthorized mixed-citizenship American families denied access to key social institutions in both of their countries of membership.

The Cumulative Effects of Structural Disintegration

Structural disintegration has consequences that reverberate throughout the family. Many individual instances of structural exclusion often seem small, even inconsequential, but they compound over time and across the different institutions for which access is barred, adding up to significant disadvantage and disintegration for immigrants and their immediate family members. The inability to access or apply postsecondary education leads to fewer opportunities for unauthorized immigrants' well-compensated employment. Lack of authorization for legal employment makes them vulnerable to exploitation, unjustified dismissal, and ongoing financial precarity. And the bureaucratic exclusion of unauthorized immigrants cuts them—and, often, their family members—off from legal protections and the social safety net. The primary by-product of structural disintegration is erasure, systematically rendering unauthorized immigrants invisible in the society in which they live, love, and labor. For unauthorized mixed-citizenship couples, this erasure of the noncitizen spouse from and invisibility to official institutions places heavy burdens on the still-visible citizen spouse. As Trish put it, "Everything falls on me." In many cases, only the citizen spouse can gain access to educational, economic, legal, and bureaucratic institutions; when she does not qualify as an individual, the whole family is excluded.

The structural disintegration unauthorized couples face bleeds into other aspects of their lives, shaping their opportunities, relationships, and ability to socially and emotionally connect with their "normal" friends and neighbors. I interviewed Trish and Alberto on a warm summer day. We sat in their front yard in the shade, Alberto swinging in a hammock, as their one-year old boy bounced up and down in a jumper chair. Their small, charming house is in an old neighborhood in the town where Trish has lived almost all of her life. From this vantage point, Trish has been able to observe how the adult lives of the kids who grew up with her have been so different from her own. For Trish, the stark difference between her young family's opportunities and those of her peers made her question the extent to which they could be considered an "American" family.

When I asked Trish and Alberto about whether or not they felt like an American family, Alberto said he did, but Trish disagreed. "I think that, for him, he feels more American because he has more than he did before. And for me it's like, I know what we could have if we had more. And so I worry about things he doesn't worry about because—I don't know why. But, for example, for him to get a license or for him to, you know—all the things are in my name and if he was to have papers, he could make more money and I could maybe stay home with the kids more; or I worry about him getting pulled over because if he were to get a license he would have to put his fingerprint. And if he puts his fingerprint, then he has the chance of getting deported," she said, glancing nervously at Alberto as she explained that he had been caught and released at the border the first time he attempted to cross. "And the car insurance is higher because he doesn't have a license. I don't know, there are just a lot of little things that put more stress on me because I feel more like everything is on me." Trish continued, "As far as things financially, legally, and things like that, if he had some kind of citizenship then things would be a lot easier." She sighed, "People just don't understand why doesn't he find a better job? Or why doesn't he just, you know, get time off or go on vacation? We don't get those kinds of benefits that other regular families do," she said, shaking her head. "We wouldn't be having this stress right now if he just had this privilege—or I wouldn't have this stress right now. I feel like most of the stress falls on me."

Trish has been able to keep her family somewhat structurally integrated in the US through the access her citizenship affords. But Alberto's inability to access those same institutions holds the family back from the progress Trish feels they could otherwise make. The combined stress of her extra burden and the precarity of Alberto's status has strained Trish's relationships with Alberto, her broader community, and the country as a whole, leaving her to feel only partially American.

Many US citizen spouses in unauthorized families echoed Trish's sentiments regarding the added burdens they carry and their families' exclusions from many aspects of the "American dream." Not only is "everything on them" as the US citizens, but their collateral structural exclusion clearly demonstrates to them that, for unauthorized families, the limits of one partner's unauthorized status overpower the benefits of the other partner's citizenship. With regard to structural integration, the unauthorized status of one family member becomes a "master status" for the entire family, shutting out noncitizen *and* citizen family members from access to essential institutions.[28] Forced to confront the limitations of their citizenship through their structural disintegration, many unauthorized mixed-citizenship families come to question their place in American society and the extent to which they truly belong.

CHAPTER 6

Parenthetical Belonging

SONIA WAS BORN AND RAISED in San Diego. She is the child of
Mexican immigrants, and her experience as a first-generation American
perfectly traces the traditional arc of integration and inclusion defined
and refined by scholars over the past century. These integration scholars
have noted a number of different "types" of integration that, in combination, lead to full incorporation into a country's mainstream, including
cultural, structural, socioeconomic, spatial, and linguistic integration,
among others.[1] Sonia satisfies almost every measure of integration, and
then some. She is a first-generation college student and graduated from a
top California university with an accounting degree. She owns her own
home in a community she loves. She votes regularly. She speaks perfect
English, earns a good income in a solid white-collar industry, and likes
to take kickboxing classes and walk around the mall in her free time.
While she is proud of her Mexican heritage, she does not think of herself as Mexican. She is American, and she sees her life as the fulfillment
of the hopes and sacrifices her parents made in search of the "American
dream."

But on one dimension of integration, Sonia has "failed," and it has
sent her life into a tailspin. Rather than marry another equally integrated American, Sonia fell in love with and married Sebastian, a Mexican citizen who came to the US at the age of 15 to join his parents who
had previously migrated from Michoacán, Mexico, to Southern California. Sebastian attended high school in San Diego and adjusted quickly
to his new life, performing well in his schoolwork and qualifying for the
National Honor Society, among other accomplishments. Unfortunately,
Sebastian struggled to continue his education after high school due to
his unauthorized status. He took courses at a local community college

for a few semesters, but as he realized that his limited access to key so-cial institutions extended beyond higher education to the workforce, he dropped out of community college and began work in construction in-stead. Over time, he became a skilled carpenter and worked with the same company for nearly a decade.

When Sonia and Sebastian met, they both felt like Americans. As Sebastian put it: "I am Mexican, but in my mind I am American be-cause I basically grew up in the United States." At one point, he even believed he had become an official American. Sebastian's parents had applied to adjust his status to permanent residency, and within a few months he was given a driver's license, ID, Social Security number, and a certificate of citizenship. He only found out later—when he tried to re-turn to the US after traveling to Tijuana on a day trip—that his lawyer had given him fraudulent documents. His use of these documents at an official port of entry was interpreted as a fraudulent claim to US citizen-ship and, as a result, Sebastian has been permanently barred from any future legal immigration status in the US.

When he lived in the US, Sebastian's unauthorized immigration status significantly impaired his ability to integrate into key dimensions of main-stream American society. He was excluded from critical structures—such as institutions of higher education, banking systems, and many occupa-tional sectors—that facilitate social and economic incorporation. His unauthorized status also limited him in his ability to be civically and po-litically active, as many civic institutions require formal US membership for participation. And although, according to integration theorists, Se-bastian's marriage to an integrated US citizen should have helped him overcome these barriers and fully integrate,[2] both Sebastian and Sonia experienced the complete opposite outcome: Sebastian's—and, by proxy, Sonia's—formal exclusion from American society.

Sebastian's most recent deportation in 2015 forced Sonia to choose between her family and her integrated status in the US. Desiring to keep her family together, Sonia and her daughter, Dulce, relocated to Mex-ico with Sebastian. By prioritizing their relationships with Sebastian, Sonia and Dulce were pushed out from the core of American society to its periphery, literally and figuratively, resulting in their individual and collective disintegration from the only country to which they felt they belonged. Sonia, Sebastian, and Dulce have all struggled with their forced spatial and structural disintegration resulting from Sebastian's deportations. But the most devastating effect of formal rejection by the US government has been their forced social disintegration and exclusion from US society, as it has hampered their ability to develop and maintain meaningful relationships in both the US and Mexico. Perhaps even more importantly, it has disrupted the American identity that both Sonia and Sebastian embraced as their own.

Nation-states have an interest in supporting social integration and encouraging their official members to identify with a national identity. States need citizens to uphold, sustain, and legitimize the sociopolitical order, and they use the construct of citizenship to help secure the support of their constituents.[3] Through citizenship, modern states become membership organizations as well as territorial organizations;[4] as a result, developing and reinforcing a national identity is an ongoing project of modern nation-states. This dual interest has transformed citizenship into both an institutionally controlled legal status *and* a social identity.[5] For most members of modern states, citizenship is not merely a legal status but tangible evidence of a deeper individual identity vis-à-vis their place in the world. The success of many states' efforts to develop a strong national identity has often backfired, in the sense that many territorially present noncitizens also develop a strong affinity with the national identities of the states in which they live but to which they do not officially belong. This expansion of citizenship from a status to an identity has resulted in a deeper struggle by states, their residents, and their official members to determine who belongs in their specific society and define what "belonging" means.[6]

In the context of immigration, national identity is paramount, and determination of whether or not an immigrant "belongs" in her new country of residence is most often based solely on her formal relationship to that country via citizenship.[7] While citizens and noncitizens alike may push back against these strict boundaries around national identity, the state has the ultimate power in defining national membership, as it is an identity grounded in law, the product of a legal fiction created for the benefit of the state, not its members.[8] This tension manifests clearly in the conflict between the individual nature of citizenship—which allows states the most control over determining which individuals should officially belong—and the basic organizational unit of society, the family—which mediates the citizen-state relationship. Most citizens in any country have parents, siblings, spouses, and children who are all citizens, too, and therefore do not encounter this tension. But citizens with a noncitizen parent, sibling, and/or spouse live with this tension every day. As a result, citizens with noncitizen family members often experience contradictions in their citizenship identity, as their individual sense of belonging in and to a country is challenged by institutional authorities who insist that their families do not fully belong.[9] These large and small reminders of their family's noncitizen status can lead to an internal shift in the way mixed-citizenship family members understand and manage their citizenship and familial identities.

The dissonance between individual and familial sense of belonging and national identity can create conflict for all members of mixed-citizenship families. Although the individual members of mixed citizenship marriages rarely choose to fully reject either their citizenship or familial identities, they often face situations in which those identities appear to be incompatible and struggle to reconcile them. These identity conflicts can directly affect individual and familial social integration, as measured by both sense of belonging and self-described identity.[10] Given that each couple I interviewed included an "insider" (citizen) and "outsider" (noncitizen) spouse, their responses revealed interesting functions of individual- and family-level characteristics and statuses that directly contribute to social (dis)integration. Interestingly, a lack of status does not impede couples' ability to socially integrate and to feel a strong sense of belonging to their country of residence. But the formal rejection of a family's reunification claim—which couples interpreted as an official declaration of their inability to belong to the United States—does shape a sense of belonging for both partners, citizen and noncitizen alike, in *both* of their countries of membership.

Legal Status and Social (Dis)Integration
within and across Borders

For mixed-citizenship families, social integration, sense of belonging, and identity on both personal and familial levels are variable, rather than fixed, phenomena. Citizens' and noncitizens' interpretation of their place in American society fluctuates based on changes in individual characteristics and experiences, but also—and often to a greater extent—based on their intimate partners' ability to socially integrate.

For couples granted legal status in the United States, their legal acceptance as a family has increased their sense of belonging in the US, both on an individual level and as a family. US citizen spouses feel *even more* American following the formal legal acceptance of their spouse by the government; noncitizen spouses granted legal status express similar feelings of belonging and acceptance in the US, often seeing their Americanness as inevitable as that of their US citizen spouses. Both partners feel individually American; they also agree that their families are American, regardless of their individual or familial ethnicity, previous immigration status, gender, where they live in the US (or outside the US), or socioeconomic status. In short, the legal validation of these families provides the ultimate evidence of not only their right to belong in the US but of the fact that they have always belonged.

A number of couples describe their family's belonging to the US as a visible, more accurate representation of what America truly is because of their mixed national origins and ethnic diversity. Mark was a regular customer at the fast-food restaurant where Susana worked. After months of brief chats at the counter, Mark finally got up the nerve to ask Susana on a date. Now—many years, a wedding, and two children later—Mark, a White, US-born man, believes the family he has created with Susana, a Mexican-born Latina woman, "is more a mirror of America than a lot of other families just because that's—there are so many backgrounds in America. That's kind of what we're about now, so our family portrait is much more the picture of an American family than what it maybe used to be fifty years ago." As Mark sees it, his family is a physical representation of the American populace's increasing diversity.

Ryan, a US-born Latino man with Mexican ancestry whose wife, Gloria, is from Mexico, expressed similar sentiments about his family: "I think more and more that's what America is, right? It's people from all around the world coming to the States." Nicole, a White, US-born woman married to Jorge, a Mexican-born man, echoed this idea, explaining how she thinks her family embodies "an American story." She sees "the US as such a plurality of different types of people and citizenship statuses and ethnicities and backgrounds and everything," the exact kinds of diversity her young family embodies. Will also evoked America's immigrant story, past and present, in reflecting on his mixed-citizenship family's place in America: "I just consider ourselves American, like any other family. Mayela's just first generation; I'm probably tenth generation. So that's that." For many couples with legal status, their families' diverse backgrounds represent a microcosm of multicultural America and provide clear evidence of their inherent Americanness.

But families whose family reunification applications have been rejected by the US government feel definitively un-American, despite the fact that they, too, embody the celebrated diversity of modern America. Formal rejection by the state leads couples to feel officially and definitively spurned, not just by the state but by society at large. Among the couples I interviewed, most rejected US-citizen spouses and their partners discussed their individual and familial exclusion from the US and described feeling compelled to abandon the American identity with which most of them had previously identified. US citizens in rejected families did not distinguish between their ongoing US citizen status and their families' inability to acquire that same status. Rather, they saw their family reunification denial as an indication of their individual social rejection and disintegration from the US.

Camille, whose husband, Giovanni, was deported to Guatemala two years after they married and shortly after the birth of their first child, felt that, in practice, she was deported with Giovanni. "When he was deported, so was I. And it's like, sure, they didn't kick me out necessarily. I can come back whenever I want. But they took away my freedom by separating me from my husband." Giovanni's deportation forced Camille to choose between her family and her country because "there's no way we can be together unless we all leave the US. That's the thing—they've arranged it so beautifully so that we can't stay where we feel home is."

When I first interviewed Camille, she wanted to feel American—and was perceived by Guatemalans as American—but she felt that identity no longer applied. I asked her, "Do you feel like an American family when you're together in Guatemala?" and Camille immediately responded, "No." But then she thought for a minute and continued, "I mean, yes, in the sense that I want to do things the American way," something Giovanni wanted, too. But everything else in their life served as a stark reminder to them that they were not in the US anymore. "We live in a house that lets dirt come in under the doors. There's no screens on the windows. We have to hand-wash our clothes. We have to hand-wash our dishes. We don't have a kitchen sink. We don't have running hot water. All these things that are typical in American households are not in our house."

While everything about her life at the time felt incredibly un-American, others in Guatemala still immediately identified Camille and her family as outsiders. "We stand out like a sore thumb because of the way we speak and the way we dress. I mean, everyone looks at us like Americans. Yet we don't have the money they expect us to have. We're not there just on vacation. We're trying to live and scrape our way through and being dirt poor." Thinking back to my original question, she paused, then concluded, "Yeah, in so many ways I feel like I should feel American still, but I don't. I don't feel Guatemalan, either. I just feel like no nationality." Camille's daily living conditions diverged so strongly from what she understood to be American—and reinforced the painful fact that she and her family had been barred from living together in the US—that she was unable to feel like an American anymore, even if she wanted to. But her family's obvious difference from typical Guatemalan families also prevented her from feeling Guatemalan, leaving her with no national identity to claim and no country to call her/their own.

Julia—reeling from five years of collateral deportation after her husband, Santiago, "voluntarily deported"—still felt American as an individual, but the US government's rejection of her family made it obvious to her that her family was not American, an offense she was slow to for-give. "It's interesting when you said, like, do you still feel American? I do, but I take it so personally—personally from the government and from the law and USCIS. It's just kind of an ugly monster to me, and it's my home and it's my country, but I feel unwelcome. And now I live here," in Mexico, more than a thousand miles away from her family and the life she left behind, "because I can't live there with who I wanted to. It's a very weird feeling to have that from your country. Unwelcoming. And un-accepting of your decisions. Even if I decided to marry some-one who was 'illegal.'" Not only had Santiago been spatially, structur-ally, and socially disintegrated from American society, but Julia had, too. Although the US government had only expelled her husband from the country, Julia felt that his rejection directly extended to her as well.

Christian expressed similar feelings, responding with an unwavering "No" when I asked whether or not he and Sharon considered themselves an American family. Before an error on Sharon's citizenship application resulted in the cancellation of her permanent residency and a lifetime bar from legal status in the US, they both felt proudly American, indi-vidually and as a family. But Christian and Sharon's permanent rejec-tion from legal status in the US had devastating consequences for them as a family, destroying their American identity and sense of belonging to the US along the way. Following up on Christian's flat rejection of an American identity, I asked them, "Had you been able to naturalize, do you think you would have [felt like an American family]?" "Yes," Christian said, as they both nodded. "And that would have been the end of the story?" "Yes!" they both exclaimed.

Although their rejection by the US spurred them into activism that they feel has positively affected their lives, that same rejection has had a profound negative impact on their sense of belonging. Christian ex-plained, "I don't feel like an American; *I actually identify myself as un-documented*. When somebody asks, I tell them we're an undocumented family." He elaborated on what he means by that: "My wife is Mexican-American, and I make sure that I identify her as Mexican and rejected by the United States. I [also] consider myself rejected by the United States." This rejection has made Christian reevaluate his relationship with the US, his desire to continue living in the US, and the validity of the historical narratives he was taught in school about the US and the promise of America. "There's some of that battle that I mentioned earlier, some of the cynicism mixed with being grateful that I can advocate. Part of me wants to go find an American flag, rip it up, burn it, and take off and go to Mexico and renounce my citizenship. And then there's the other part that's kind of glad that I can stay here and I can fight injustice. That happens. Sometimes I feel like we're stronger" because of the family-level immigration challenges they have faced. "I just think of our history and the wars that were fought and kind of this idea that I grew up with about how people fought for my freedom. They didn't fight for *my* freedom. On Independence Day, I make posts on Facebook about how our family isn't free and other injustice in America and that kind of thing. There's that kind of mix, and I feel like, because my country and culture is rejecting my family to a degree, that it's rejected me." When Christian finished describing how and why his American identity has permanently ruptured, I asked Sharon if there was ever a time when she felt American, to which she replied, "No. Even today, I don't feel American. Even if God ever provides a way for me to become a citizen, I don't know that I ever will."

For Sharon and Christian, their legal rejection from the US and the stripping of Christian's American identity has been both indisputable and irreparable. Sharon and Christian also talked about how their official rejection by the US brings the divisive power of the border into their social interactions with friends and neighbors. "For me, the concept of the border is ever present," Sharon explained. "Something that is a physical barrier, geographically, turns into a relational barrier—a very real and a very painful one. So I guess it's kind of like something that has its own life in everyday encounters. When you have people that love you and care about you, and they don't mean any harm, but they will start talking about 'those illegals' and saying things like that. And they don't even think that that could be you. And then the border becomes a real [barrier] between you." Christian nodded vigorously, adding, "I have good friends who know about our situation and still use that term—talking about 'those illegals' and that situation. And, I'm like, 'You know, you're talking about me. I'm right here.'" Their official rejection as a family from the US forced Sharon and Christian back into the category of an "undocumented family" and introduced an additional social barrier that hinders their social integration.

Esther and Chuy have felt the effects of this social barrier since moving as a family to Mexico following Chuy's deportation. Chuy said that, when he lived "on the other side" (in the US), he felt "proud to say that I was Mexican." But now that he lives in Mexico, he questions that identity—or what he thought that identity meant—saying, "I don't think I'm Mexican, man." Esther chimed in, "He didn't even know what left and right was in Spanish." Chuy nodded, telling me how a White American friend of his who speaks fluent Spanish once told him, "'You don't even know Spanish.' I go, 'What do you mean? I know Spanish.' He's like, 'Nope.' And then, once you're here, you literally see that you're not Mexican," Chuy lamented. Unable to speak the "proper Spanish" and unfamiliar with so many aspects of daily life in Mexico, Chuy feels the opposite of belonging. This difference is as obvious to Esther and Chuy as it is to the Mexicans they encounter on a daily basis. While they can feel some sense of normalcy inside their home, Esther says that as soon as they're around other people, "You feel like you don't belong." And, Chuy adds, the locals "make you feel like that, too." Their children also faced bullying and other threats when they tried to attend local Mexican schools, leaving Esther no choice but to enroll them in schools in the US. This change requires more than an hour-long drive each way (plus the border wait) every schoolday, spatially disintegrating their family each day and further reinforcing their lack of belonging in both countries.

The biggest frustration for Chuy is that he was sent back to a "home" he never knew. As someone who was brought to the US with unauthorized status as a young child, Chuy did not remember anything about his first years of life in Mexico, nor did he have any meaningful connection to extended family there. And he realized when he was in custody prior to his deportation that there are thousands of other deportees being sent back to Mexico with the same level of detachment to what is purportedly their "true" home. Chuy explained, "I met a lot of people when I was in custody that are actually in the same shoes as I was.

They were raised over there [in the US], they didn't choose to go across the border. They didn't choose to be on that side. We were taken over there, and for all the rest of our lives we got used to the American way and then they send you somewhere where they say you were born that you don't even know. You don't even know how life is. It sucks." When I asked Chuy if he felt that his daily experience had changed now that he was living in a country where he did have citizenship and where he officially belonged, he shrugged. "Honestly, it doesn't make any difference. I thought I would have more privilege here, because you're in your country, or what not. I don't see it as home. I don't see it like—I don't. Home, to me, is the US, honestly." Chuy and Esther both feel like unintegrated immigrants living in Mexico, even though it is supposedly the country to which Chuy truly belongs.

Sebastian and Sonia also feel like an immigrant family in Mexico. Although Sebastian lived in Mexico until his mid-teens, he feels like his twenty years in the US transformed him into someone who Mexicans no longer recognize as one of their own. "It's hard for me because I am Mexican, but in my mind I am American," Sebastian explained, "because I basically grew up in the US. I lived twenty years in the United States, and I feel—I feel attacked. When I was in the US, there was obviously discrimination because of my Mexican roots. Now that I'm in Mexico, the same thing happens because of what I have lived and where I have grown up. I am Mexican, but my own people see me as different. Why?" He paused. "Because I carry two different cultures with me, and it is difficult for people to understand the schooling I have. Two cultures, two languages. Truthfully, I feel like I'm from a different planet. There are times that I wish people could understand, but they obviously can't because they haven't lived it, what I have lived." Although Sebastian thinks some people might not understand why or how he feels more American than Mexican, it is his truth. "Deep down inside, I feel more American, even though I am Mexican. And, if I say it in public, lots of people will criticize me and see the worst in me. But I know they are not going to understand me because I know what I carry inside of me. It's as if I had two different people rolled into one, an American and a Mexican."

After being in Mexico for almost a year following his most recent deportation, Sebastian still feels like "an outcast—I feel the looks people give when you are a foreigner." Sonia is even more aware of standing out, as her accent in Spanish exposes her "nonnative" speaking status, while speaking in English in public calls attention to her difference even more explicitly. Even in places where she feels like she shouldn't stand out, other people notice her difference immediately. "I was attending Zumba classes here and, right off the bat, someone comes up towards me and tells me, 'You're from the other side, huh?'" Sonia and Sebastian still feel like an American family, and a Mexican-American family, but not a Mexican family, despite the fact that Mexico is their only country of membership in which they will ever be able to live together as a family. As Sebastian said, "What I feel like is that I am not in the right place." He sighed. "I can say it this way, I don't feel accepted by my own people. And, like I've said, I feel inside, deep inside me, that my culture and my roots have also been American, and that I am a mixture of cultures and languages and traditions." Julia expressed a similar division of self that ultimately contributed to her divorce from Santiago: "I realized that, really, a lot of the emptiness that we've had in our relationship, or the hole that I have that cannot be filled is just having—I have two separate lives that cannot come together."

Many families with legal status in the US also feel that they embody a mixture of cultures, languages, and traditions. But rather than having "two separate lives" that they cannot bring together, these families' diverse backgrounds and experiences help them feel full social belonging in both of their countries of membership. In contrast to her experience with Santiago, Julia's marriage to Sergio has produced the fusion of two lives rather than their division. As Julia explained, "We're this great mix of both cultures, both customs, and I think that's the best way to live. . . . It's just a nice little melting pot of love and happiness." Though Sergio and Julia still live in Mexico, his ability to be a part of her full life and her ability to do the same with him have completely transformed Julia's experience as a member of a mixed-citizenship marriage.

Jiancarlo and Sondra described a similar merging of worlds, histories, and lives through their relationship. Jiancarlo explained to me that
the theme of their wedding was *"Unión de Desiertos"* (Union of Des-
erts) because "we felt that we were from two parts of the same desert,
divided by a border. There was a lot of symbolism in the way we even
got married, in the sense that it was a union of those two different des-
erts, the two different families, the two different cultures." And they
feel that unity as they travel back and forth between the US and Mexico. "We live in both [countries] and our ways of life are dual in that
sense. It isn't either/or for us," Jiancarlo explained. Chuck and Melodia also feel equally at home and a part of both of their countries. Thus,
rather than describing themselves as an American or a Mexican family, Chuck thinks they are a "completely binational family," not just legally but also "culturally and everything else," adding that this sense of
belonging holds even when they travel deep into Mexico or the US, not
just in the border region where they live. Melodia agrees. "It's like both
places feel like home." Judy, a stay-at-home mom who lives in a border community with her husband (Franklin, a pastor) and their daughter, feels the same way. "I almost forget we are being in two countries,
I guess. Because I feel like this [Mexico] is home, and I am from the
United States and that is [also] home." For couples with legal status in
the US, their official membership in the US has allowed them to feel like
full members in both spouses' countries of citizenship. This holds true
for couples living within *and* outside of the US.

As Aylin and Jared acknowledge, this privilege is as much a reflection
of their class position as it is of anything else. When I asked them how
they would describe their family-level nationality, they—like many other
couples—struggled to find the right term. They feel neither fully American nor fully Mexican, but Aylin also worries that adopting a Mexican-
American identity would lay claim on a history of struggle and oppression that they have not experienced. Aylin first suggested "binational,"
but decided that was not specific enough, either. "I actually think that
we are very much—we're very bourgeois class. We're just a very bourgeois couple. Maybe that's a good way of describing us." Jared agreed,

"We're part of the overeducated class. If there's the undereducated class, we're part of the overeducated class." "In a way," Aylin continued, "that confers this very weird international citizenship that's enabled not only because we're both citizens from these countries but also because we're specifically middle-class citizens"—"Upper-middle class," Jared interjected—"upper-middle class from these countries." Because of that privilege, Aylin "wouldn't like to say we're Mexican-American only because," she feels, "Mexican-American couples are not allowed to" live as freely as Aylin and Jared do.

Both Aylin and Jared recognize that their access to this "international citizenship," which is facilitated by their ability to travel freely in each other's countries of citizenship *and* travel together to other countries around the world, is more a product of their social class position in both countries rather than some inherent feature of their mixed-citizenship union. Aylin's experience has differed so significantly from the "typical" Mexican-American story in large part because of her privileged class position in Mexico, which afforded her more opportunities in Mexico prior to her move to the US and enabled her to move to the US with a valid visa. Similarly, Jared's socioeconomic class status in the US qualified him to sponsor Aylin's green card application and solidify their international bourgeois status permanently. The access to a binational—even international—lifestyle that Aylin and Jared and other couples receive as a result of their family-level legal immigration status creates opportunities for both spouses to meaningfully integrate into both of their respective countries of membership.

Official governmental approval of these couples through their acquisition of legal status plays a key role in supporting individual and familial social integration and sense of belonging. Jorge, who was a doctor in Mexico before he immigrated to the US on a fiancé visa to marry Nicole, highlighted the importance of "legal certainty" in shaping his personal sense of belonging in the US. He said, "Citizenship I don't think will make me feel more a part of the US. I think it's more of the legal certainty. Maybe my personality is that I came to the US and I just feel part of the work, I feel part of the place I started working at. It's this weird place of, again, being aware from time to time that I am from somewhere else, that I am learning a new system, but at the same time liking it and feeling like, yeah, this could have been my home the whole time."

This sense of belonging to the US even holds for families with legal status in the US but who have chosen to live primarily outside the US. According to his wife, Leticia, Mario changed significantly once he secured permanent resident status in the US, even though they continue to live as a family in Mexico. Part of this stems from the fact that Mario had been working previously without authorization in the US, and residency gives him legal authorization to work, thus eliminating a huge risk to their family stability that he faced before. But Leticia also saw that Mario changed with regard to his sense of belonging and sense of entitlement once he had official status in the US: "He changed a lot when he became a resident. Yes, people do change. One minute they gave him his papers and he became a resident, and then he's like, 'Oh, now I have a place here.'"

Chuck and Melodia both felt an added sense of belonging and peace of mind following their naturalization in each other's respective country of citizenship.[11] Melodia described this dual status change as transformational: "I just feel at peace, because I'm thinking, 'Whatever happens, I know that we're okay in both places.'" Chuck added, "I guess it's just a feeling of integration and being more at peace—[Melodia: 'Secure']—in both countries." As a result of this legal belonging, Chuck and Melodia are confident that their family belongs culturally and socially in both countries, describing themselves as a "binational" family. They see their official status as citizens of both countries as a key factor in facilitating their social integration in both countries, a measure of belonging that remains constant no matter where they live.

Couples' experiences of formal acceptance or rejection confirm the findings of many researchers who have noted the key role of legal status in shaping integration opportunities and outcomes across a number of dimensions.[12] For couples receiving formal approval by the US government in the form of a successful family reunification claim, the acquisition of legal status not only increases their access to spatial and structural dimensions of American society but also serves in and of itself to confirm that they already belong as a family in the US. Interestingly, and somewhat counterintuitively, acquiring legal status in the US also enhances these couples' social integration in their other country of membership. While integration toward the "mainstream" of one country has traditionally been understood as a process accompanied simultaneously by disintegration from the previous society of residence, this is not necessarily true, especially in the case of mixed-citizenship families with legal immigration status in the US.[13] Individual members of these legally authorized families can use their social and cultural capital and experience as citizens to draw their noncitizen spouses toward inclusion on multiple dimensions. This process can happen in both countries simultaneously and to an equal degree.

The formal legal rejection of families leads to their social disintegration from American society, whether those families continue to live in the US or are forced to leave. Both partners—including the US citizen spouses whose individual status and legal claim of belonging to the US has not technically changed—interpret their legal rejection by the state as a denial of their claim to an American identity. Notably, this alienation from US society extends to social estrangement within their other country of citizenship, too. While one might think that social disintegration from US society would push mixed-citizenship families toward social integration in the non-US citizen spouses' country of citizenship, the experiences of couples in this study suggest the opposite. Rejected families still living in the US cannot meaningfully connect with their other country of membership without leaving the US for at least a decade and, in some cases, permanently. Rejected families living outside the US find themselves with limited access to incorporation into their new country of residence. In many cases, this is due to the non-US citizen's lack of the social capital and experience necessary to navigate social and cultural institutions, practices, and expectations. Their social inexperience in these countries is also compounded by a real or perceived difference—on both the part of the "repatriated" citizen and their "native" counterparts—that only reinforces the idea that these mixed-citizenship families are too foreign to belong in their new country of residence, even if some family members can claim official legal membership to that society through citizenship. The effects of families' formal rejection by the US government are the exact opposite of those of formal acceptance. Accepted families experience enhanced social integration in both of their countries of membership while rejected families suffer social disintegration from both of the countries with which they have individual-level citizenship ties.

Liminal Social Integration

Couples with an "undetermined" status in the US—those with current unauthorized status but who have not yet pursued and/or received a final decision regarding their eligibility for family reunification (see chapter 3)—do not fit the pattern described above. While I find unauthorized status to be a key factor in limiting opportunities for spatial and structural integration (as demonstrated in chapters 4 and 5), it does not seem to have the same effect on couples' social integration and sense of belonging. Although the rejected families discussed above feel definitively excluded and disintegrated socially, families living within the US with unauthorized status but who have not pursued any family reunification decision feel the opposite. Overall, these unauthorized families express a strong sense of belonging to the US and a perception that others in their communities equally perceive them as belonging (with some caveats). Consequently, formal rejection of a couple through the denial of their family reunification claim, rather than the lack of legal status, appears to be the driving factor in families' social disintegration.

When I asked Kate and Juan if they felt like an American family, Kate immediately responded, "Oh yeah. I think so," to which Juan added, "I think so, too." As Kate put it, "I see ourselves as just any other family, any other American family." Many other couples echoed this feeling of "normalcy," of living as any other "normal" American family does. Seeing other mixed-ethnicity and mixed-race couples in their communities also makes couples feel like they belong. Kat and Beto, who live near Seattle, feel that region in particular, home to "tons of interracial marriages and intercultural marriages and everything," has welcomed them as an American family. Because he lives "the same style as an American," Beto also feels comfortable embracing an American identity for himself as an individual and for his family, despite his lack of official legal status. William and Berenice also noted that an increase in inter-ethnic couples in their community has helped them feel American and, they think, helps others perceive them as American, too.

Even before Tenoch adjusted to a legal immigration status, Juliette told me that they were a "normal" American family. She saw her family's "normalcy" in terms of how she and Tenoch struggled as a couple to help their family succeed.

> Maintaining the relationship is just the same as anybody else, whether they're married American-American, citizen-citizen, no matter what country, it's the same exact thing. Like, do we have enough to make a living? Do we have enough to have food on the table? Are we happy in the things that we're doing as a family and individually, working or, you know, do we have dreams that we want to do together? That's what every family's concern is, it's not whether or not you're completely documented or whatever. So, I think, that's probably the base of it all is that we're just a normal family.

Rodrigo described his and Carmela's familial belonging to the US in comparable terms, explaining that the US "is a country that opened opportunity to me, and the only thing you need is the willingness to work and with that you can get everything that you want." Juliette found her family's conventionality in their common effort to meet their family's basic needs, and Rodrigo saw his family as normal because they can work hard and strive for opportunity just like everyone else.

Of the unauthorized families living in the US that I interviewed, all expressed a sense of belonging, at least on some level, and most felt that the American identity described them better than any others (e.g., Mexican, Latinx, and/or a hyphenated identity). But some couples did express a more circumscribed American identity due to the limitations their lack of legal status places on their daily lives. Trish believes that she and her family simultaneously are and are not just like any other family in their small-town American community. Trish explained that sometimes, "like when we're going out on a date together," she feels they are just like any other family. "But when I look at other people and their families, and they are like, 'Oh yeah, let's do this or that,' I don't know. Like going on vacation is different. Paying our bills is different. There are a lot of different things that have just become [part of] our lives. So, yeah, going out together is fine, I think. We feel okay. But just normal day-to-day life," she sighed, "if you talk to someone else, our life is very different." Trish could not overlook the practical, daily challenges her unauthorized family faces that differentiate them from other, legally authorized families in her community. Yet, despite these differences, she feels that both she and her family can and do belong in the US. Their claim on an American identity, while tentative, has not yet been fully rejected and, therefore, could still be fully legitimized through official legal approval. Unauthorized families living in the US still find hope in their partial US citizenship and its implication of social belonging, something that rejected families no longer see. In this sense, unauthorized families express a sense of belonging to the US and a level of social inclusion much closer to that of legally authorized families than those that have been officially rejected.

A major difference between these unauthorized couples' social integration and that of couples who have received official legal approval through family reunification involves their (in)ability to socially integrate into the non-US citizen spouses' country of citizenship. For example, while Kate and Juan both willingly described their family as American, they did not feel they could embrace a similar identity as a Mexican family because, as Kate put it, "it's just hard living here in the United States to really feel part of that culture." None of these couples had lived together outside of the United States, which produced for many of them an inability to imagine what life would be like for them there and whether or not they could also belong as a family in those specific national contexts. In this sense, the lack of legal status impedes their ability to socially integrate into both countries of membership, although it does not seem to interfere significantly with their sense of belonging in the US, their country of residence.

The other notable difference between unauthorized couples living in the US and their legally authorized counterparts is the liminality of their status.[14] While these couples have not yet been officially rejected as American families by the US government, they are well aware of the fact that they have not yet been legally accepted as American families, either. Before Tenoch successfully adjusted to an authorized immigration status, Juliette and Tenoch saw themselves as "just a normal family"; but she added the caveat that Tenoch's deportability introduced uncertainties in their life that other families with legal status did not face: "So, the only difference is, I guess, normal American citizen families don't have to worry about if someone's leaving—getting kicked out of the country." Chandra described her family as both American and Mexican, but feels her family, especially her children, would benefit most from being able to grow up in the US. Yet she noted that Pancho's unauthorized status means this might not be a long-term possibility for them as a family, making it hard to feel fully American and plan for a life together in the US. "I don't feel like there's one culture in our house that's more important than the other one," Chandra said, "or that one nationality is more important than the other one. I want to raise our kids here. I prefer to raise our kids here, but that's mostly because [Pancho] left Mexico for a reason. So, that's how I prefer it." But, she added, they also recognize that you cannot always "count on plans."

These unauthorized couples' complicated, yet generally positive, sense of belonging in the US and perception of their social integration echoes many other scholars' findings that social citizenship, membership, and inclusion in both a local and national context are not determined by one's formal individual (or familial) legal membership.[15] Individuals and families given opportunities to participate in local and national social life naturally develop ties and relationships that encourage an increased sense of belonging and affiliation with the local and national identity. This is true whether or not families have an official legal status. While families' lack of legal status implies their potential future formal exclusion from society, their lack of legal rejection simultaneously supports a hope in their future formal inclusion in society. This hope enables unauthorized families to identify and embrace opportunities for social inclusion in the US, even if that inclusion remains tentative.

Social integration uniquely shapes overall integration processes and outcomes in three key ways. First, as with other aspects of integration, family-level legal status directly influences individual social (dis)integration and sense of belonging. Citizens, who by definition compose national society and by their nature at minimum legally "belong" to a country, actively abandon that notion and feel individually rejected and ostracized when the government formally rejects their immediate family member. While the state frames this familial rejection in individualistic terms and reinforces its commitment to citizen family members,[16] the effect of that rejection has legal, social, and identificational impacts for all family members, regardless of their (non)citizen status. Citizens can and do experience direct social disintegration as a result of the treatment of their family members under the law.

Notably, citizens' social integration and sense of belonging can also be augmented by the positive treatment of their family members under the law. When citizens' spouses receive official, legal approval to live, work, and thrive in the US, the citizens—as well as their spouses—experience a stronger sense of belonging to the US, even when they already felt socially integrated prior to that decision. Both of these results suggest that, rather than functioning as a dichotomous outcome, social (dis)integration functions on a spectrum in which both citizens and noncitizens can move toward or away from social integration at any time based on factors outside of their own individual characteristics and experiences.

Second, family-level legal status functions differently for social integration than for other dimensions of integration. Unlike other facets of integration (e.g., spatial, structural, civic, and political) for which possessing legal status appears to be the primary determinant of integration, social integration is shaped more by the *absence* of formal legal rejection by the US rather than by the receipt of official legal status. This distinction means that individuals and families who confront structures of exclusion in multiple dimensions of their daily lives due to unauthorized status can still find meaningful spaces, relationships, and interactions that encourage and reinforce social integration and a strong sense of belonging. The findings here echo those of other scholars whose research confirms that official legal status is not necessary for social integration,[17] nor does possession of official legal status guarantee social integration.[18] Rather, it is the act of formal rejection that triggers social disintegration for noncitizens and citizens alike. Socially integrated individuals and families invest more in their communities across many measures; thus, recognizing and supporting all families living in the US—not just those with legal immigration status—strengthens those families and the communities in which they live.[19] Pursuing policies that formally and informally reject and ostracize families without legal status will continue to create instability for those families and their broader communities.

Finally, the effects of social integration reach beyond the specific society in which (dis)integration occurs to shape social (dis)integration processes in other national contexts, as well. This seemingly counterintuitive finding that mixed-citizenship families' increased social integration in the US actually facilitates their increased social integration into their other country of membership challenges traditional notions of assimilation.[20] These traditional theories of assimilation assert that individuals must shed their "otherness"—which can include language, cuisine, and cultural practices and traditions—before they can socially integrate with the "mainstream." This process of "acculturation" implies a natural and simultaneous dissimilation of immigrants from their countries of origin.[21] Yet the experiences of mixed-citizenship couples suggest the opposite—that the social integration of both spouses in one country can coincide with the simultaneous social integration of both spouses in the other country.[22] Likewise, social disintegration from one country inhibits social integration in another country, even for individuals and families with citizenship ties to both places. Social integration cannot be forced; when individual and familial social experience is grounded in trauma, rejection, and difference (and often in the absence of official acceptance and recognition in the new social context), the conditions necessary for social integration are absent, too.

The difference in sense of belonging as expressed by unauthorized families and rejected families also provides an interesting case for understanding how identity management processes work at both the individual and familial levels.[23] Unauthorized families, and the citizen members of unauthorized families specifically, do experience conflict at times between their identities as individual (non)citizens, members of an unauthorized family, and willing creators of those intimate family relationships. But because their official familial status vis-à-vis the state has not yet been determined, both citizen and noncitizen family members can reconcile these identity conflicts and find meaningful spheres of social belonging in the US. Formal rejection leaves no room for hope, intensifying seemingly unresolvable conflicts between familial and national identity and leading both partners to undergo long-term identity change. Legal outcomes do much more than determine opportunities for individuals and families; they shape deeply personal understandings of who one is and who one can become. For this reason, the decision not to "play" the family reunification game discussed in chapter 3 can be important not only to preserve the possibility of future legal status for mixed-citizenship families but also to preserve crucial individual and familial identities.

The findings in this chapter demonstrate yet again that family mediates the integration experience at every level: spatially, structurally, socially, and everywhere in between. In the concluding chapter, I discuss the implications of these findings for individuals, families, and nation-states as they each struggle to assert and sustain their own legitimacy, their right to self-determination, and the defensibility of the claims they make on each other.

Conclusion

ABOUT A YEAR after I began collecting data for this book, I received a grant enabling me to pay a very small incentive ($10) to participating couples. I wanted to make sure the couples I had already interviewed also received their incentive, so I began contacting each of them. When I messaged Chandra, whom I had interviewed with her husband four months earlier, her reply shocked me: "It's interesting that you contacted me today because this morning my husband was actually taken into custody by immigration. Looks like we get to do battle."

My heart dropped as I read her message. I knew Chandra had given birth to their first baby—he was only six weeks old—and, as a new mom myself, I could not imagine navigating all of the exhaustion of the immigration enforcement system with a newborn. Chandra and Pancho lived and worked on a ranch in southern Utah, and with Pancho in custody and unable to work and Chandra home with a newborn, the ranch owners told Chandra that she would have to find new housing (and a new job). In one day, their lives had been turned upside down.

I offered to help in whatever way I could, contacting immigration lawyers I knew to ask for referrals and even helping them figure out a place to stay in Mexico if he were deported. Over the next few months, we maintained regular contact. Chandra kept me updated on Pancho's hearing schedule and explained her lawyer's plan for getting Pancho out on bail in the short term and fighting the deportation order in the long term. She also asked me about life as an American in Mexico. We talked about ranches near my house by the border, the feasibility of cross-border life, and what kinds of documents she could start getting in order to help support their case to fight his deportation. We also tried to navigate the immigration bail bond system and scoured the internet for information on charities that might be able to help Chandra and her family with food, bail funds, work . . . anything.

Three months after Pancho's arrest, over the same weekend as Donald Trump's presidential inauguration, the judge assigned to Pancho's case granted him release on bail. Chandra was thrilled. They had a lot to celebrate and a lot of memories to make up for: during that three-month separation, they had missed celebrating their first anniversary, Pancho's birthday, and their baby's first Christmas. Once Pancho was out of detention, they also began waiting. With their next court date set for 2022, they are still waiting for a final decision on whether a judge will cancel Pancho's deportation order or if they will be forced to uproot their family and try to find a place outside the US where they are allowed to live together as a family. While their love is strong, they will yet discover if it is strong enough to overcome the cruelest aspects of US immigration law.

In chapter 1, I introduced Chandra, Pancho, and four other couples whose lives followed drastically different trajectories because of their standing with regard to US immigration law. The law left Chandra, who did not earn sufficient income to sponsor Pancho for permanent residency, unprotected from the threat of deportation and family separation. Chandra and Pancho's relationship, which began with so much hope and possibility, has come to be defined as much by its vulnerability before the law as the depth or "legitimacy" of their love.

Molly met and married Hector in Mexico, where they had both lived for more than a decade. Shortly after they married, Molly successfully sponsored Hector for permanent residency in the US. They moved into a small home a few miles north of the border and traveled regularly to Mexico to visit friends and family there. About a year after they moved to the US, things were going well: Molly received a significant promotion at her job, they had new a baby, and another baby was on the way. But just a year later, Hector was arrested, charged, and convicted of a felony. He spent four years in prison in the US; upon his release from prison, he was deported and barred from legal reentry into the US for at least ten years. With Hector out of prison, Molly moved their family back to Mexico again. In the five years since Hector's deportation, they have tried hard to find ways to keep their relationship strong. Molly works just across the border in the US, and their two older kids go to school over there, too. Hector cares for their three younger children and keeps things running smoothly at home. Most of the time, everything seems pretty great. But when the older kids have events at school or Molly's family invites them up for Sunday dinner, Hector cannot join them. He always has to stay behind. They are hopeful that, after his ten-year wait is up, he will be allowed to enter the US again to go to Molly's family reunions, attend his children's school presentations, visit Molly at work, and be fully present in his children's lives. In the meantime, they wait.

Berenice, who broke up with William multiple times while they dated, worried about how her unauthorized status in the US would affect him. "I broke up with him because I was like, 'I don't want to put anybody into this, especially a gringo, with this immigration thing.'" She felt like William did not understand the implications of unauthorized status, and she did not want to pull him into unauthorized life blindly. She also worried he would think she just wanted to marry him for papers—"you heard that a lot"—which was not her motivation at all. She decided it would just be easier to end the relationship. But William, determined not to lose Berenice, began researching everything he could about what it meant to have unauthorized immigration status and how it would affect their life together. Ultimately, they both decided that the benefits of building a life as a family outweighed the risks and forged ahead into the uncertainty together, hand in hand. Although Berenice's status remains unresolved and deportation is a real possibility, she and William have decided to live their lives to the fullest despite the unknowns, hopeful that a viable path to legal status presents itself in time.

All three of these couples live with some combination of forced (and indefinite) waiting, (fear of) separation, and disintegration.[1] As we have seen throughout the book, though, not all mixed-citizenship couples face such challenges and uncertainty. Historically, tens of thousands of mixed-citizenship couples successfully qualify for family reunification every year.[2] Brett and Mariana, after their chance encounter in the

Cancun airport and years in a long-distance relationship, finally decided to "tie the knot." With the help of a lawyer, they secured a fiancée visa enabling them to finally live together. Now they can travel to visit family and friends in Mexico and the US, rather than using all of their vacation days crossing borders to see each other. While they have settled in the US for now, they envision a future in which they can live and work wherever they choose on either side of the border.

Grace and Lucas, whose relationship has been geographically binational from the beginning, now split their time between the US and Mexico, working together at an American university when school is in session and living in Mexico during their long winter and summer breaks. They are thrilled to be able to share both of their worlds with their one-year-old daughter and hope she will come to know and love both of her countries as much as they do.

For Grace and Lucas, Brett and Mariana, and many other couples, US family reunification law has facilitated their access to "the best of both worlds" in both of their countries of citizenship. Their experiences substantiate the important truths that family reunification is achievable and its benefits are significant and long-lasting. Juliette, my friend whose experience motivated this research, helped transcribe some of my interviews, and she balked at this realization when she listened to Grace and Lucas tell their story. In the interview, when I asked Grace and Lucas about their experience applying for Lucas's permanent residency, they mentioned complications with timelines—coordinating residency requirements with Lucas's academic fellowships in the US and France, scheduling their dissertation defenses, navigating the unpredictable academic job market, and finalizing postgraduate plans—and finding the right time to adjust from a temporary to permanent immigration status. But they never expressed any doubt that the government would approve their application for family reunification.

After listening to Grace and Lucas recount their experience with the US immigration system, Juliette sent me a series of text messages conveying her complex reaction: "Wow. Hearing the difference in emotional experience with the system from this couple who seem ok financially and had proper visas through school, etc., compared to mine and that of my friends is night and day. We—and my friends—had experiences where our husbands had multiple entries and either lost a hard-to-get-visa or never had a chance in hell to get one. We are all lower-income families hovering around the poverty level for our household sizes." Knowing the psychological toll that the threat of rejection takes on unauthorized families, Juliette expressed that hearing Grace and Lucas "discuss the bureaucracy as a nuisance with disdain but really otherwise unaffected is mind boggling. I am currently helping a friend out emotionally (as much as possible) because she is so afraid. The depression and anxiety that followed me is also what I've heard from others." Juliette knew that this vast difference in experience was not arbitrary, nor accidental. "It's so intriguing to see the class difference, education difference, opportunity-from-home-country difference. Astounding," she continued. "It's like the United States became the high roller club, and based on the hand you were dealt you get special treatment."

Her flurry of messages stopped for a moment, and I sat reading and processing what she wrote, thinking of how to respond. "I know" felt insufficient. "I'm sorry" did, too. How do you find words to apologize for all of the pain your government has inflicted upon your friend? And how do you acknowledge that, had she and her partner had more social and economic capital, their experience might have been completely different? As I struggled to collect my thoughts, my phone chimed as another message from Juliette appeared on the screen. "I would have loved to speak so gracefully and with more confidence about our outcome while waiting for it all to play out," she wrote. "So often I felt that I was lacking faith. But really it's all about not wanting to have forms of oppression placed on your future because of obeying and sustaining the law, being subject to corruption. A major part of wanting to 'get right with the law' was propelled by wanting the best for our family, but also my religious understanding about being in good standing with the law. I thought/hoped it would be an easy process since all we wanted was to pay our dues and reconcile. But," she said, "it's thrown in your face over and over again that privilege is not on your side."

Juliette recognized in these conflicting encounters with the same legal system a trend that I had noted in my interviews with mixed-citizenship couples and my analysis of the laws governing these couples' access to family reunification: there is no such thing as an even playing field. Like Juliette described it, families' access to legal status and family reunification has more to do with their luck at having a higher socioeconomic status than their right to a purportedly universal privilege of US citizenship.

The class-based preferences built into the US family reunification system shape the lives of mixed-citizenship couples in dramatically different ways. Punishments directed toward US citizens and unauthorized immigrants from lower socioeconomic backgrounds prevent those families from accessing family reunification. Rather than being a program of family reunification for all Americans and their noncitizen family members, the current US immigration system uses family relationships as a way to facilitate the legal immigration (or adjustment to legal immigrant status) of middle- and upper-class noncitizens and the partners of middle- and upper-class US citizens. These class-based distinctions are further exacerbated through the process of engaging with US immigration laws—a citizen-driven process that introduces additional opportunities for better-educated and well-resourced families to work the law to their benefit and further their systemic advantage. The implications of these inequalities and their consequences—for individuals *and* families—cannot be overstated.

Unequal access to family reunification and legal immigration status in the US has significant and long-lasting effects on families and their integration. While policymakers often claim that laws directed toward immigrants do not affect citizens, mixed-citizenship families' experiences prove definitively that such is not the case. Every US immigration law produces consequences experienced at the family level. Sebastian explained it well: "Obviously the themes that we are discussing are very broad and there are so many things I would like you to ask me or to be able to discuss in more detail, but it is not simple. This is life—not just one person's life, but in our case, three lives. And there are many, many families that are in the same situation. Together we are, I believe there are millions of people that are going through this situation, and it is a separation of families." He paused. "A separation of families, and the one who is paying the consequences, in this case, is my daughter." Sebastian explained that his daughter does not understand why he cannot do all of the fun fatherly things he used to do with her. "She asks me things that I cannot explain to her, things that are impossible to me. And this makes me feel impotent. It makes me angry and sad to not be able to give her something so simple but, at the same time, impossible for me to give to her in the moment that she asks me for it. It is something so simple but so meaningful for my daughter. When I was living in San Diego, I would wake her up, dress her, and walk with her to school. It is something so simple that I cannot do today." Sebastian's inability to integrate into American society because of his unauthorized status and subsequent deportations have not only affected his relationship to his wife and daughter but his wife's and daughter's ability to fully integrate into American (and Mexican) society, as well. As Sebastian said, his status does not just affect him individually, but it affects his entire family.

Sebastian and Sonia's experience is not unique. Their experiences, and those of the other couples discussed throughout the book, demonstrate that the institution of the family mediates the process and experience of integration. Because "families are meant to be lived with," as Sonia said, the spatial dissimilation of one family member generally leads to the spatial dissimilation of all family members. Individual access to social, educational, economic, governmental, and other institutions key to structural integration also filters through the family. And structural integration facilitates incorporation on many other dimensions, including social integration and belonging.[3] Mixed-citizenship families able to integrate spatially and structurally feel like they belong to the US and that other Americans also see them as part of (and representative of) America. But families barred from fully integrating on spatial and structural dimensions also face exclusions that inhibit them from integrating socially, too. These effects—both positive and negative—impact all members of mixed-citizenship families, regardless of their individual citizenship status.

Because the family is a central institution through which integration happens, American laws and policies that punish immigrants contribute toward the alienation and disintegration of immigrants *and* their citizen family members. Denying legal immigration status to the spouses of US citizens is a policy of disintegration—forcing either the dissimilation of the entire family from society or the dissolution of the family itself.

Too often, we overlook the true consequences of US policies that force family disintegration, separation, and dissolution. Once immigrants have been deported, their ongoing experiences and struggles frequently disappear from media coverage and public discourse. But the effects of "removal" on immigrants and their family members—both those who leave the US and those who stay behind—reverberate through every aspect of their lives, often for generations.

Members of the same immediate and extended family can have disparate access to legal status, creating legal inequalities and suffering that flow between and across family relationships. Reeves described to me the starkly contrasting outcomes of US immigration law in her husband's family, in which two brothers adjusted from unauthorized to legal immigration status and two other brothers could not. All four brothers entered the US without authorization, crossing the border from Mexico into the US and settling together in Chicago. Erick's oldest brother married a US citizen and was able to adjust to a legal immigration status and, in time, naturalize. Erick, too, became a permanent resident after adjusting his status following his marriage to Reeves. But Erick's two other brothers—Chepo and José—who, at different times, preemptively "self-deported" back to Mexico after run-ins with the police, both suffered a very different fate. Chepo, who had to leave behind his wife and children when he left the US, fell into a severe depression as he accepted the reality that he would likely never live with—or perhaps even see—his family again. Less than a year after he returned to Mexico, Chepo committed suicide. Four years later, when José was forced to leave the US, he, too, took his life. Repatriation and its consequences—family separation, shame, hopelessness—were the driving factors behind their deaths. As Reeves observed, "It is striking to me that the men in this family had two paths, and these paths were so determined by their options for legally remaining" in the US.

Every family I interviewed who had experienced deportation—either their own deportation or that of close family members—described significant, long-lasting consequences of enduring the brutality of US immigration law. Among the ten couples I interviewed with a spouse who had personally experienced deportation, "voluntary" removal, and/or permanent bars to legal status, interviewees reported depression and anxiety, alcoholism, drug abuse, and divorce as struggles stemming directly from their banishment from the US. We cannot ignore the ruthless reality of US immigration laws that devastate American families every day. Nor can we ignore the after-effects of the punishments inflicted by the law, which linger long after the deportation act is complete.[4]

A number of the laws causing this irreparable damage can be easily amended to minimize (if not eliminate) the unnecessary burdens and suffering borne by many mixed-citizenship families. Additional policies could be implemented to further support mixed-citizenship families while their applications are in process and/or while those families are living abroad. A few such policy changes and recommendations include the following:

Bars to Reentry. The three- and ten-year bars to reentry instituted in the 1996 Illegal Immigration Reform and Immigrant Responsibility Act (IIRIRA) have directly contributed to the separation of millions of American families. In the twenty-five years since the implementation of this policy, researchers have found no clear evidence that the bars discourage unauthorized immigration or protect the US from national security threats (the purported goals of the policy), although they have found significant evidence of the bars' devastating consequences for American families.[5] One option—though its effects would reach far beyond mixed-citizenship couples—is to repeal the multiyear bars to legal reentry currently applied to almost all unauthorized immigrants upon leaving the United States. Repealing the bars to reentry would help many mixed-citizenship families adjust to legal immigration status without facing years of separation and/or forced relocation outside the US. A more limited approach would involve changing current law to allow all unauthorized spouses of US citizens to adjust to legal status from within the United States. (This exception currently stands for the unauthorized spouses of US citizens who overstay a valid visa but not for those who have entered the US without a visa.) If readmission through a port of entry remains a necessary bureaucratic or symbolic step, arrangements could be made to allow such processing at international airports based within the United States once applicants receive final visa approval, satisfying the letter of the law without invoking the bars to reentry.

Minimum Income Thresholds. The IIRIRA also introduced minimum income thresholds that citizens must meet in order to qualify to sponsor a spouse for permanent residency.[6] Designed to help prevent immigrants from becoming "public charges," this policy actually contributes to the economic instability of thousands of mixed-citizenship American families. These minimum income thresholds should be repealed. Failing that, the potential earnings of the noncitizen spouse being sponsored should be included toward meeting the minimum income thresholds. Disqualifying American citizens from family reunification because they earn low wages perpetuates income inequality and punishes US citizens for circumstances that are often beyond their control. It also prevents them from increasing their family income and economic opportunities by prohibiting their reunification with an additional wage earner. The current policy on its own does not protect the US government from an unnecessary financial burden because immigrants with legal status are already disqualified from accessing most welfare benefits. Instead, the US is likely augmenting its welfare costs by preventing low-income mixed-citizenship families from increasing their familial earning potential through family reunification. Family reunification should not be a citizenship benefit accessible only to citizens with "sufficient" means.

Permanent Bars for Fraudulent Claims of Citizenship. The permanent bar to legal entry to the US associated with "falsely claim[ing] to be a US citizen for any purpose or benefit under [. . . any] federal or state law" exceeds its intentions and severely punishes many mixed-citizenship families.[7] While part of the determination of a false claim requires an immigration officer to ensure that the noncitizen "made the false representation knowingly," the burden of proof for immigration officers is low and the ability of noncitizens to challenge the accusation of a false claim is nearly impossible.[8] Although the law is designed to deter individuals from making false citizenship claims, it works in effect to punish individuals who found themselves in a situation in which they could be accused of making a false citizenship claim, whether or not that was their intention. The permanent bar to legal admission to the US associated with this charge most severely burdens mixed-citizenship couples who, as a result, are permanently prevented from living together legally within the United States, essentially forcing the exile of US citizen spouses and children or the dissolution of the family. While making a false claim to citizenship is a serious offense under some circumstances—such as fraud and willful misrepresentation, conditions to which this rule was previously limited—lawmakers should at minimum create a waiver similar to the Extreme Hardship Waiver that would allow noncitizen spouses of US citizens subject to this permanent bar to appeal for relief. A return to the narrower definition of a false claim of citizenship (in force prior to the IIRIRA), which was limited to fraud or willful misrepresentation, would further remedy the current policy failures, but this should be in addition to the creation of a waiver rather than in lieu of one.

Standards for "Legitimate" Relationships and Families. In the thirty-five years since Congress passed the International Marriage Fraud Amendments in 1986, advancements in communication technology have drastically altered the ability of individuals from different countries to meet and develop deeply intimate relationships without ever physically sharing the same space. Couples living on different sides of the country (or in different countries) can maintain intimate relationships and "see" each other many times a day, something with which we are all now deeply familiar after having lived through the COVID-19 pandemic. And, as many of the families I studied who were forced to separate or live dislocated lives across borders prove, legitimate marriages and families often look very different from the limited definition of "legitimate" marriage enshrined in the IMFA.[9] Lawmakers should update the IMFA to reflect these advances in modern love and family to create a more inclusive and accurate definition of "legitimate" mixed-citizenship marriage. Additionally, Congress should also expand the definitions of "family" and "marriage" to better accommodate modern American families and, at minimum, create a waiver that allows couples and families to petition for family reunification with relatives—such as common-law spouses, parents-in-law, and grandparents—whose connection to citizens falls outside of the relationships currently acknowledged in US family reunification law.

Temporary Authorization for Mixed-Citizenship Families Applying for Family Reunification. The disparate treatment of mixed-citizenship families seeking reunification extends to their treatment while their family reunification applications are under review. Couples living in the US seeking to adjust the non-US citizen partner from a (current or expired) visa to permanent resident status can apply for work authorization and permission to travel outside of the US while their application is under review. This means that, while their application is moving through the different stages of review and approval (lasting anywhere from months to years), couples can maintain connections with their family living abroad, and noncitizen partners can support their families through legal work. Couples applying for family reunification through consular review (either because the spouse is living outside the US or because the spouse entered the US without authorization) must wait until a final positive determination is made regarding their application before the noncitizen spouse can travel across borders or work in the US. While they wait, these couples often endure financial strain and lengthy separations. Giving all mixed-citizenship couples the same access to family togetherness and the legal labor market will help them flourish rather than force many mixed-citizenship couples to endure unnecessary extended hardship stemming solely from drawn-out administrative processes.

Access to the US without Requiring Permanent Residency. Under current US immigration law, the only visas enabling temporary or permanent entry to the US based on a family relationship with a US citizen are permanent residency and fiancé(e) visas. Both of these visas have residency requirements that oblige recipients to live in the US for most or all of the duration of their status.[10] Permanent residents of the US can lose their residency status if they live outside of the US for more than six months at a time. Many mixed-citizenship couples who choose to live outside of the United States cannot access visas that would allow the temporary entry of the noncitizen spouse to the US based on their relationship.[11,12] This means that mixed-citizenship families must apply for family reunification and live most of the time in the US or potentially never travel to the US together as a family. Congress should create a new nonimmigrant visa category that enables the short-term travel of citizens' immediate family members to the US to recognize the fact that mixed-citizenship families choosing to live primarily *outside* the US would still like to be able to travel to the US together for limited periods of time. This would allow many more mixed-citizenship American families to maintain strong ties to the US even when living abroad.

As policymakers consider every policy option, they must remember that laws targeting immigrants affect citizens, too. Policymakers should shift their attention away from punishing unauthorized immigrants and toward supporting and preserving American families. Modifying existing policies and developing new policies to provide opportunities for mixed-citizenship American families to succeed will reduce the unauthorized immigrant population while generating significant benefits for these families and the communities in which they live.[13]

The experiences of mixed-citizenship couples suggest that modifying current policy and developing new laws within the existing individualistic legal framework of (non)citizenship will not resolve all the conflicts their mixed status generates, for themselves or for the nation-state. This is because mixed-citizenship families, by their very nature, challenge the individualistic citizenship regime and the state power it upholds. Mixed-citizenship families pose a threat to states seeking to exert ultimate control over their membership and borders.[14] As single family units composed of individuals from different countries, mixed-citizenship families are not fully immigrant families, nor are they fully native families, and their attempts to belong as a family unit (not just as individuals) in one or both countries call into question the social, political, cultural, and moral separations that international borders are designed to reinforce. Citizens who choose to marry noncitizens wrest control from the nation-state in deciding who belongs and who does not by challenging the state to accept or reject them as a family, not just as individuals. In managing mixed-citizenship couples, states must either declare the entire family unit welcome in society (even if the noncitizen spouse might not otherwise qualify for membership as an individual) or dismiss the family altogether, including the citizen spouse who has always officially "belonged."

Any system of citizenship that ignores the primacy of family relationships in determining the experience of citizenship and access to its associated privileges will continue to generate problems for mixed-citizenship families and society at large—including the alienation of citizens from society, the erasure of crucial contributing members of communities due to their unauthorized status, and the destabilization of the family as the key organizing unit of society. To resolve the conflict between individual-level citizenship and the family-based organization of social life, states must recognize the importance of families to their long-term viability and the role of the family in shaping citizens' lived experience. States will have to acknowledge the grave costs of the current citizenship regime to their own stability and their citizens' well-being as it sows division among its citizens and effectively creates a second-class citizenship by barring some citizens from accessing their promised rights. States will have to abandon a hypocritical system that legally favors and privileges families in some situations while blatantly ignoring family relationships and stability in others and adopt, instead, one that recognizes the right to family life across all legal settings.[15] If states do not take these necessary steps, the foundations upon which their power and legitimacy rest will continue to crumble.

One way forward in addressing this issue could be found in shifting how the US government recognizes family-level citizenship status. Right now, mixed-citizenship American families experience the "lowest common denominator" problem with regard to US citizenship and immigration law: each mixed-citizenship family unit has only the rights and privileges associated with the *least*-entitled family member's status, whether that be as a legally authorized immigrant, an unauthorized immigrant, or a nonimmigrant living outside the US. For example, if one family member does not have the right to live legally in the US, the family itself has no right to live legally in the US. The "lowest common denominator" problem produces many of the consequences discussed in this book in which US citizens cannot practically access their citizenship privileges because of a family member's noncitizen status.

What if, instead, our citizenship and immigration laws functioned under a *highest* denominator system? What if individual-level citizenship status afforded family units the rights and benefits promised to the *most*-entitled family member? Such a solution would recognize the citizen's right to family life promised by the Constitution but denied through decisions such as *Kerry v. Din*. It would promote the inclusion and incorporation of mixed-citizenship families. It would fortify the citizen-state relationship by investing in the well-being of the citizen, including her family. Extending citizens' rights, privileges, and protections to their family units would strengthen millions of American families without significantly increasing risks to the American state.

Precedents for such an approach to citizenship exist within the United States' own history. From 1855 to 1922, the wives of US citizen men automatically qualified for citizenship as a result of their marriages to US citizens.[16] While women's citizenship was largely symbolic prior to women gaining the vote in 1920—and automatic citizenship for the foreign wives of US citizens ended in 1922—there is no evidence that granting citizenship to these foreign wives for nearly seventy years threatened or weakened the US in any way, even after those women could vote. Rather, this policy facilitated the integration of the wives of US citizen men (and thus the integration of their families, too), and it explicitly recognized the right of the US citizen to family life. This experiment in family-level citizenship demonstrates that a "highest denominator" system could work to support millions of mixed-citizenship American families at little cost to the government and without risking national security. Even if foreign spouses of US citizens merely received legal permanent residency automatically, mixed-citizenship families and the country as a whole would benefit tremendously. Stability would replace uncertainty, and families would be free to fully invest in an American life together.[17]

A "highest denominator" approach is one way policymakers could overcome the individualist problem of citizenship and reintroduce the family into official citizenship policy. I add my voice to those of scholars such as Yasemin Soysal, Judith Butler, and Elizabeth Anderson, who argue that individualist approaches to social contracts like citizenship fall short of creating systems that properly acknowledge our infinite interdependencies and establishing the conditions necessary to achieve true equality.[18] Mixed-citizenship couples represent just one example of this truth. Until we adopt a new system of national membership that prioritizes our social dependencies over hyper-selectivity and state power, we will all continue to suffer the consequences.

Epilogue

IN JUNE 2020, in the midst of the pandemic and a wave of protests across the US supporting the Black Lives Matter movement, Camille, Juliette, and I came together (over Zoom) to think about everything we have been through since Juliette's wedding ten years ago.

Camille's husband, Giovanni, was deported to Guatemala in 2011. She soon moved with their baby boy to Guatemala to live with Giovanni, and they all lived together there for two-and-a-half years. Camille and Giovanni had another child and tried to make their marriage and life in Guatemala work, but Camille reached a breaking point and moved back to the States in early 2014 with her two small children to finish her college degree (she had one semester remaining when Giovanni was deported) and try to find a way to resolve their immigration situation. Ultimately, there was no way for Giovanni to legally return to the US, and Camille filed for divorce in 2015.

Juliette worked tirelessly for seven years to try to adjust Tenoch from an unauthorized to a legal immigration status. Finally, in 2017, the government granted their hardship waiver and approved Tenoch's residency application. While the fear of deportation and family separation has receded with Tenoch's acquisition of legal status, it has not resolved all of their problems. They are still paying off their debt from legal fees and immigration applications; they are also trying to unlearn the unhealthy coping patterns they adopted in the face of their deportation fears.

And I am still waiting for a resolution to our story. Ramón and I married in 2012 and lived together in Mexico while he worked and I finished graduate school. We applied for his residency in 2018 shortly after I accepted a full-time academic position at Brigham Young University in Utah. Two years later, his application is still unresolved, with no clear timeline indicating when he will be able to officially live with me and our children in the US.

The conversation that follows is a snapshot of our thoughts and feelings regarding what Camille, Juliette, and I have been through personally and what we have survived alongside each other as we have navigated the complexities of mixed-citizenship family life. It has been edited for clarity and length.

> JULIETTE: It's interesting when I reread what you wrote with our interview even just a few years later I was like: "Wow! I sound so desperate and shook up." And I was! I was. Even now, I get triggered by a lot of things and I'll just have to sit down and have a cry out. And I'm like: "Man, people don't get it." [laughs]
>
> CAMILLE: It is ridiculously tough. And I think that's what so many people don't understand because so many times the breakup of the family is a choice. You know? It's hard enough when it's a choice. But when it's launched at you, it's debilitating. All three of us been "fortunate" enough to feel that on extreme levels. That's the only way I can describe it. When Juliette was talking about reading our blurbs in the book, it's true. It brought back everything. I was like, "Oh my gosh!" When I started reading it, I didn't think it was me, necessarily, because you don't use our names. And I was like, "Wow, this person was going through exactly what I was going through." And then I realized, "Oh my gosh, that's me!" [laughs] It was really weird taking a look at it from an outside perspective and realizing how difficult it really was.
>
> I think my biggest frustration through all of it is when my husband was an unauthorized immigrant and incarcerated, nobody cared if the kids got to be with him, if he was part of their lives, or anything. Until I tried to get a divorce. And then, suddenly, they're like: "Well, what about visitation rights? When is he going to see the children?" And I'm like, "You don't care! You don't care when he sees the kids because you've had opportunities to make that possible." But because we were married, it

wasn't a big issue. Then the second that we're divorced, suddenly, it's like: "Oh, red flags! What's going to happen to the kids?" . . .

JULIETTE: Your rights as a citizen were totally trampled underfoot when it was about him being deported. And then it was like, "Oh hey, let's trample on her rights a little bit more. Because we are going to focus on the fact that he is a father and his kids were born here, or whatever."

CAMILLE: Suddenly [the US legal system] cared that he was their dad. And I was like: "No, no, no. Where were you before? Where was all this before?" And it was—

JULIETTE: Maybe you would have been able to stay married had they cared a little before.

CAMILLE: Yeah. Well, they were just fine with me being deported with him. They deprived my children of their right to a father. And me the right to my husband that supposedly I had. I always felt like I had that right. But that was the most frustrating thing, because I finally said: "Alright, you win. Look, you made it so my family can't be together. Congratulations! You did it, America." And then they were like, "Oh wait, wait. What about his rights? Does he get time with the kids? What will happen to the kids if they don't have time with him?"

JLL: You're like: "You should have asked yourself that before you forced him to leave." What kind of contact do you have with Giovanni now?

CAMILLE: He and I only really talk if there is a problem. I'll send him pictures of the kids. And he'll say: "Hey, can I call?" And I say yes. And he doesn't. So he's talked to the kids maybe two or three times this year.

JLL: Wow.

CAMILLE: Because he just doesn't call any more.

JLL: How are your kids doing with that?

CAMILLE: Because they haven't really had their dad, they're okay. But my daughter is old enough now that she understands that she doesn't have a dad. And so when things go bad that day, she starts crying, saying she misses her dad. But she misses the concept, you know? She misses that her family is not complete. That there's supposed to be a dad there. . . .

JULIETTE: Sorry, I'm asking lots of questions. [laughs] Would you definitely say, because I know being a child of divorce, and we know that couples always have issues anyway. But would you definitely say that the government caused the result of this situation to be divorce?

CAMILLE: That's kind of a complicated situation, but the deportation did not help. His [one-year] incarceration was probably the biggest issue, but because we weren't in the States afterwards, he couldn't get help for whatever it was that he was dealing with. I don't even know half the stuff that he went through in jail, and he didn't even tell me some of it until after we were divorced for a while. So there are serious issues that he was trying to deal with all by himself. And we didn't have the money, we didn't have the capacity, we didn't have anything to be able to go and get the psychological help that he needed in order to heal from that experience of not just being incarcerated but being kicked out of the only country he knew. He was much more American than he was Guatemalan. He didn't know any of his family there. . . . It wasn't a good situation. And I do think that, because we were deported, we weren't able to get the help that we needed in order to heal from all the other things.

JULIETTE: Even going back all the way to what the system looked like when he first arrived as a kid, I wonder how that fit into the choices they made as a family. And I can't speculate that. But just knowing the stress that we have felt as a family at just the *idea* of the problems that could come, has just really played into my kids' lives a lot, and their choices that they make and how they respond to difficult situations even.

JLL: Can you elaborate on that a little bit? Or give an example?

JULIETTE: Just even a small thing is any time my oldest daughter hears anything about "the wall," she gets really: "If I were president, I would rip it all down." That's what she says all the time. And that's directly because of what she understands from immigration affecting our family. Our other daughter has had nightmares all the time just because she is an empath and she picks up my stress. So the times in my life when I was in highest stress, she was really little, and she'd cry a lot, worried that our family was going to be ripped apart. And I'm like: "No, it's not going to happen." But you know? Even now thinking about how Tenoch can apply for citizenship this year, and my oldest daughter has been learning about citizenship in third grade. And so she's kind of like: "I'm enamored with this stuff that my dad gets to do! All the things!" And it's just interesting to see where you don't think it's going to affect them but then it pops into their lives and they'll bring it up at the weirdest times.

So, now with the backdrop of this pandemic and everything that's happening, it's interesting to think about what this next process [naturalization] is going to look like. I'd like to say: "Oh yeah, I'm hopeful that it'll all work out and that he won't just have to be a resident his whole life." But, my sister, as the sponsor,[1] has had a real issue lately. I guess I didn't really read into what that entailed as well as I thought I did, and when Tenoch's appendix burst in February, she kept asking about insurance and things. I was like: "Well, I don't think we can apply for emergency Medicaid, so you might have to come in at this part." And she's like: "Okay, we will talk about that later." And when we talked about it later, it was her saying, "I want a handle on this now. What's the plan? We need a mediator because I can't afford his medical bill." I was like, "Well, that's not what I meant." But reading back into it, technically she was supposed to be able to help him stay above the poverty line, and if we wanted to we could sue her if she didn't. I was like, "We're not going to sue you!" But if anything goes wrong with this citizenship stuff that will definitely put a hinder on our relationship. Not on my side, but I know on her side. He can still gain it through those hours of working experience and whatnot, but that'll be ten years. And they could change that, too.

CAMILLE: So much uncertainty in all of it.

JLL: Yeah. It's interesting because I think a lot of people would assume that the uncertainty finally ended when he got residency,
right? That that would be the point where you're like, "Finally!"
And to a certain extent, of course that was probably a significant
change for you all, and I would love for you to talk more about
how that affected you psychologically. But it's not the end at all.
Most likely—we'll have to follow up and see—even getting citizenship isn't necessarily going to be the end of everything.

JULIETTE: Yeah. You know, no one accounts for the fact that you
don't get to grieve your fear. You can have some coping mecha-
nisms, and people can help you keep going when you have anxiety or whatever. But there's not really ever a chance to just be
like, "Let me process this as it's happening." So when we got his
residency, I was elated. I was very excited. I would keep talking
about all the new possibilities. But what happened was that it
opened a door for him to grieve things that he wasn't able to
grieve before. Like knowing that he was now able to travel to see
his family—two years too late [his brother had died two years
earlier]. I think that just, it was like the anvil dropped. So that relief was very short-lived for us. We got home in October [2017],
and he was totally just depressed. He would say things like: "It's
just a piece of paper. It doesn't mean anything. I didn't win the
lottery." And I was like: "Ugh! I just did all this crap, come on!
Be happy." But . . . he felt really incredibly guilty for his brother's death. So, there was a brief moment that we were very, very
happy, and it's just been high stress ever since.

He's been able to get some of that out, and going back home
to see his family definitely helped. But he still talks about the
time that he came [across the border, and after a scary encounter
near the border] his whole entire group started going back. And
he's like: "Well, whatever, I'm going to keep going." . . . And I
said: "Well, why weren't you afraid?" He said, "I don't know if
it *wasn't* fear, but it was just that I had nothing to go back to. I
had no college opportunities, unless I had money, and the only
way to get money was to go where the money was." His plan was

go work, get the money, go back [to Mexico] and finish school so he could have a chance at life. But then we met, and he's like, "Well there goes that idea!" But it is interesting because he had applied for a visa, and they wouldn't give it to him because he had no property in Mexico, no money, no funds. His mother had recently passed away, and he was already 23. So they told him, "You really have no ties here [in Mexico]. You have no reason to come back." And he's like, "I'm trying to do this the honest way!" His visa application was denied.

But I think as it comes to that relief, am I happy that it's done? Of course. Is he? Hopefully. Sometimes he is totally indifferent. But I feel like the stress, the damage, was done. The problems we dealt with psychologically like Camille mentioned, have totally altered the people we are. Like who we thought we married . . . that person has changed. And some of that came because of sorrow in the family, but most of it came because we were always being chased by this idea of insecurity. All the time. Every decision I made was based on asking myself, "How will this affect our case?" I've been with a therapist now for a year, and I was just barely able to talk about some of that two weeks ago. And she was like: "Wow. Okay, hearing you say that has opened my mind as to what you went through." And I was like: "This is the iceberg—the tip of the iceberg." So, yeah, I don't know that I've felt the actual relief and just that sigh of the burden being taken off. I haven't really gotten that moment.

CAMILLE: I think that's the thing, too. Just because, and I don't know completely. We never got to the point of getting citizenship. But it can't go back and erase all the pain and hardship and all of the hurt it caused before. That's always there. Like Juliette said, it changes who you are. What kind of person you are. For good or bad, but it's there.

JLL: Yeah. As you know, I've been thinking about these things a lot. But a year ago when I was writing my book proposal, and I put this section in, I pitched it as, we're all going to talk about what had happened after we had all experienced a decision one way or another. And here we are almost two years after we applied [for Ramón's residency] and nothing. Nothing has happened. And I never, ever imagined that we would still be in this unknown situation. We picked one option for our application so that Ramón could still leave the US since he had his visa. So we initially applied to adjust his status through the consulate in Mexico. That way, he could still use his visa and travel back and forth. He would be able to be with his dad, who is chronically very ill, and we don't know how long he will be around. But Ramón's visa expires this month, so we have had to completely restart our application and apply to adjust his status from inside the US instead of outside. So, right now, Ramón can't leave. The other day, he asked me: "What happens if something happens to my dad?" And I was like: "You can't go." And I hate that. So much. I feel like it's my fault. But we tried so hard, and for a year and a half, that's where we were. We were trying but—my father-in-law has made it a year and a half, which is great, because we didn't know if he was going to make it that long. But to feel like I have to keep Ramón from his family . . . or, you know, what if his mom gets sick? There's this pandemic going on, and he can't leave. For him to have to choose between being able to be with us—his wife and children—or being able to be with his family, it's terrible. I hate being in that position. And we have basically the best-case scenario. He had a visa. As I was interviewing couples for this book, I always thought: "We're so lucky." ("We" as in my family.) I've seen what happened to both of you, and I always felt like, "It's going to take paperwork and time, but it's going to work out for us." And I guess I never could have anticipated Donald Trump, but also we are in a situation that I never imagined.

And it has been such a strain for us. It's been so hard. Ramón hasn't been able to work in the US for these two years. And we went through almost a year of extended periods of separation; for the first five months, my daughter and I were here, and he was there. I think it really traumatized her. There are things that she says and does where I realize that it was so hard on her, and it was temporary and it was pretty much something we chose. That was the option that we chose because that was the option we thought would be better. And to think about how quickly the consequences of these laws, and even just the consequences of forcing people to wait, really seeps into our relationships and into our minds and changes us, like you said, Juliette. It's a conclusion that I never anticipated. I hate it. I thought that my whole argument was going to be like: "The system is broken, but it works for some people." And I thought that Ramón and I were in part of the "some people" that it works for. But it turns out that it's really easy to break the system even more.

JULIETTE: I was just thinking about that couple [Grace & Lucas] that really flipped the switch for me in your transcriptions. Like, "Aw, man. They keep using the word bureaucracy and how annoying that is, but they have no hard connection to the problem." When you said, "We did everything right, and yet here we are." That just hit me because [crying] knowing about Ramón's dad and the situation there . . . I've been triggered by that a lot. I've had several conversations with my family about you, Jane, because in 2014, in May, Tenoch's grandma died, and like Ramón and his dad, Tenoch was really, really connected to her. So that was really emotional for him, and he couldn't go [to the funeral]. And then July of that year we got our waiver denial. And it was very ambiguous—the biggest argument they made is that I made 51 percent of the income. And therefore, losing 49 percent wasn't a big deal. [laughs] And then, in August, his dad passed away of a heart attack, and he couldn't go. The next year, after my oldest son was born, I had really bad postpartum depression, probably tied in to all of this. And then Tenoch's brother was murdered in October of that year. And then my grandpa died that December of 2016. When I went to his funeral, the kids stayed with the babysitter. Tenoch had work, and he didn't come. He could have asked it off, but he didn't. And after the services were over, I just completely lost it. And all these people kept coming up and saying, "I'm sorry for your loss. Your grandpa was so special." But I wasn't crying for him. I was bawling my eyes out, and my sister sat by me and she said, "I wish Tenoch could have this moment, too." Because he never got closure. And so I think about that with your family, and I think about . . . [crying] how the only thing, wrong thing, Tenoch ever did that we want to criminalize in this country was coming here without papers. The only record he had was speeding violations. And yet, as a country, we took away his human right to grieve with his family. And to pursue a better life. Just because of an imaginary line.

JLL: It truly is inhuman what we do. The laws are basically set up to make it legal to treat people who aren't citizens as less than human. I don't think we see or understand enough of the true cost of that approach. And of the cost to our society. Obviously, you and Tenoch are feeling that more than society as a whole. But we are hurting ourselves. We are hurting our communities by denying people these basic rights. By denying their humanity. By making their contributions to our society invisible and trying to force them to hide or to police themselves, like you were saying. You had to think through every decision you made and ask yourself: "How is this going to affect our case?" You internalized the law, and you were policing your own actions. They didn't even have to be there. You were doing it for them because the consequences were so great. I really want people to hear these stories and to not just say: "Gosh, that's so sad for them." But to recognize that, indirectly, what we are doing to families, what we're doing to noncitizens, we're doing it to ourselves. And we are all paying the price of that.

I want to invite you both to take a minute and just think about where you were ten years ago. It's almost Juliette and Tenoch's anniversary. Let's go back to remember that time. What did you think things would be like right now? So, ten years later, what were you imagining things would be like? Both of you. You were beautifully pregnant, Camille.

CAMILLE: Not beautifully, but I was definitely very pregnant. I remember the picture of us from that night. Now I guess it's my turn to get all emotional. Ah . . .

JULIETTE: We definitely didn't think we would be sitting here crying.

[laughter]

CAMILLE: Yeah! I was supposed to have a dozen more kids, I'm sure. When I got married, I was supposed to have a Happily Ever After. Like my parents. They had been married for about a trillion years. We were going have kids and [Giovanni's two older children] were going to be with us. And we would definitely have a house by now, for sure. I had in my head all these plans to be just . . . the little typical American family. Things would be perfect. And . . . they're not. [laughs] My kids are supposed to have a dad. [crying] And he can't even be bothered with them anymore. I can't say that I'm completely sad about that because we've definitely been blessed in a lot of ways. But we should have been a together-forever-happy family, and that is not what we have. We're a happy family, but we're missing family members. And we weren't supposed to be.

JLL: Yeah . . .

CAMILLE: My eyes are so wet.

JLL: [laughs] Is it raining in Arizona?

CAMILLE: It is! Inside, of all places. It's so weird! [pause] If I could go back . . . I could see a lot of people reading this and thinking that, had I known what would happen, I wouldn't do it. And I can definitely say that because I have my kids, I would do it all again in a heartbeat. Not because it wouldn't rip me apart. Because it has. But because they're worth it. My family is worth it. And it would have been really nice to feel like my country was on my side. But you know, it just taught me that my citizenship, my children's citizenship, my vote, my desires, all of those things, are nothing. They get lost. I don't know whose matters, but it's not mine. . . .

JLL: I'm interested, Camille, in how all of this changed your relationship to the US. I know you have alluded to that in different ways. You are living back in the US again but, like you said, along the way they forced your family to separate for you to be able to do that. And I'm interested in what it's like for you now.

CAMILLE: The United States has a lot of programs in place to help struggling individuals. And I have to say as individuals because those supports start to go away when family is in the mix. But the truth is, I came back here because I understand and I know how to live here. But I don't feel any ties anymore. I am an American, but I've never had my country be there for me, in that sense. So it's really hard to feel like—I guess I do feel emotional when I see the Statue of Liberty, when I see what our forefathers fought for. What America should be right now, but it isn't. I definitely feel that. I know that we fought for something that should be different from what it is right now. We've had people fighting for equal rights for women, for people of color, against racism, and even for immigration. We've had so many people fighting these battles already and we're still fighting them. And it's disappointing. I'm disappointed, America. [laughter] I guess that's what it is.

JLL: Thanks. Okay, Juliette, you're up.

JULIETTE: I have a bajillion thoughts rolling in my head. Just like, everything she says I could have a follow-up line. I'll try to keep it focused. Ten years ago, I didn't know how naïve I was with regard to what we were going to be up against. In my mind, it was going to be so easy to get all of that taken care of, it wouldn't be a problem. When we were getting married, I was like, "Well, everyone I've talked to in this situation, either college friends who married immigrants or friends or whatever, they've all taken care of it themselves." None of them had the same situation, but I still thought it would be fine. Over the course of everything that happened, I lost my . . . my naïve virginity, my virgin naïveté. Just realizing, like Camille said, that no one was going to come up to bat for me.

When we got married ten years ago, the sky was the limit. I was so excited about things I was going to do with dance and possibly getting my master's degree for either performing arts or for arts administration. But literally getting through Tenoch's case became my life for seven years. I have a master's degree in survival. [laughs] The personal development and growth that we thought we would have hasn't happened. Tenoch was taking English classes for so long. He wanted to study physics and chemistry and had a goal of like: "I want to be a physics teacher!" And now he fights this: "I'm too old now!" I thought we would have been visiting Mexico by 2015, and at least five times by now. Introducing the kids to their cousins and uncles and aunts. When Tenoch went, all he did was take pictures of people and places that were special to him or to show them fun things that he wanted to teach them about . . . And he's like: "It just wasn't the same. Yes, it was good to go back but, without my family, it wasn't the same." We didn't have enough money to all go together. Our credit cards that I used for immigration are still— they're in deferment right now and we're trying to settle because we haven't been able to pay it. So yeah, it's just like, you've been fed this idea your whole life about the heroic people that gave you your freedom and gave you everything that is America and everything that you got, to live and grow up and get an education. It was this idea of, because you're in America, there's this dream. And you can make things happen. But that's only true if you're a certain person—you're a certain type of people. Dictated by who? I don't know.

CAMILLE: I just have to echo that. We grew up knowing that we are free. I grew up knowing I was free to choose who I married, when I married them, how I married them. And the color of someone's skin and where they are from never mattered. Because we had been through all of that already. We had already fought for it . . . and because good men and women died, I could do whatever I wanted. I was totally free to make that choice, to make that decision. I remember talking to one of my professors, after I had come back [from Guatemala]. And I remember expressing to her the difficulty that I was in right in that moment. I don't remember what the whole conversation was—I'm sure she was upset at me for being late to class, and I was like, "I'm sorry! I was up till midnight or one o'clock trying to help my husband feel better and trying to help my toddler go to bed. Because of all this." And she said: "Well, you put yourself in that situation. Like, think about it. That is what people are going to see when they hear your situation, they're going to say, 'You put yourself in that situation.'" And part of that is true. I made my choice. I chose to marry this man even though I knew he was an undocumented immigrant. And even though I know I knew it would be hard because he had already been married and had two kids. So, yes, I did put myself in that situation. But I wouldn't have done it had I really not thought that America was behind me. That my decision mattered. Because that is what I grew up believing. That we live in a free country where my country is going to support and sustain my rights because that's what has been fought for, and my rights matter. Instead, what America did was turn around and said: "You put yourself in this situation." They washed their hands of me. We're spoon-fed this story that we can make anything happen here. And you can only make it happen if you're the right people. And who are those people? I have no idea.

JULIETTE: I thought I was the right people.

CAMILLE: That's what we're supposed to be!

JULIETTE: So this is interesting with what you're saying. When we were moving, or starting to pack up, trying to figure out whether to move back to my hometown this spring, I started to ask Tenoch, trying to make sure I don't push him to do things that he doesn't want to do. And I'm just questioning him now, "Had I not pushed for this [legalizing his status] so hard, would you have applied to try to get status here?" And he was like: "Probably not." I still have to do a follow-up question on that, but he was like: "I can see, now that we have a family, what some of those benefits are. But for the process, was it worth it? I don't know." That's what he said. And that just started my wheels turning. Why did I fight so hard, and say, well, this is what we have to do? One, I've been taught to obey the law. So I was like, let's get you in legal status so we don't have problems as a family. Two, I wanted him to have the benefit of this country on his side. I fought so hard. When we first met with a lawyer, they said wait and apply in 2012. So, we started with the lawyer in April 2012, and by July or something they were saying: "Wait, there's this waiver that you can apply for pardon here and wait here, so you don't have to leave the country." Because at that point we had heard all the stories of everyone being away from their families for several years waiting for that pardon. And so I was like: "Okay, let's do that."

After we got denied the first time, we thought about going to Mexico. And I remember talking with Jane, and being like, "Hey, we could come live in Mexico with you all!" I sometimes wonder if we had decided to just go the other route [and live outside the US], and me learn how to adapt—like Camille said—to a different country and live a different way, I wonder what that would have done for our relationship, to share something that was his instead of feel like I've been hoarding him here the whole time because of the government. There's just a lot that makes you question your reality, makes you question: "Is this country really worth all that and a bag of chips? Was it really worth my sanity and our stable relationship to keep us in lockdown, basically?" We were on lockdown in the US until his status was all sorted so that he could go again to see his family. I don't know what that would have been like, but people shouldn't have to choose that. You shouldn't have to choose between relocating your entire family or separation. You shouldn't have to choose between waiting for your life hardship to show up so that you can file that paper. Everyone has hardships. We know that. We know that as a country—there's no one exempt from hard things. And they didn't even have a rubric. They didn't even have anything even that could outline what counted and what didn't [for the hardship waiver]. It was just based on whose desk it landed on and what mood they were in, and if their perception of life and their perception and understanding of what you were going through, was going to trigger them enough to say: "Yeah, that's pretty hard." It's insane. What mind games are we playing here?

CAMILLE: Life is hard enough anyway. Let's take our marriages, and let's remove all this immigration mumbo jumbo. We would still have difficulties. It's two different people making things work. It's bringing kids into the equation. It's not like we would miss out on that hard thing, right? I think a lot of times it's easy for people to turn and look the other way because it's not them. I wish people—I hope that when people read your book, Jane, that they envision being woken up in the middle of the night with a phone call that their husband's not coming home. Ever. What it would feel like to have your children only meet their father through a screen because you're not allowed to go in and see him. And to have to abandon my country in order for our family to be together. None of that makes sense. . . .

JLL: I've been thinking about how would I answer this question of where I imagined myself ten years from now, ten years ago, and I don't really know. We were dating, and I was hoping that we would get married, but we didn't get married for two more years. I think the thing that would be different is that, I thought that ten years later our future would be more certain. It was an uncertain time, but it was a hopeful time. I had lots of hope for my future, even though I didn't know exactly what it was going to look like. But I thought it would look good. And I thought: "Gosh, by the time I'm 37, things are going to be pretty worked out. Those next ten years are going to look really concrete." And things are more uncertain now than ever.

I think that, among our many tactics in punishing immigrants and their family members, keeping you in this endless limbo is its own kind of torture. Having that final decision of deportation is brutal. I don't think there's anything worse than that. But you have an answer, and then you can at least go from there. Of course it's awful. And that's not the outcome that you want. But I almost feel like, at some point, people would rather just have a final answer than to not know. Because that going back and forth between hope and fear and hope and fear and that uncertainty is so restricting and debilitating.

CAMILLE: And you [never] feel protected and safe. That's one thing that I haven't felt in a really long time. It's this lack of safety because my family can be wrenched from me at any moment. How do I protect them from this? How do I shield my children from what it was actually like to have their dad be deported?

JLL: And it almost feels like what you read about the psychology behind domestic violence, when victims can't get away from their abusers or keep going back to them. It feels like you are put in a situation where you have to keep trusting your abuser because there's no one else to turn to. There's no other system there, but you inherently feel like you could never trust them again because of the abuse that they inflicted on you.

CAMILLE: Yes. But there's nowhere else to go.

JLL: Exactly. Where are you going to go? What else are you going to do? There's nothing else, so the choice is between nothing and potential protection. But also potential abuse.

JULIETTE: Jane, I have a question for you: Having done all this research, and talked to dozens of families, and now finding yourself in a place that you didn't anticipate, having, like you said, done everything "right": Do you feel like you have taken on any of their emotions with your own situation? Do you fear things that you might not have anticipated but you've connected it with other people's experiences?

JLL: I feel like my brain is split in two. There's the logical side of my brain that says, "We're following the law, we're doing everything the right way. It's just taking time, and it's taking more time because someone has intentionally manipulated the system to make it take longer. One way or another, it's going to work out eventually because, based on the law, everything should be in our favor." So that's the logical side of my brain. But the other side of my brain just goes crazy imagining all the things that could happen.

And it feels like the law is changing. It *has* changed, actually. They've changed the requirements for a number of things, like how much income you should have to be able to guarantee that your spouse won't become a public charge. You also have to be able to prove that you have health insurance or that within thirty days of getting to the US that you'll have health insurance. All of these crazy things. And, luckily, so far, we can meet all of the new requirements because I have a really good job. But if I was applying now as a grad student, we wouldn't qualify. And I just have this fear that the laws are going to keep changing to the point where we no longer qualify, even though we did before, and that by deciding from the beginning or trying from the beginning to obey the law, by not applying until he qualified to apply—if you're living outside the US, you can't have residency because you're supposed to live at least half the year inside the US. So we never applied all those years that we were living in Mexico because we weren't living here. I was so familiar with the law and so familiar with the fact that you could lose everything over something seemingly tiny that I didn't want to ever run that risk. And now I feel like there are lots of people who did that, who lied and said they were living in the US when they weren't, who applied when it was easier, and it worked out for them. And now it's unclear if it will work out for us. I'm still generally hopeful, but it's hard. Wait times for cases to be processed have tripled since we applied. And this was before coronavirus.

So I have this huge fear that they're going to change the law again to the point that we no longer qualify, right before our eyes. And so in some way I've felt more prepared because of all these stories that I've heard from people. And I do feel like, at least, worst-case scenario, we have lived in Mexico, we can go back. But it would be a lot harder. It would be *a lot* harder. Especially because the city where we lived is less safe than it was before, or at least it certainly feels less safe to me now. And now, because I have a career, it would be a lot harder to lose my job, which would happen if we move.

JULIETTE: Of the families you interviewed, how many have you followed up with? Have you been able to follow their patterns, see where they are now?

JLL: Just over half. I've been in touch with them or we're friends on Facebook or whatever and I've been able to see what happened. I'd say that, long-term, most people have been able to get status—even a couple of families that I knew who were deported, waited the ten years, reapplied, and have been able to get back to the US. But it's not a cure-all and the consequences are still there. There's this one family that I interviewed [Vicente & Herlinda], and it took probably fifteen years from when she was deported for her to finally get her green card. And there were certain things, like buying a house, where they were at least fifteen years behind in some of these basic things that affect their long-term security and happiness. Interestingly, I have talked to them since they moved to the US, and I asked the wife what the biggest difference was for her, and she said, "Time." They're together as a family so much more now. When they were living in Mexico, he was commuting across the border every day, so he was gone all the time and the kids were going to school in the US and now that they don't have to do that anymore, they have so much more time to be together. It's called family reunification for a reason. It's about helping families be together, and the government literally just arbitrarily decides which families deserve to be together and which ones don't.

JULIETTE: That's talking about just the pure physical being together part. But even doing these processes the way the system is now, you have barriers to psychological togetherness, too. I think about how I changed jobs every two years in that ten-year period. And I wonder how much of that came from just a fear of instability, a fear of "I don't know what's going to happen." You can't focus. So there's a question of time, like how long does it take to speed up the process? What's going on here? But then there's also a question of, why aren't we taking into account not only the physical separation but the psychological division? When people get married, it's usually because they have a common idea, right? We might have different thoughts and methods to get there, because we're all a universe, every person is a universe. But then you throw into the mix this idea of like: "Well, should we apply for this immigration thing?" And if you agree on it, cool. But then the government comes back and throws in your face: "We don't care about your unity right now. We don't care what your dreams are. We don't care about how good community members you are. We don't care what you've done for society or for your family, like your kids or whatever. We don't care about that. We care about making sure we have money and that we save face with all of our politics."

CAMILLE: How can the United States protect the individual but not the family? They've done a really bad job. And maybe that's what needs to be looked at, is how can we protect the family? Versus how can we protect the country from immigrants or how can we protect our lands? Or commerce? You know, all of these things that don't actually matter. Because studies have been done to show that a country is made or broken by the family. So, how can we protect our families? What is the government doing to ensure that our families have rights and our families are protected?

JLL: The other question is, How much does America have to lose? How much is America at risk by just letting our families be here? Is the threat really so great that it is worth it to disenfranchise millions of citizens and their families to make them invisible or literally banish them from the country, just for this potential to *maybe* protect us from some as yet unidentified threat to our country? The harm we are doing to ourselves is so much greater than any threat we are averting.

And we have all felt that harm directly. I think we can all say confidently that we have all experienced some level of depression directly related to this and all of our partners have, too. We have all suffered mental anguish.

JULIETTE: It's been a ride. I'm watching where we are right now and how the financial distress coupled with the mental distress and then coupled with the trauma that just happens to everybody. I'm afraid this whole situation will get us separated anyway. That's been on my mind a lot. We did all of these things, and I pushed strongly for a lot of things based on my fear of family separation and our family unit falling apart based on my own life. And yes, we are here working through it, and we're trying really hard and we have bad days and good days. But I'm just like, "How did we come to this point?"

Description of Methodology

Citizenship is an invisible status and, often, an invisible identity. As such, mixed-citizenship couples can strategically reveal or hide their mixed-citizenship status from others.[1] While immigrant or noncitizen status may be more evident in some countries with very small immigrant populations, such is not the case in the United States, in which one in every eight people living in the US was born abroad and nearly half of those foreign-born immigrants have become US citizens through naturalization.[2] Because of mixed-citizenship couples' "invisibility," finding couples who met the study participation criteria proved my greatest struggle in data collection.

In order to identify qualifying couples, I employed a purposive snowball strategy through the use of my personal and professional networks. I personally knew one or both spouses prior to this research project in twenty-one of the couples I interviewed; some I knew only superficially, others I knew quite well. I was linked to twenty-four more couples through my personal networks and the recommendations of other study participants. I connected with the remaining eleven couples through professional and social media networks, including private Facebook groups designed around cross-border or binational living whose membership included individuals in mixed-citizenship families. More than 90 percent of the couples I approached to participate in the study agreed to be interviewed. I found that many couples were eager to share their stories, especially with someone who understood the complexities and chaos of navigating the US family reunification system.

Through my research, I sought to answer this primary question: Why do some mixed-citizenship families succeed and others fail in their quest for family reunification? Because current US immigration law treats visa overstayers differently from those who crossed the border without inspection, it was clear to me early in the project design that I needed to limit the study to mixed-citizenship couples with noncitizen spouses from countries for which visa overstaying *and* entry without inspection (EWI, which is heavily dependent on a country's geographic proximity to the US) are viable options. As the top source of both legal permanent residents and unauthorized immigrants, Mexico was an essential source country to study; mixed-citizenship couples with a Mexican spouse compose a majority of families (50 of the 56 couples) included in this study. I also included a smaller cohort of couples with roots in El Salvador (five families) and Guatemala (one family) to help expand our understanding of the mixed-citizenship experience beyond the US-Mexico context while still enabling comparisons between legally present, unauthorized (visa-overstaying and EWI), and "extraterritorial" families.[3]

Of the 56 couples I interviewed, 32 were living within the US and 24 were living outside the US (23 in Mexico and 1 in Guatemala). Families living within the US included those who were currently unauthorized (8), formerly unauthorized (9), or who had maintained continuous legal immigration status within the US (15). Families living outside the US included those whose non-US citizen spouse had experienced deportation or removal from the US (9), those with authorized or "pre-authorized" status to enter and/or live in the US[4] (9), and those whose noncitizen spouse has no official relationship with the US (6).

To the extent possible, I also sought to ensure participant variation in other important individual and familial characteristics, including gender, class, age, ethnicity, sexual orientation, and parental status.[5] Of the 56 couples, 20 included a male US citizen partner and a female noncitizen partner, 35 were composed of a female US citizen partner and a male noncitizen partner, and one included a female US citizen partner and a female noncitizen partner. The class and educational backgrounds of both the US citizen partner and the noncitizen partner varied across the couples (and, often, within couples), with the following distribution: working class (15), mixed working-middle class (19), middle class (12), mixed middle-upper class (5), upper class (4), mixed working-upper class (1). Of the noncitizen participants, 15 did not finish high school, 18 had graduated from high school, 4 had some college experience, 12 had a bachelor's degree, and 7 had a master's, professional, or doctorate degree. Of the citizen participants, one did not finish high school, 10 had graduated from high school, 10 had some college experience, 26 had a bachelor's degree, and 9 had a master's, professional, or doctorate degree. Participants' ages ranged from early twenties to mid-sixties, with most participants between the ages of thirty and forty-five. Most of the couples had similarly aged partners, although one couple had partners with an age difference of over twenty years. Of the US citizen partners, 24 were Latinx and 32 were non-Latinx White. Most couples had been married between five and ten years at the time of the study, although the length of their marriages ranged from being newlyweds of just one week to having been married for more than thirty years. Additionally, two couples were engaged to be married and applying for a fiancé(e) visa at the time of our first interview.[6] At the time of our first interview, 47 couples had children and one couple was expecting their first child. (More details about each couple can be found in Appendix B.)

I conducted open-ended, semi-structured interviews with each couple. In all but six cases, the couples were interviewed together.[7,8] My goal for the interviews was to understand how the couples' interactions with the law have shaped their relationships within their families, their communities, and their countries. I asked questions to learn more about how the couples met, what their initial notions of family and citizenship were, and if (and how) those notions have changed as a result of their experiences navigating the legal processes of family reunification. I also asked questions to explore how previous orientation toward and experiences with the law shaped each spouse's interpretation of their family reunification process and their current orientation toward the law. In order to better understand couples' sense of belonging, I also asked them to describe their families and how they perceive themselves in relation to US society and the non-US citizen spouse's home country. The duration of interviews spanned from one to three-and-a-half hours; most interviews lasted between one-and-a-half and two hours.

I first interviewed 15 of the participating families in 2012 and 2013.[9] I conducted interviews with the other 41 couples between 2016 and 2018.

Whenever possible, I conducted the interviews in person (40 of 56 interviews). In these cases, I interviewed most couples in their homes, but I also conducted a small number of interviews in cafes, parks, and other public areas, as well as three interviews in my home. The geographic location of some participants (particularly those recruited online) made face-to-face interviews impossible; in these instances, we interviewed over Skype, Facetime, or phone (16 of 56 interviews). I recorded all interviews with the participants' permission. I conducted interviews in both English and Spanish, depending on the interviewees' preference. Once completed, all interviews were transcribed and coded. To protect their identities, I use pseudonyms for all participants; in some cases, I also needed to change other potentially identifiable information about study participants, such as their place of employment, to protect confidentiality.

In addition to in-depth, semi-structured interviews, I also conducted extended ethnographic analyses of six families participating in the study. I chose these families based on their theoretical relevance to my research questions. I followed some of the families as they navigated the US immigration and family reunification system: Karen and Jo (outside the US) as they applied for a fiancée visa, Juliette and Tenoch (inside the US) as they applied for the Extreme Hardship Waiver and legal permanent residency, and Chandra and Pancho (inside the US) as they dealt with ICE detention and a deportation order. I followed two additional families living outside the US and dealing with the aftermath of deportation, one well into its decade-long bar to reentry (Vicente and Herlinda) and one shortly after deportation (Camille and Giovanni). The final family was living in the US with current legal status as one partner applied for US citizenship (Diana and Leo). I was able to spend multiple days following most of these families through their day-to-day routines; with all of the families, I checked in regularly to learn about changes in their legal situations, as well as general family updates. I also had more sporadic contact post-interview via our connection over social media, email, etc., with more than half of the other families who participated in the study.

While I do not quote them directly in this project, the findings I present here are further contextualized by additional interviews I conducted (primarily in 2012) with couples whose profiles did not ultimately qualify them for inclusion in this study,[10] as well as informal conversations with mixed-citizenship couples I have met in the years since I stopped conducting official interviews in 2018. I also bring to this project my own experience as a US citizen in a mixed-citizenship marriage, living outside of the US and traveling regularly between countries (during data collection) and, later, living in the US and applying for family reunification (while writing the book).[11]

Following the work of other qualitative migration scholars, I employed an inductive analytical strategy to look for trends and recurrent themes across interviews.[12] After the interviews were transcribed, I read through each interview individually and coded it for themes. I first coded printed copies of interviews by hand and later used the online qualitative data management program, Dedoose, to manage my data analysis. Once I had coded the interviews separately, I compared similarly coded portions across all interviews to identify common trends, which compose the main findings presented in each chapter of this book.[13]

Interview Guide[14]

Background Questions (for both)
—Where were you born/raised?
—What is your job/educational background?

How did you two meet?
—Where and when?
—How long have you been together?
—When did you decide to marry? What contributed to that decision/ how did you decide?

What was the process of getting married like?
—Wedding plans, family considerations, visas, borders, etc.

Daily Life
Each of you, describe a typical workday/weekday for me.

Tell me a little bit about your relationship:
—What do you like to do together? What kinds of activities do you do separately?

—Do you have cultural and/or linguistic differences?

—How do you make decisions in your family?

—What was the last thing you had a disagreement about? Why?

—Do you think your different citizenships affect your relationship? If so, how? Are there benefits to having different citizenships? Disadvantages?

—Do you have other couple friends (mixed-citizenship or not)? What are they like? Do you think you are similar to them or different from them? How? Can you tell me about an experience you have had as a couple that you don't think would happen to same-citizenship couples?

Do you see yourselves as a cohesive family unit? Do you feel like you belong in your respective extended families? Your respective hometowns? Your respective countries?

How would you describe your family's nationality? Do you feel like your family belongs in the country where you live now? (why/why not?) What if you lived in [other spouse's country of citizenship]?

In your experience, do you think there is a difference between the way people perceive you in terms of your national origin and the way you are perceived racially (both individually and as a couple)? What role does race/ethnicity play in your mixed-citizenship experience?

How do you keep in touch with your extended families?

Do you have children?

—Have there been any new issues related to your different citizenships that emerged as a result of becoming parents?

—Do you teach your children about their different national heritages? Have your children been to both countries?

—Do you/your children have dual citizenship? What does having another citizenship mean to you? In relation to your first citizenship?

What does the border mean to you? Do you feel its presence in your daily life? How?

What role does the border play in your relationship?

Immigration History and Perspectives

(non-US citizen spouse) Did you immigrate before you met your spouse?

[Yes]—Walk me through that decision: What was life like for you before you immigrated? What were your expectations? What was your immigration process like? What was life like for you once you had immigrated? Did/do you feel like you belong in the US? If you had to do it all over, would you make the same decision to immigrate? Why/why not?

[No]—Was your decision to immigrate motivated primarily by your relationship with your spouse? How did you decide that you would immigrate? What was that process like? Did/do you feel like you belong in the US? Did you consider having your spouse move to your country of citizenship? (follow-up with spouse)

—As you were growing up, what did being [your nationality, e.g., Mexican or American] mean to you? Did you feel [your nationality]? Why/why not? What did it mean to be a citizen of your country? Have your feelings changed since meeting and marrying your spouse? In what way?

(US citizen spouse) What did you know/think about immigrants and immigration before you met your spouse? Has your relationship with him/her changed your understanding of/feelings toward immigration? How? Do you feel like you and your family belong in your community/the US?

(both spouses) As you were growing up, what did being [your nationality, e.g., Mexican or American] mean to you? Did you feel [your nationality]? Why/why not? What did it mean to be a citizen of your country? Have your feelings changed since meeting and marrying your spouse? In what way?

Official Visa Application Process

Have you applied for permanent residency?

—Describe decision to (not) apply, process, outcome.

—Did you seek help from any organizations (e.g., Catholic charities) or individuals (immigration lawyer, etc.) while preparing your application? What was your experience with them? Do you think it was helpful?

—What kinds of questions were you asked in the interview? Any that stand out in your mind?

—How do you feel about the process and your family's outcome?

—Have there been any health outcomes (positive or negative) that you attribute to your immigration outcome?

(if they live outside US) Describe your experience of leaving the US. (US citizen spouse) What was it like for you to leave the US? Had you lived outside the US before? Do you think of yourself as an immigrant now? What has your experience in this new country been like? How do you think it compares to your spouse's experience as an immigrant in the US? (noncitizen spouse) What was it like for you to come back to your country of citizenship? Do you feel like you belong here? Do you feel like your family belongs?

(All) Are you living where you want to live (both individually and as a family)?

Experiences with the Law

—Before you got married/applied for a visa, did you have other experiences with the law or law enforcement? (Speeding ticket? jury duty? go to court? etc.)

—Describe an encounter you've had with the law.

—What have your friends and relatives said to you about the law/law enforcement?

—What did you think about the legal system in your country?

—How did those experiences affect your approach to the visa application process?

—Given your family's immigration experience, have your feelings toward the law/law enforcement changed? If so, how?

—What are your feelings about law enforcement now? In US vs. country of residence/spouse's country of citizenship?

—Are you politically active and/or active in your community? If so, in what ways?

What aspects of your current family situation (work opportunities, income, family size, where you live, etc.) do you think are a direct result of your mixed-citizenship family status?

What are your thoughts on immigration law in the US? In noncitizen spouse's country of citizenship?

—Have your feelings about US immigration law changed since you got married?

—Do you think American politicians are thinking about families like yours when they discuss immigration reforms/policies?

—If you could change anything about US immigration law, what would you change? If you could change anything about the law, particularly immigration law, in [immigrant spouse's country of origin], what would you change?

Have you heard of DACA/DAPA? (If no, give brief explanation)

—What are your thoughts on the policy? Have you or anyone else in your family benefitted from DACA? Does your family qualify for DAPA? If so, would you apply for it?

Brief Background on Study Participants

Entry Format: Citizen & Noncitizen (Country of Birth) (place of residence at the time of the first interview; year of first interview; immigration status at time of first interview)—additional information about couple's story. Chapters in which couple is mentioned. (Interview language)

Angelica & Ramses (Mexico) (Mex. border; 2012; Deported)—They were neighbors in Mexico and met following divorces. Angelica acquired permanent residency through her parents during high school and later naturalized, but she grew up primarily in Mexico. Ramses was taken to the US without authorization as a child and spent most of his childhood and adolescence in the US. He is more fluent in English and American culture than Angelica, but she is the US citizen. Ramses voluntarily deported in his early twenties after run-ins with the police. They have struggled in their relationship due to his inability to travel to the US and with the difference in their income earning potential because she can work in the US and earn dollars. They have two children and divorced in 2018. Chapters 1, 2, 5. (Spanish and English)

Anne & Cesar (Mexico) (US West; 2012; Formerly Unauthorized)—They met in the US. At the time, she didn't speak Spanish and he didn't speak English. They faced a number of challenges when applying for family reunification, due to suspicions around the "legitimacy" of their marriage and lack of some important original documents from Mexico. In their interview, the consular officer told them to be sure to have a baby before their two-year follow-up; they ultimately had eight children. They also discussed racism and discrimination that their children have faced from teachers and peers. Chapter 2. (Spanish)

Antonio & Lizeth (Mexico) (Mex. border; 2017; No Status)—They met online. They were both living in Mexican cities on the US border. When they married, she moved to his town, but she still has most of her life (family, friends) in her hometown and spends most of her time there while he is at work. He commutes across the border every day to work, which adds hours to the time they spend apart every day. Chapter 4. (Spanish)

Brett & Mariana (Mexico) (US Southwest near border; 2017; Authorized)—They met at an airport while he was studying abroad in Mexico City and had an on-and-off relationship for many years. When they finally decided to get married, they applied for the fiancé visa. (They had only been married for a week when I interviewed them!) Brett is a therapist and talked about working with children who have been directly affected by family-level unauthorized immigration status, including (collateral) deportation. Mariana works in marketing and really struggled with having to leave her job in order to marry Brett. Chapter 1, Conclusion. (English)

Camille & Giovanni (Guatemala) (US West/Guatemala; 2012; Deported)—They met while Camille was serving as a full-time volunteer in Giovanni's community. Giovanni had criminal charges pending when they got married. At some point, Giovanni missed a court date and a warrant was put out for his arrest. About eight months into their marriage, when Camille was heavily pregnant with their first child, Giovanni was pulled over for speeding, arrested, detained, forced to take a plea, and served a year in jail before being deported. Camille and their young son followed Giovanni to Guatemala, but she had to travel back to the US for extended periods of time to work. They had another child in Guatemala, but shortly thereafter Camille decided she had to return to the US. They divorced in 2015. Preface, Introduction, Chapter 6, Epilogue. (English)

Carlos & Estrella (Mexico) (US West/Mexico; 2012; No Status)— Carlos and Estrella met in a small rancho in Mexico where Carlos's aunt and uncle live. They dated long-distance, then married in Mexico and settled into a home in a border town. A year later, they had to move away from each other while waiting for Estrella's residency application to be approved, during which time she gave birth to their first child. Now they live in the US with his family and, after living apart for so long, both have struggled to find a new balance in their relationship. Chapter 4. (Spanish)

Carmela & Rodrigo (Mexico) (US West near border; 2017; Unauthorized)—Carmela and Rodrigo met at a club. Carmela has two children from a previous relationship, but Rodrigo has fully taken on the role of being their dad. Rodrigo, from Mexico, has no authorized immigration status in the US, and his lack of status has complicated their daily lives, how they move through the border region where they live, and the plans they can make as a family. Carmela, an engineer, does not think she could qualify for a hardship waiver because she is Mexican-American, speaks Spanish, and could do her job in Mexico, too. Chapters 4, 5, 6. (Spanish)

Cathy & Samuel (Mexico) (US South; 2013; Formerly Unauthorized)—Cathy is an elementary school teacher whose student introduced her to Samuel, his soccer coach. Samuel was deported to Mexico but then received a humanitarian visa to support Cathy as she underwent surgery for a brain tumor weeks after giving birth to their first child. While Samuel was in the US on the humanitarian visa, they applied to adjust his status. Through that process he was granted permanent residency; he has since naturalized. Chapter 3. (English)

Chandra & Pancho (Mexico) (US West; 2016; Unauthorized)—They met on a ranch where they both worked. When I interviewed them, Pancho had been in the US for more than ten years; they had been married for less than a year and were expecting their first child. Chapters 1, 6, Conclusion. (English and Spanish)

Christian & Sharon (Mexico) (US Southwest; 2016; Unauthorized/Formerly Authorized)—Christian and Sharon met at their church. Sharon came to the US with her parents and siblings as an early adolescent. Christian and Sharon applied for a hardship waiver, which was approved, and Sharon became the first permanent resident in her family. When applying for citizenship, though, they committed an error that led to the cancellation of her residency and a permanent bar from ever possessing lawful immigration status. Following this rejection, they became ardent activists and organizers for immigrant rights. Christian even ran for Congress on a platform of immigration reform. Chapters 3, 4, 6. (English)

Chuck & Melodia (Mexico) (Mex. border; 2017; Authorized)—Chuck and Melodia met at work; they were both managers at a factory in northern Mexico. It is the second marriage for both, although Chuck is much older than Melodia (he has adult children her age). They lived in the US briefly when Melodia was waiting for her residency application to be approved, but have lived in Mexico for most of their marriage. Chuck was the only US citizen I interviewed to have acquired Mexican citizenship through his spouse (some others had dual citizenship prior to marrying or qualified through their parents). Chapters 3, 6. (English and Spanish)

Daniel & Pachita (Mexico) (Mex. border; 2016; Authorized)—They met while Daniel was conducting full-time volunteer work for his church in Pachita's hometown. They reconnected after he returned home and had a very short courtship. She is from southeastern Mexico and he is from the US West, but they have lived together in northern Mexico for most of their courtship and marriage (they lived briefly on the US side of the border after they married while waiting for Pachita's permanent residency to be approved). Daniel commutes across the border every day for his job as an information systems manager. They have adopted three children (one in Mexico and two in the US), and have encountered a number of complications as they have navigated legal guardianship and adoption in both countries. Chapter 2. (Spanish)

Diana & Leo (Mexico) (US West; 2016; Authorized)—They met in the US through a service project with their church. Leo had a tourist visa when they married and his status adjustment was relatively easy and straightforward. She is a dental hygienist and he has worked in a number of different industries. They have three small children. Following the unexpected death of his father, they have helped his mother and siblings come to the US (and overstay visas while waiting for Leo to naturalize, at which point he can sponsor them for permanent residency). Chapters 2, 3. (English)

Dina & Salvador (Mexico) (Mex. border; 2017; No Status)—Dina was born in the US but spent all of her life in Mexico. They met in their hometown as youth; Dina was good friends with Salvador's sister. Both work for the local government in Mexico. They lived together with their three daughters just across the border in the US for a time (Salvador lived there on his tourist visa because he was still working in Mexico). His visa was canceled because of suspicion that he was working in the US. Now, Dina and their daughters live with Dina's mom on the US side of the border so their children can attend school in the US, a citizenship right Dina never enjoyed. Salvador lives alone in Mexico, but his wife and children visit him daily. Chapters 3, 4, 5. (Spanish)

Elias & Susana (Mexico) (Mex. border; 2017; No Status)—Elias and Susana met at church as teens. Elias was born in the US but grew up mostly in Mexico. Susana had a tourist visa, so they married in the US and lived in the US for a while shortly after their marriage, when Susana was pregnant with their first child. After their son was born, they moved back to Mexico and Susana's visa expired. They were under the impression that she did not qualify for residency after having lived without official status in the US, so they did not apply for any visa for nearly twenty years. She has only recently applied for a tourist visa, which was approved. (Spanish)

Emily & Benjamin (Mexico) (US West; 2012; Formerly Unauthorized)—Emily and Benjamin met at a restaurant where they both worked, Emily as a hostess and Benjamin in the kitchen. They were married for quite a while before applying to adjust his status. During that time, Benjamin left the US to attend a funeral and came back again without authorization. Because they married prior to the full implementation of the 1996 IIRIRA, Benjamin was able to adjust his status without facing the ten-year bar. Before Benjamin acquired permanent residency, Emily described feeling like they were a normal family most of the time but experiencing moments in which their precarious status suddenly became relevant again (and still felt somewhat precarious given that Benjamin had not yet naturalized, even though he qualified, and therefore still had to renew his residency every ten years). (English)

Enrique & Carolina (Mexico) (US West near border; 2016; Authorized)—Enrique and Carolina met in Mexico in grade school. Both of their families are highly politically connected and very wealthy. Enrique went to an elite boarding school in the US, and his father would not let him apply for US citizenship (through his mother) until he turned 18. They have two children and described their experience living in two countries as enjoying the best of both worlds. Chapters 3, 4. (English and Spanish)

Esther & Chuy (Mexico) (Mex. border; 2017; Deported)—Esther and Chuy met in high school and married while still in their mid-teens. Chuy was brought to the US as a child, and they both grew up in an immigrant farming community in the US West. Chuy was arrested by ICE in front of his child, and he was moved to a distant detention center and then deported before his lawyer had time to file the necessary paperwork to challenge his deportation. Esther and their three younger children moved to Mexico with Chuy. Although both have Mexican heritage, neither of them feels like they belong in Mexico, as individuals or as a family. They have five children and separated in 2018. Chapters 3, 4, 5, 6. (English)

Felicitas & Hugo (Mexico) (Mex. border; 2017; Authorized)—Felicitas was born in the US but grew up in Mexico. She is a therapist, and Hugo is a mechanic. Hugo has acquired permanent residency through his marriage with Felicitas, but failed the language requirement of the citizenship exam. They take turns each night, with one spouse sleeping in a mobile home they rent in the US to help their kids attend US schools and the other spouse staying in their home in Mexico, to which Felicitas's therapy practice and Hugo's workshop are both attached. (Spanish)

Felix & Genoveva (Mexico) (Mex. border; 2016; No Status)—Felix and Genoveva met in high school and married, against their parents' wishes, just before Genoveva turned 18. Felix was born in the US but relocated to Mexico when his mother was deported (he was six months old). He now commutes to the US to work in high-end construction. They have a two-year-old daughter and struggle with the daily separation they face from Felix's commute to work. Although Felix's income is much higher than what he could earn working in Mexico, he still does not earn enough money to sponsor Genoveva for family reunification. Chapter 2. (Spanish)

Georgina & Moises (Mexico) (US West near border; 2017; Formerly Unauthorized)—They met at a bar in Mexico before Moises ever migrated to the US and dated on-and-off in both countries for many years before marrying. Georgina, who has enjoyed free movement and regularly traveled between the US and Mexico from her base in a US border town, described how her understanding of what being unauthorized means has evolved, and she has had to learn how to respect the fact that he could not cross borders even if she could. They applied for and appealed rejected hardship waivers multiple times before finally securing permanent residency for Moises in the US, enduring a year-long separation while their final appeal was processed. They also discussed how navigating US immigration laws compounded other challenges they faced as couples, including their struggles with infertility. Chapters 3, 5. (English and Spanish)

Grace & Lucas (Mexico) (US Midwest/Mex. interior; 2017; Authorized)—Grace and Lucas met while they were both pursuing PhDs; Grace was in Mexico collecting data for her dissertation, and Lucas was based at a university in Mexico City (his family also lives there). They discussed how they had an "easy" path to permanent residency but still struggled to coordinate visas and timelines while participating in academic fellowships within and outside the US. They also discussed their experience fostering a newborn baby who they were in the process of adopting and their goals to share both of their cultures with her. They now work at the same US university and split their time between their conservative college town in the US Midwest and Mexico City. Chapter 1, Conclusion. (Spanish and English)

Jaime & Rita (Mexico) (Mex. border; 2018; Authorized)—Rita and Jaime were neighbors and met as Rita and her small child were recovering from a difficult separation with the child's father. Jaime's parents are also mixed-citizenship and, although he grew up mostly in the US, he didn't actually get his citizenship until he was a teen. Rita acquired legal permanent residency through Jaime and has since naturalized. They have lived in the US and Mexico, but prefer Mexico. They have three children. Chapter 4. (English and Spanish)

Jared & Aylin (Mexico) (US Midwest; 2017; Authorized)—Aylin has a PhD in political science and Jared is a high school teacher. When we spoke, they had been married for less than a year, a decision they made in part to protest the 2016 election result. They described themselves as "international bourgeoisie" and expressed complicated feelings of what it means to be an immigrant because of recognizing the privilege they have both enjoyed in both of their countries of citizenship (and beyond). Chapters 2, 3, 4, 6. (English)

Jessica & Julio (Mexico) (US West near border/Mex. interior; 2017; No Status)—Jessica and Julio met in Mexico at a salsa dancing class while Jessica was there for an extended vacation before going to graduate school in Italy. They fell in love, and Jessica decided not to go to Italy. They have had a binational relationship for over fifteen years, but only recently officially married so that Jessica could sponsor Julio's son from a previous marriage for residency in the US. Julio still owns his business and lives two-thirds of the year in Mexico, traveling to the US on a tourist visa. Jessica works full-time in the US and spends two-thirds of the year in the US. They each spend about one-third of the year living in the other's country. Chapters 2, 3, 4, 6. (English and Spanish)

Jiancarlo & Sondra (Mexico) (US Southwest; 2017; Formerly Unauthorized)—Jiancarlo and Sondra both grew up in border towns, he in the US and she in Mexico. She and her mom overstayed their tourist visas when she was a teen. The couple met in college and decided to marry "by the state" two years before actually being married "by the church" (and living together as a married couple) because of Sonia's need to adjust her status and be able to work. Chapters 2, 3, 5, 6. (English)

Joanna & Joel (Mexico) (Mex. border; 2017; No Status)—Joanna and Joel met at church. They both grew up in Mexico (she grew up in a border town with a dad who commuted to the US to work for most of her life; he grew up in the interior of Mexico and moved to the border region during college). Getting residency would be fairly easy for them, but the subsequent need to move to the US and work there would introduce complications in their comfortable life. Joanna commutes to the US every day with her dad for work, and Joel works at a bank in Mexico. Chapter 4. (Spanish)

Jonah & Selene (Mexico) (US West; 2017; Authorized)—Jonah and Selene met in their doctoral program. Because Selene's student visa required her to return to her country for at least two years before she could qualify for a different visa, they experienced extended separation from each other and later had to live in Mexico with their baby at the end of/following the completion of their doctoral degrees. Jonah now works at a university in the US, and Selene and their daughter were only recently able to return to the US to live with him. (English)

Juanita & Heriberto (Mexico) (US West; 2017; Formerly Unauthorized)—Juanita and Heri are both immigrants. Heri migrated with his brother to the US without authorization as a child; they came to reunify with their mother, who had migrated years earlier. Juanita's father migrated alone and was later able to bring his family to the US following his status change through IRCA. They met in high school—Heri, a strong student, helped tutor Juanita, a new arrival to the US, as she adjusted to the language and culture. Heri is now getting his PhD. Although Heri has been able to adjust his status through Juanita, he says that the psychological trauma of being unauthorized lingers and that he experiences both fear and guilt due to his mother and brother's ongoing unauthorized status. Chapters 3, 5. (English and Spanish)

Judy & Franklin (Mexico) (Mex. border; 2016; Authorized)—Franklin migrated from southern Mexico to the border region to train as a pastor. He met Judy at their church, where her father was also a pastor. Franklin believes people should—and can—do things "the right way" with regard to immigration. He is now the pastor of their church; though they have lived in the US, they prefer living in Mexico. Chapters 3, 6. (Spanish and English)

Julia & Santiago (Mexico) (Mex. border; 2013; Deported)—Julia and Santiago met working in a fast-food restaurant in Julia's hometown. Shortly after they married, they submitted an application to adjust Santiago's status and got a letter telling them to leave the country instead. They struggled for five years dealing with the aftermath of "voluntary removal" and the ten-year bar. After exhausting every possible option to lift Santiago's bar to reentry (including appealing to their congressional representatives and even Oprah) and finding no way to overcome the emotional and relational costs of deportation, they ultimately decided to divorce. Chapters 2, 3, 4, 6. (English and Spanish)

Julia & Sergio (Mexico) (Mex. border; 2017; No Status)—Shortly after Julia's divorce from Santiago, she met Sergio at the international school where she works (she teaches art and he runs the school's tech). Sergio already has a tourist visa, enabling him to travel freely and be with Julia's family, something she never enjoyed with Santiago. Fearing that the family reunification process would take many years, they applied shortly after they married and are now feeling uncertain about their pending move to the US since his residency application was recently approved. Julia is also pregnant with their first child. Chapters 2, 4, 6. (English)

Juliette & Tenoch (Mexico) (US West; 2012; Unauthorized)—Camille, a former roommate of Juliette, set the couple up. Tenoch was up front with Juliette about his unauthorized immigration status from the beginning, which Juliette appreciated. They were married for seven years (with three kids and another on the way) before he was able to adjust his status. Juliette's severe depression and anxiety, brought on in large part by the fears and stresses of unauthorized life, "helped" them qualify for the hardship waiver and reunification. Preface, Chapters 2, 3, 4, 5, 6, Conclusion, Epilogue. (Spanish and English)

June & Stefan (Mexico) (US West near border; 2016; Formerly Unauthorized)—June and Stefan met at work, married young, and had five children when I interviewed them ten years after they met. They underwent a decade-long effort to adjust Stefan's status, describing feelings of freedom and liberation when their hardship waiver and residency applications were finally approved. June is a homemaker and Stefan works in the service industry. Chapters 3, 4, 5. (English and Spanish)

Karen & Jo (Mexico) (Mex. border; 2017; No Status)—Karen and Jo met in southern Mexico; Jo was working as an artist and activist, and Karen was there studying an art collective and activist movement. After living together for more than a year in southern Mexico, they moved to the Mexican border so Karen could commute to a fellowship in San Diego while they waited for Jo's fiancée visa application to be processed. Chapters 2, 4. (English and Spanish)

Kat & Beto (Mexico) (US West; 2016; Unauthorized)—They met when she was working at Target and he was there as a contractor working on a remodel of the building. Beto was previously married and has children from that marriage; their first child together was born days after our interview. They discussed how unauthorized status can make you especially vulnerable before the law, which some people can weaponize against you. They felt unsupported in their quest for the "American dream" and unprotected by the law, even when they were victims of a crime. Chapters 5, 6. (Spanish and English)

Kate & Juan (Mexico) (US West; 2016; Unauthorized)—Kate, an elementary school teacher, and Juan, a machinist, met online. This is Kate's second marriage to an immigrant; the first ended terribly after she discovered that her spouse was only in it for the papers. Juan is from Mexico City and has other siblings living nearby in the US. There does not seem to be an option right now for Juan to adjust his status, and while they are optimistic about the future, it feels very uncertain. They recently bought their first home and had their first child. Chapters 5, 6. (English)

Leticia & Mario (Mexico) (Mex. border; 2017; Authorized)—Leticia was born in the US, but both Leticia and Mario grew up in Mexico. Mario is a long-haul trucker in the US; he worked without authorization on his tourist visa for many years and now continues to do the same work as a permanent resident. They do not want to live in the US, even though it is a requirement of his residency status; instead, they continue to live in Mexico with their young daughter. Chapters 3, 6. (Spanish)

Lucy & Javier (El Salvador) (US West; 2012; No Status)—Lucy, a nurse, met Javier while she was volunteering in El Salvador with some other recent nursing school graduates from her college. After a short, in-person courtship in El Salvador, they spent more than a year apart while working and waiting for Javier's fiancé visa to be approved. Javier had never been to the US before arriving for his wedding. They now have two children and are trying to help Javier's mother and sister immigrate to the US, too. Chapter 4. (English)

Marcos & Petrita (Mexico) (Mex. border; 2012; Authorized)—Marcos and Petrita, in their sixties when I interviewed them, met decades earlier at a dance in Petrita's hometown. Marcos grew up in the California fields with parents who were agriculture workers (they were also a mixed-citizenship couple). Petrita has permission to be in and live in the US; they choose to live in Mexico, though they visit the US regularly. Their children have settled in both countries. (Spanish)

Maria & Sebastiano (Mexico) (US West; 2017; Authorized)—Maria's parents are Dominican and Puerto Rican. She grew up in Puerto Rico and has had the unique experience of being a citizen since birth but still feeling foreign in the US. Sebastiano is Mexican and acquired permanent residency through Maria. Their experience with family reunification law has been straightforward, but they both spoke of specific instances when they and their children have experienced racism and discrimination because of the color of their skin and/or their accents. (Spanish)

Mark & Susana (Mexico) (US Midwest; 2013; Formerly Unauthorized)—Mark and Susana met at the fast-food restaurant where Susana worked. Susana did not have legal immigration status, but applied for the hardship waiver and to adjust her status through Mark. She had to wait in Mexico for four months while her hardship waiver petition was under review. While she was gone, Mark stayed home with their two small children—their lawyer said it would look like more of a hardship if he stayed behind with the kids while she was gone. Her application was approved. Chapter 6. (English and Spanish)

Molly & Hector (Mexico) (Mex. border; 2016; Deported/Formerly Authorized)—Molly grew up on both sides of the border with her missionary parents and met Hector when they were living in Mexico. Molly and Hector initially qualified for family reunification and lived in the US for the first few years of their marriage. At some point, Hector was arrested and convicted of a crime that required four years of prison time followed by deportation and a ten-year bar before he could reapply for legal status/entry to the US. She works full-time in the US while he cares for their five children. Chapters 1, 3, Conclusion. (Spanish)

Nicole & Jorge (Mexico) (US West near border; 2012; Authorized)—
They met in the US through a weekly volunteer program at their church.
Jorge was trained as a doctor in Mexico but did not really love it and
decided not to try to re-certify to work as a doctor in the US. Nicole
was finishing her PhD in English and caring for their infant son when
we first spoke in 2012; Jorge was working in biotechnology. They had
an interesting experience dating across the border (but within an hour's
drive of each other) and also faced a number of challenges qualifying
for the fiancé visa and, later, in the transition period from fiancé visa to
permanent residency, during which time Jorge could neither work nor
leave the country. Chapter 6. (English)

Rebekah & Miguel (El Salvador) (US West/Australia; 2016; Authorized)—Miguel's sister, who met Rebekah while living in the US, encouraged Miguel to contact Rebekah when he traveled to the US for
a "working holiday." He is Salvadoran by way of Australia, where his
parents sought refuge when he was a small child, shortly after the beginning of the Salvadoran civil war. Once Miguel was in the US and
met Rebekah, they connected quickly and decided to become engaged
and marry before his visa expired. Their family reunification application was straightforward and they easily secured approval, especially
after the immigration officer heard Miguel's Australian accent. Chapter 1. (English)

Reeves & Erick (Mexico) (US East; 2017; Formerly Unauthorized)—
Reeves and Erick met while working at a restaurant. After Reeves graduated from college, she moved away and they broke up. They kept coming
back together, though, and finally decided to marry. Erick was unauthorized, and when they decided to apply to adjust his status, Reeves said
that she anticipated that their marriage would dissolve if the application and hardship waiver were denied. Erick's application was approved,
and they have continued to progress as a family and now have a daughter. Reeves said that class differences have been their biggest struggle
as a couple, as her upper-middle-class childhood trained her to see the
world and pursue its opportunities in a very different way than Erick's

childhood experience in poverty in Mexico and then as a young adult with no status in the US. Chapter 5, Conclusion. (English and Spanish)

Ryan & Gloria (Mexico) (US West; 2016; Authorized)—Ryan and Gloria were introduced by mutual friends at a New Year's Eve party in Mexico. Ryan celebrates his Mexican heritage and, although their primary residence is in the US, they continue to live as much as possible in both countries. Gloria had a tourist visa to the US when they married, and subsequently their family reunification process went smoothly. They love being a part of both countries and cultures and being able to share it all with their children. Chapter 6. (English and Spanish)

Sabrina & Joaquin (Mexico) (Mex. border; 2017; Permanently Barred)—Sabrina, who works in local law enforcement in the US, met Joaquin at a party at her cousins' house when she was in Mexico visiting them. She grew up in southern California and traveled regularly across the border to visit family and friends. They began dating immediately and moved in together within two months of their first date, but they did not formally marry until almost a decade later, well after the birth of their child. Due to an unplanned encounter in a car at the border, Joaquin was permanently barred from legal status in the US for "claiming" he was a US citizen. While Sabrina is accustomed to the cross-border commute, they have struggled to maintain their closeness as a family stratified across borders, especially as it has more directly affected their son. Chapters 2, 5. (Spanish and English)

Sandra & Esteban (Mexico) (Mex. border; 2012; "Self-Deported")—Sandra and Esteban met in Tennessee while Sandra was working as a volunteer through her church. Sandra grew up in Mexico, just a few yards from the US border, and regularly traveled/lived in both countries. Esteban immigrated as a young adult to the US in search of a better-paying job. They married in San Diego but decided very soon after to have Esteban voluntarily leave the country and process his status change from Mexico. In Mexico, they only found a comfortable lifestyle after Sandra took on full-time work in the US and Esteban stayed home to care for their young son. Neither of them prefers this arrangement, but it was the only way they could earn enough to pay for Esteban's immigration application. As a result, they have decided they must wait until Esteban's status is resolved before they have more children. Chapters 3, 5. (Spanish)

Sonia & Sebastian (Mexico) (Mex. border; 2017; Deported)—Sonia and Sebastian met at a club in a California border town where they had both lived for many years. Sebastian has experienced multiple deportations following his permanent bar to reentry after presenting papers at the border that he had been falsely told were evidence of his citizenship. After his last arrest for unauthorized status, he was jailed for three months pre-deportation (and threatened with years of imprisonment if he tried to return), so they decided to relocate their family thirty miles south in Mexico. Sonia continues to work in the US and their daughter attends school in the US. The daily separation they experience as a family and their individual and collective lack of integration in their new town have left them feeling truly alone. Chapters 2, 4, 5, 6, Conclusion. (English and Spanish)

Thomas & Lola (Mexico) (US West; 2016; Authorized)—Lola, a Mexican-trained lawyer turned US-based waitress, met Thomas, a city employee, at the restaurant where she worked. Lola came to the US on a tourist visa and gave birth to her only child shortly after settling in the US. She has always maintained a legal presence in the US (although, for a time, she violated that status by working). Thomas unexpectedly died in his sleep just a few years after he and Lola married; his sudden passing has shaped Lola's sense of belonging in the US in interesting ways. Chapters 4, 6. (Spanish)

Trish & Alberto (El Salvador) (US West; 2016; Unauthorized)—Trish met Alberto at a party when she traveled to California, where she had lived for a time, to visit her friends. They dated long-distance and then Alberto moved closer to Trish. After they married, they settled in Trish's hometown near her family. Trish has experienced a number of serious health issues requiring surgeries, and all of their children have been born more than a month premature. These health struggles have increased the stress she feels as she bears the burden of providing stability for their family because of their different citizenship statuses and as they have struggled to pay off the debt Alberto accrued in funding his initial migration journey to the US. Chapters 2, 5, 6. (English and Spanish)

Vicente & Herlinda (Mexico) (Mex. border; 2012; Deported)—Vicente and Herlinda met at a party while he was in Mexico for a family reunion. They dated long-distance for less than a year, after which Herlinda moved with her young son to the US to join Vicente. When her tourist visa expired, Herlinda's renewal request was denied. Anxious for Herlinda's prompt return, Vicente arranged for her to enter the US without authorization. She was deported three years later on his fiftieth birthday. They have spent the last decade living in Mexico during Herlinda's ten-year bar to reentry. Chapters 3, 4, 5, Epilogue. (English & Spanish)

Will & Mayela (El Salvador) (US West; 2016; Authorized)—Will and Mayela met in college. Mayela moved to the US from El Salvador as a middle-schooler when her family fled the civil war—they came to the US on tourist visas and later qualified for Temporary Protected Status. They live in the US and both feel American, but also discussed navigating the complexities of race, identity, and adoption at the individual and family levels. Chapters 3, 4, 6. (English)

William & Berenice (El Salvador) (US West; 2013; Unauthorized)— William and Berenice met through mutual friends. Berenice migrated to the US from El Salvador in her late teens and began working immediately. William is generally conservative but described how his views on immigration have evolved as a result of marrying someone who was unauthorized. They said that, as a couple, they do not feel limited by Berenice's status, but they have more concerns when thinking about having a child and how those dynamics would change. Chapter 1, Conclusion. (English)

Yuliana & Mateo (Mexico) (Mex. border; 2016; Deported)—Yuliana was born in the US, but Yuliana and Mateo both grew up in Mexico. They met in grade school and were junior-high and high-school sweethearts. During high school, Yuliana moved with her family just across the border to the US. They kept dating and, at some point, Mateo decided he had to cross to be with her. They lived in the US together and had two children when he applied to adjust his status; his application was denied, and they are in their eighth year of waiting out his ten-year bar to reentry. Chapters 3, 4, 5. (Spanish)

Notes

Preface

    1. Though admittedly infinitely *less* "easy" under the Trump administration.

Introduction

    1. *Kerry v. Din* 2015: 1.

    2. Lee 2013; Abrams 2007, 2013; Colon-Navarro 2007.

    3. Abrego 2014.

    4. *O'Bannon v. Town Court Nursing Center* 1980.

    5. *Kerry v. Din* 2015: 14–15.

    6. *Ng Fung Ho v. White* 1922: 259; *Baumgartner v. United States* 1944: 322.

    7. In re *Chung Toy Ho and Wong Choy Sin* 1890: 398; *Obergefell v. Hodges* 2015: 576.

    8. For this reason, many federal policies in the US—encompassing everything from tax and estate law to housing and health care regulations—all contain measures that explicitly benefit families over individuals.

    9. Joppke 1998, 2010; Muría and Chavez 2011.

    10. Herzog 2011; Marshall [1949] 1998.

    11. Bredbenner 1998; Cott 1998.

    12. It is important to reiterate that only some mixed-citizenship families—those of adult male US citizens—qualified for this automatic family-level citizenship program. At best, US citizen women in mixed-citizenship marriages maintained their legal citizenship status with limited practical access to the benefits of citizenship; at worst, they lost their citizenship altogether (Volpp 2006; Bredbenner 1998).

    13. Women's and children's "derivative" citizenship flowed from that of their husbands and fathers.

    14. Bredbenner 1998; Cott 1998.

    15. Chacón 2007; López 2008.

    16. At least with regard to immigration and citizenship issues.

    17. Rawls 1971, 1985; Marshall [1949] 1998.

    18. Butler 2020; Anderson 1999. The majority decision in *Kerry v. Din* perfectly exemplifies this absurdity, maintaining that the citizen continues to

have free access to all of her rights, even while accessing one right (country/husband) necessitates her abandonment of the other.

19. Ngai 2004; López 2015.

20. Brubaker 1992; Torpey 1997.

21. The fictional nature of citizenship has several consequences, including the fact that citizenship is not a uniform concept, politically or practically (Bloemraad and Sheares 2017). The content and quality of citizenship varies drastically between nation-states, which generates additional global inequalities whose consequences are distributed purely based on the accident of birth (Bhabha 2004; Schachar and Hirschl 2007). Citizenship has institutionalized inequalities among countries, creating an additional "wealth gap"—of rights, economy, freedoms, and mobility—between citizens of affluent or welfare-rich countries and citizens of poor countries or those with weak (or nonexistent) social safety nets.

22. Cf. Abrego 2019; Boehm 2012; Bonjour and de Hart 2020; Castañeda 2019; Dreby 2015; Enriquez 2017b, 2020; Gomberg-Muñoz 2015, 2016, 2017; Haynes 2017; Rodriguez 2016; Schueths 2012, 2015.

23. Butler 2020: 41.

Chapter 1: The Same, but Different

1. Coontz 2006.

2. Swidler 2001; Hull 2006.

3. Arriaga et al. 2018; Parks 2017.

4. Kobayashi, Funk, and Khan 2017.

5. Sprecher, Wenzel, and Harvey 2018; Parks 2017.

6. Larsen and Walters 2013.

7. Vasquez 2015; Vasquez-Tokos 2017; Muro and Martinez 2016, 2017; Qian and Cobas 2004.

8. Skinner and Hudac 2017; Harris and Kalbfeisch 2010.

Chapter 2: The Right Kind of Love(r)

1. Immigrants who enter the US without authorization tend to have lower income and less education: also, they are almost exclusively immigrants from Mexico and Central America (Henderson 2014; Migration Policy Institute 2016).

2. Low-income workers are disproportionately less educated, female, and non-White (US Census Bureau 2016c).

3. Demleitner 2003; Hawthorne 2007; Lee 2013; Ngai 2004.

4. Who qualified as "White" shifted many times during the period in which this overarching policy reigned, but it generally tended to facilitate migration from Western European countries (López 1997; Molina 2014; FitzGerald and Cook-Martin 2014).

5. FitzGerald and Cook-Martin 2014. These policy changes did not eliminate racial and national origin preferences in the application of US immigration

law, as they prioritized the legal migration of noncitizen family members of individuals who were citizens at the time the law was passed; in 1950, 89.5 percent of the US population was White (Gibson and Jung 2002). Country-level quotas limiting the total number of immigrants from a specific country in any year also created unequal family reunification access from countries with large populations and/or large immigrant communities in the US; these inequalities persist and have grown in the nearly seventy years since the INA was passed.

6. Nearly half of all immigrant visas issued between 2016 and 2018 went to the "immediate relatives" of US citizens (Bureau of Consular Affairs 2018).

7. Permission to immigrate is not automatic for these immediate family members, but their applications usually are processed within six months to two years.

8. Kandel 2018; Motomura 1995.

9. King 2010: 510.

10. Before 2013, mixed-citizenship same-sex couples (married or not) did not qualify for family reunification. Married same-sex couples can now access family reunification following the repeal of the Defense of Marriage Act (DOMA) in 2013. Unmarried couples—same-sex and heterosexual—still do not qualify for reunification.

11. Friedland and Epps 1996: 436.

12. Hawthorne 2007: 818.

13. Demleitner 2003; Hawthorne 2007; King 2010.

14. Degtyareva 2011.

15. Bergquist 2007.

16. US Census Bureau 2019; Hawthorne 2007; King 2010.

17. King 2010.

18. Enríquez 2015.

19. Demleitner 2003.

20. Pear 1986.

21. Gigolo Act, Section 3.

22. Ibid.

23. Richins 1988.

24. INA Sections 204(b), 205(b), and 235(a).

25. Harvard Law Review 1986.

26. *Lutwak v. United States* 1953.

27. IMFA Sections 2(b)(1) and 2(d)(3).

28. IMFA Sections 2(d)(1)(A)(i)(I) and 2(b)(4)(B).

29. IMFA Section 2(d)(4)(B)(i).

30. IMFA Section 2(c)(2).

31. IMFA Section 3(a)(1).

32. IMFA Section 5(a)(2)(e).

33. Rae 1988: 188n57.

34. Immigration Marriage Fraud 1985: 84.

35. Ibid., 71, 84.
36. Ibid., 27–28.
37. USCIS Fraud Referral Sheet 2004.
38. Immigration Marriage Fraud 1985: 72.
39. Ibid., 87.
40. Harvard Law Review 1986: 1239, 1243.
41. Ibid., 1246.
42. Lynskey 1987: 1093; Lipsky 1980. Furthermore, as AILA president Coven noted during the IMFA congressional hearings, divorce is almost as common as marriage in the United States, and the presumption that the duration and success of marriages between citizens and noncitizens would diverge significantly from those between two citizens is not logically defensible (Immigration Marriage Fraud 1985: 89).
43. Bernstein 2010.
44. Luibhéid 2002.
45. Nock 2005: 22.
46. Cianciarulo 2015.
47. Ibid. A 2017 opinion of the Ninth Circuit Court of Appeals confirms that "nonimmigrants" with Temporary Protected Status (TPS)—including those who entered the US without inspection—should be considered legally admitted (not unauthorized) for the purposes of adjustment to permanent legal immigration status and can adjust their status from within the US (*Ramirez v. Brown* 2017). The US Supreme Court is reconsidering this decision in its Spring 2021 session with the case *Sanchez v. Mayorkas.*
48. IIRIRA does allow couples facing the multiyear bars to reentry to apply for an Extreme Hardship Waiver (EHW), which waives the bars to reentry for successful applicants. In order to qualify for a waiver, couples must prove significant hardship for the US citizen spouse and children above and beyond the financial and emotional costs of deportation itself (Fix and Zimmerman 2001). Originally, the noncitizen spouse had to leave the US to attend their consular interview before finding out if the EHW had been approved, introducing significant risk to any unauthorized couple's attempt to adjust to legal status. The Obama administration implemented a policy to allow couples to apply for the waiver *before* leaving the United States for the consular interview, which has eliminated some of the risk of applying for the waiver (Skrentny and López 2013). But for families whose waiver application is denied, they must either remain unauthorized and at risk of deportation within the United States or leave the US and wait out the multiyear bar to reentry.
49. Cianciarulo 2015; Kelly and Dalmia 2011; Mercer 2008; Enchautegui and Menjívar 2015; Lofgren 2005; Lundstrom 2013; Martínez de Castro 2013.
50. Unauthorized spouses of US citizens who have been convicted of an "aggravated felony," as defined in the IIRIRA, are often subject to additional penalties to legal reentry and, in some cases, are permanently disqualified from

obtaining any legal authorization to enter the United States (Abrego et al. 2017; Coonan 1998). Additionally, changes enacted through the IIRIRA subject any non-US citizen who admits to have "fraudulently" claimed to be a US citizen (or has been accused of doing as much by an immigration authority) to a permanent bar from legal entry to the US (Taylor 2009; USCIS 2018). Before the IIRIRA, only immigrants convicted of intentional fraud and willful misrepresentation faced the permanent bar, but changes in the IIRIRA broadened this policy to affect many more immigrants, including those who unintentionally or unknowingly make a fraudulent claim to citizenship. There is currently no waiver available to challenge this permanent bar.

51. Bureau of Consular Affairs 2015: 2; emphasis added.

52. Fuentes 2003.

53. Murray 2013: 1.

54. Ibid. The US has a visa waiver agreement with thirty-eight countries (75 percent of which are in Europe) that allows citizens of those countries to travel to the US as tourists without first attending a consular interview in their home country in which applicants must meet the standards listed above. Access to the US and the opportunity to overstay a visa in the US is obviously much easier for individuals from these countries, although a purported requirement for countries to remain qualified in the waiver program is a low visa-overstay rate (less than 2 percent; US Code §1187, Section 217(c) of the INA).

55. Menjívar, Abrego, and Schmalzbauer 2016; Warren and Kerwin 2017.

56. Baker and Rytina 2013.

57. Golash-Boza and Hondagneu-Sotelo 2013.

58. Hwang and Parreñas 2010.

59. This is a sliding scale based on family size. A sponsor who is single or married with no children would have to meet the income thresholds for a household of two (the citizen sponsor plus the immigrant spouse/fiancé[e]); sponsors with children and/or other dependents must prove sufficient income for a household that includes themselves, all of their dependents, and the immigrant spouse being sponsored.

60. Hayes 2001. While a third party could step in as financial sponsor of the noncitizen spouse in case the citizen's income is insufficient, the third party must be willing to accept legally enforceable financial responsibility for the visa applicant for the duration of her stay within the United States (even if the marriage dissolves). Financial responsibility remains in force until the immigrant (a) becomes a citizen, (b) accrues forty quarters (ten years) of employment history in the United States, (c) returns to her country of citizenship, or (d) dies (USCIS 2013). Securing an outside sponsor under these conditions can be very difficult, especially for citizens with low social capital.

61. Although this income threshold disproportionately punishes unemployed US citizens and those working in low-paid, service-sector jobs, it does not perfectly correlate with class and education levels. For example, as a graduate

student, my fellowship and student employee income did not meet the IIRIRA minimum income threshold, either.

62. A "public charge" rule by the Trump administration, which took effect in February 2020 but was vacated by the US District Court for the Northern District of Illinois in November 2020, further exacerbated these inequalities by broadening the criteria determining which green card applicants are likely to become a public charge (USCIS 2020). For permanent residency applicants being sponsored by a spouse, this rule would include an analysis of the citizen spouse's income and personal use of social welfare programs in determining the potential that the noncitizen spouse is likely to need/be eligible for any public assistance programs. Immigrants whose sponsors' income exceeds 125 percent of the federal poverty level but is less than 250 percent of the federal poverty level (in 2020, that's $32,750 and $65,500, respectively, for a family of four) are considered at greater risk of becoming public charges and could be denied visas on those grounds (Kight 2020).

63. ASPE 2016; Center for Poverty Research 2016.

64. USCIS 2021.

65. FRED Economic Data n.d.

66. US Census Bureau 2016b.

67. US Census Bureau 2016a.

68. Chauvin and Garcés-Mascareñas 2014.

69. Hayes 2001; LeMay 2007.

70. Reiter and Coutin 2017.

71. Bunting 2015; Darian-Smith 2015; Lee 2013.

72. Golash-Boza and Hondagneu-Sotelo 2013.

73. Hawthorne 2007.

74. FitzGerald and Cook-Martín 2014.

75. Hwang and Parreñas 2010.

76. Mathema 2017; Migration Policy Institute n.d.

Chapter 3: Navigating the High Stakes of US Family Reunification Law

1. Lynskey 1987; Mercer 2008.

2. Abrams 2007.

3. García 2006.

4. Carron 2015.

5. Marshall and Barclay 2003.

6. Silbey 2008.

7. Merry 1990; Sarat 1990; Nielsen 2000; Salcido and Menjívar 2012; Hirsh and Lyons 2011; Pasquetti 2013; Ng 2009; Abrego 2011; De Hart, Van Rossum, and Sportel 2013; Kulk and De Hart 2013; Menjívar and Bejarano 2004.

8. Cowan 2004.

9. Ewick and Silbey 1998.

10. This is especially the case with unauthorized families in the US whose application denials generally trigger deportation or "voluntary removal" orders and, upon leaving the US, the ten-year automatic bar to reentry (López 2017a).

11. Delgado 2009.

12. Unauthorized spouses of US citizens who entered the US without inspection must attend their visa interview in their country of citizenship, but when they leave the US to attend the interview, they automatically become subject to the ten-year bar to legal reentry to the US. The only way families can avoid this bar is to secure an EHW.

13. Between 1996, when the EHW was introduced in conjunction with the IIRIRA, and 2012, noncitizen spouses would not be informed of whether or not their waiver application had been successful until after attending their consular interview outside of the US. This threat of long-term separation or relocation outside of the US kept many mixed-citizenship families from applying for family reunification and the EHW at all. In 2012, President Obama issued an executive order enabling families to learn whether or not their EHW application had been approved *before* leaving the country for the consular interview (Skrentny and López 2013). This significantly reduced the risks for families seeking family reunification who would otherwise be subject to the ten-year bar. (Note: unauthorized spouses of US citizens who overstayed a visa can be interviewed at INS offices within the US, rather than having to travel to the US consulate in their country of origin. Because they are not required to leave the US before adjusting their status, they are not subject to the ten-year bar to reentry.)

14. Applying for the EHW does not force couples to pursue a family reunification outcome. It is more equivalent to an opportunity to change a "card" in their "hand" than to use their one chance to "play their hand."

15. US citizens' spouses with unauthorized immigration status who entered the US without inspection must prove that their US citizen relatives would suffer "extreme hardship" above and beyond the hardship one would expect as a result of deportation in order to qualify for a waiver to the ten-year bar to reentry. Due to Juliette's mental health crisis, she was unable to work and also struggled to be the primary caregiver of their children. Her (and their children's) need for Tenoch as the financial support of the family and as a crucial caregiver in the home strengthened their claims of extreme hardship as compared with their first application, when Juliette was the primary breadwinner and their family enjoyed good physical and mental health.

16. USCIS 2016.

17. Harvard Law Review 1986; Lynskey 1987; Rae 1988.

18. US Code §1182.

19. *Lutwak v. United States* 1953.

20. With the potential exception of their difference in age—Chuck is nearly three decades older than Melodia and has children her age. While the USCIS

agent briefly mentioned this significant difference in age during Melodia's green card interview, Chuck said that the whole issue blew over quickly after he made a brief reference to Jay and Gloria's relationship from *Modern Family*.

21. There is absolutely a gendered element to one's ability to bend this rule, as immigration officers have been culturally primed to find a woman's lack of work in the US while holding a green card as less suspicious than a man's lack of work. As long as Melodia could hide the fact of her work in Mexico from the US (or satisfactorily claim that she had performed that work remotely), her status as a wife and, soon thereafter, mother of young children provided a culturally acceptable justification for her lack of work in the US following her receipt of permanent residency and a Social Security number. Male partners in heterosexual relationships could not accomplish the same feat without facing much more scrutiny (Bouchard 2000).

22. Both partners in each of these couples came from and maintained a privileged socioeconomic status. As discussed in chapter 2, current US immigration laws preference couples (and the individuals who compose them) who can demonstrate past and current socioeconomic success. Thus, these couples' paths to family reunification—while not guaranteed—were straightforward and easily accessible at any time.

Chapter 4: (Dis)Integrated Families, (Dis)Integrated Lives

1. See *Kerry v. Din* 2015.
2. López 2017a.
3. Hagan, Eschback and Rodriguez 2008; Menjívar 2011; Dreby 2015.
4. Castañeda 2019.
5. Gordon 1964; Massey and Denton 1985; Alba et al. 1999.
6. Wright et al. 2003.
7. Hagan, Lowe, and Quingla 2011; Menjívar 2011; García 2014.
8. Individuals with lawful permanent residency (LPR) status in the US are required to reside within the US at least 180 days of every year. While failing to meet this requirement could result in the cancellation of LPR status, a number of couples I interviewed were living or had lived outside the US with LPR status and faced no negative consequences. (With regard to the gendered aspect of this issue, see note 21 from chapter 3.)
9. The couples I interviewed had mixed citizenship in the US and one of the following countries: Mexico, El Salvador, or Guatemala. US citizens have visa-free access to all of these countries and could gain legal status through their spouses much more easily than in the US. For these couples, access and spatial integration into the non-US country did not depend so heavily on the noncitizen spouse's legal status there. Such may not be the case for mixed-citizenship American families with ties to other countries.
10. López 2020a.
11. Hwang and Salazar Parreñas 2010.

12. Massey and Denton 1985, 1993; Alba et al. 1999; Alba, Logan, and Stults 2000; South, Crowder, and Chavez 2005a, 2005b; Iceland and Nelson 2008.

13. Ellis, Wright, and Parks 2006; Gabriel 2016; Spörlein, Mouw, and Martinez-Schuldt 2017; Qian, Lichter, and Tumin 2018.

14. Iceland and Nelson 2008; Gabriel 2016, 2018; Ellis, Wright, and Parks 2006.

15. Gabriel 2016: 185.

16. Novak and Chamlin 2012.

17. Brigham 2009.

18. García 2014, 2019; Menjívar 2011.

19. García 2014; Castañeda 2019; Hagan, Lowe, and Quingla 2011.

20. García 2014, 2019.

21. The IIRIRA states that any person who has been unlawfully present in the United States for at least one year is automatically subject to a ten-year bar to legal reentry in the US. Given the time it takes to meet, fall in love, get married, etc., almost all unauthorized partners in mixed-citizenship couples living in the US have been living without lawful immigration status for at least one year and would be subject to a minimum ten-year bar upon leaving the US.

22. Castañeda 2019.

23. Christian and Sharon applied for the Extreme Hardship Waiver before the introduction of the 2012 Obama executive order that allows mixed-citizenship families seeking to adjust to a legal immigration status to apply for the waiver before unauthorized family members leave the country for their consular interview.

24. Sharon, wanting to be completely honest in her application, checked the box stating she had claimed to be a US citizen in the past, assuming that she probably had checked the "citizen" box on a job application at some point during her youth and young adult life (see chapter 3). The punishment for fraudulently claiming US citizenship status is a permanent bar to legal status in the US; once imposed, the bar cannot be appealed.

25. For the distinction between "authorized" and "pre-authorized," see note 4 in the Appendix.

26. For a detailed discussion of this ruling, see the introductory chapter of this book.

Chapter 5: Institutional (In)Visibility

1. Faber and Friedline 2018; Soederberg 2012.

2. Agius Vallejo and Keister 2020; Chavez 2012; Martin 2015; McConnell 2015; Yoshikawa 2011.

3. Meng and Gregory 2005.

4. Gordon 1964: 130.

5. Gonzales 2011, 2015; Martinez 2014.

6. Scholars have developed "immigrant generation" designations to distinguish between immigrants who arrive in the US as adults (1st generation), immigrants who arrive as children (1.5 generation), and individuals born in the US with at least one immigrant parent (2nd generation; Gonzales 2015: 239).

7. Abrego 2006; Baum and Flores 2011; Osei-Twumasi and Lopez-Hernandez 2019; Rincón 2020.

8. Abrego and Gonzales 2010; Lara and Nava 2018; Amuedo-Dorantes and Antman 2017; Cho 2017; Terriquez 2014.

9. Gonzales 2015.

10. Gonzales 2015. Unauthorized couples with noncitizen spouses who arrived as adults did not highlight limited educational access as a significant structural barrier as frequently as those who had arrived as children. This is likely due to the fact that most unauthorized immigrants who come to the US as adults come seeking work in the US rather than education. Some of these unauthorized families did discuss lack of educational opportunities, but they generally did so in different terms, such as having to give up educational pursuits in order to migrate to support their parents/siblings following a death in the family or other significant loss *or* their inability to pursue further education once in the US because they had to work multiple jobs with long hours just to make ends meet, leaving no time to study.

11. Golash-Boza 2015.

12. Some states and private universities have passed policies to help relieve some of these pressures, such as California's Assembly Bill 540 (2001), which allows long-term California residents, including the unauthorized, to pay in-state tuition rates, and the California Dream Act (2011), which allows students who qualify for AB 540 relief to also apply for certain types of public and private financial aid (Abrego 2008; Enriquez et al. 2019).

13. All three received permanent residency, two of whom acquired it after successfully petitioning for the Extreme Hardship Waiver (EHW). Sharon, who has bachelor's and master's degrees, was granted the EHW and adjusted to lawful permanent resident status. Her disqualification from citizenship and cancellation of her legal status came three years later from an error on her citizenship application.

14. Even worse, all four were eventually forced out of the US through deportation or "voluntary removal" after being threatened with deportation.

15. Chauvin and Garcés-Mascareñas 2014.

16. Reyes Lola 2017; Allison et al. 2018.

17. O'Neil 2018; McConnell 2015.

18. Los Angeles Almanac 2020.

19. Singer 2004.

20. Broder, Moussiavian, and Blazer 2015. Some exceptions can be made, usually in extreme circumstances (such as when requiring emergency medical care).

21. Make the Road New York 2011.

22. USDA 2019; Ayón 2009.

23. López-Sanders 2017. The lines have been further blurred by changes imposed by the Trump administration in 2019 to deny residency applicants who "more likely than not" may become a public charge in the future (US-CIS 2020). A sponsoring spouse's prior dependence on federal welfare benefits could be used as evidence that the immigrant applicant is at greater risk of becoming a public charge (USCIS 2020). Citizens have also been explicitly excluded from federal welfare programs because of their family relationships with immigrants, reinforcing confusion and concerns regarding eligibility issues for citizens with noncitizen spouses (López 2020b).

24. Bloemraad and de Graauw 2011; Luibhéid, Andrade, and Stevens 2017.

25. As citizens, Angelica and her daughters would not be required to pay back the value of any social welfare benefits they utilized. But she could be required to reimburse the government for any benefits her husband accessed at any time before becoming a naturalized citizen (USCIS 2019). Angelica's confusion over these rules is common among many citizens in mixed-citizenship families and often leads them to intentionally avoid accessing social welfare benefits for any family member, including eligible citizens.

26. Grabell 2017.

27. Smith 2012.

28. Gleeson 2010; Gonzales 2015.

Chapter 6: Parenthetical Belonging

1. Assimilation (as a sociological concept) was first described as "a process of interpenetration and fusion in which persons and groups acquire the memories, sentiments, and attitudes of other persons or groups, and, by sharing their experience and history, are incorporated with them in a common cultural life" (Park and Burgess [1921] 1969: 736). While Park and Burgess's definition of assimilation implied movement and change for both "newcomer" groups and those in the established "mainstream," much of the work that built upon their theories in the decades that followed adopted a stricter view of assimilation as the movement of "outsider" groups in a "straight line" toward a set and predetermined (White, Protestant) American "mainstream" (Gans 1979). This "traditional" view of assimilation imposed problematic assumptions about the cultural superiority of this "American mainstream." The theory also builds on the controversial expectation that newly arriving immigrants and immigrant groups would want to shed their cultural identities and traditions and conform to the social and cultural standards of the "mainstream" (and that the "mainstream" would accommodate them).

Scholarship challenging both of these assumptions—groups' desire to abandon their own culture in pursuit of assimilation and the extent to which that effort could result in full acceptance into the "mainstream"—has flourished in the last thirty years. These works have demonstrated that maintaining strong ethnic ties in receiving and sending countries can improve immigrants' economic, labor, and education opportunities while also protecting against "downward" assimilation, or integration into social categories that fall outside of the (White, Protestant) "mainstream" (see Glazer and Moynihan 1970; Bonacich 1973; Light 1984; Portes and Manning 1986; Gibson 1988; Waldinger 1996; Zhou and Bankston 1998; Portes and Rumbaut 2001, 2006; Logan, Zhang, and Alba 2002; Bean and Stevens 2003; Smith 2006; Kasinitz et al. 2008; Telles and Ortiz 2008; Haller, Portes, and Lynch 2011). They have also convincingly argued that full integration into this racialized and classed "mainstream" is impossible for certain individuals and groups whose structural exclusion by race and/or class permanently marks them as other (Portes and Zhou 1993; Kazal 1995; Zhou 1997; Kim 1999; Waters 1999). These studies pushed the field of assimilation research in new directions, prompting some scholars to return to Parks and Burgess's broader notion of assimilation as a process of convergence between groups that involves change and adaptation by all groups and results in a new "composite culture" (e.g., Alba and Nee 1997, 2003; Alba 2005; Brubaker 2001; Jiménez 2010a, 2010b, 2017). Others have introduced alternative theories of incorporation, such as multiculturalism and transnationalism, that foreground the peaceful coexistence of multiple cultures and social practices simultaneously, with no expectation of convergence (Sánchez 1993; Kymlicka 1995a, 1995b; Glick Schiller 1999; Carens 2000; Smith 2006; Levitt 2009; Levitt and Lambda-Nieves 2011).

2. Intermarriage between "old-timer" and "newcomer" groups has been studied as a key measure of group-level assimilation by scholars since the concept of assimilation was introduced a century ago, cf. Park and Burgess [1921] 1969; Gordon 1964; Waters and Jiménez 2005.

3. Herzog 2011.

4. Brubaker 1992: 23.

5. Herzog 2011; Joppke 1998.

6. Favell 1998; Crul and Schneider 2010.

7. Zolberg 1999; Ngai 2004.

8. Aleinikoff 1986; Torpey 1997.

9. López 2017b.

10. Different approaches to understanding social integration and determining what it "looks" like have led scholars to define and measure social integration in many different ways—from both the individual and group perspectives, from both the immigrant and nonimmigrant perspectives, and based on both self-evaluations and external evaluations of integration. Unsurprisingly, the way a scholar chooses to evaluate social integration directly affects her findings and conclusions (Marrow 2013; Bloemraad and Sheares 2017). Here, I employ a subject-centered approach to social integration through an examination of citizen and noncitizen spouses' self-evaluation of both their sense of

belonging and their (non)identification with different national identities. These two measures—sense of belonging and national identity—are directly relevant to the citizen-state relationship and help disentangle the individual and familial dynamics of social integration and identity management.

11. Chuck is the only US citizen spouse I interviewed who naturalized in his partner's country of citizenship through his marital relationship. A handful of other US citizen interviewees already had dual nationality through their parents or acquired dual nationality through their parents in order to be able to marry in Mexico.

12. Dreby 2012, 2015; Enriquez 2015, 2017a; Gleeson 2010; Gonzales 2011, 2015; Gonzales and Burciaga 2018; Rodriguez 2016; Schueths 2012, 2015.

13. Mazzucato 2008; Waldinger 2015; Jiménez 2017.

14. Menjivar 2006.

15. Crul and Schneider 2010; Kasinitz et al. 2008; Gonzales 2015.

16. See the discussion of *Kerry v. Din* in the introduction.

17. Crul and Schneider 2010; Kasinitz et al. 2008; Gonzales 2015.

18. Thronson 2006; Schueths 2015; López 2017b.

19. Riger and Lavrakas 1981; Keyes 1998; Snel, Engbersen, and Leerkes 2006.

20. See note 1 from this chapter.

21. Innovative scholarship on assimilation has actually used dissimilation of immigrant groups from nonimmigrant cohorts in their countries of origin as evidence of assimilation into the host country (see Jiménez and FitzGerald 2007).

22. This appears to be possible only when both spouses have legal status (or access to it) in both countries enabling their free travel within and between both places.

23. Burke 1991.

Conclusion

1. Auyero 2011, 2012.

2. The number of green cards issued under the Trump administration dropped dramatically, primarily because of processing delays implemented before COVID-19 that have now been compounded by delays stemming from pandemic-related closures of INS and consular offices.

3. Gordon 1964.

4. Menjivar and Abrego 2012; Caldwell 2019; Cardoso et al. 2014; Kanstroom 2007.

5. Lofgren 2005; Krikorian 2007; Lundstrom 2013; Abrego et al. 2017; Trucios-Haynes 1998.

6. A 2019 Trump administration policy made these income requirements even more rigorous (see USCIS 2020).

7. USCIS 2018: Vol. 8, Part K.1.A.

8. USCIS 2018: Vol. 8, Part K.2.

9. Hirsch 2003; Schaeffer 2012.

10. Fiancé(e) visa holders must marry their US citizen partner within 90 days of entering the US on their visa; they then must apply to adjust to permanent resident status within 180 days of their entry to the US. Until their residency application has passed the first stage of processing and the noncitizen receives permission to travel, fiancé(e) visa holders cannot leave the US without forfeiting their status.

11. The noncitizen spouse could qualify for certain temporary, nonimmigrant visas, like a tourist visa, but not based on their relationship to a US citizen. In fact, being married to a US citizen could jeopardize an individual's ability to qualify for a temporary visa.

12. Noncitizens from countries with visa waiver agreements with the US do not face this issue because they can travel to the US for to six months at a time without applying for a visa. See chapter 2, note 54.

13. Bloemraad 2006; de Graauw and Bloemraad 2017.

14. Papadakis 2018.

15. Das Gupta 2014.

16. Cott 1998; Sapiro 1984; Abrams 2009.

17. I recognize that a "highest denominator" system would not address all of the failings of the current immigration and citizenship regimes. Many immigrant families, especially those whose members all have unauthorized immigration status, would remain vulnerable given that their "highest denominator" with regard to rights would continue to be significantly limited. That said, such a system would go a long way toward helping the state comply with its obligations to its official members.

18. Soysal 1994; Butler 2020; Anderson 1999.

Epilogue

1. When Tenoch's Extreme Hardship Waiver was approved and they finally could apply for residency, Juliette was not working because of severe anxiety and depression that had come on, in large part, due to the stress from being undocumented. Juliette's sister earned just enough income to act as Tenoch's fiscal sponsor for his residency application and agreed to take on the legal responsibilities that sponsorship entails. (See chapter 2, note 60.)

Appendix A: Description of Methodology

1. Arar 2016.

2. Radford 2019.

3. By "extraterritorial," I mean mixed-citizenship American couples living outside the US.

4. The term "authorized" refers to non-US citizen spouses who have acquired lawful permanent residency status and/or US citizenship following

marriage to their US citizen partner. The term "pre-authorized" refers to non-US citizen spouses who already possess a valid nonimmigrant visa (such as a tourist visa) but who have not applied for permanent residency or any other immigrant visa to the US.

5. Abrego 2008, 2011; Colon-Navarro 2007; Dreby 2012, 2015; Jiménez 2010a; Kymlicka 1995a; Menjívar and Abrego 2012; Menjívar and Bejarano 2004; Salcido and Menjívar 2012; Vasquez 2015; Waters 1999. Given that federal immigration law does not recognize unmarried cohabiting couples for family reunification purposes, members of these types of mixed-status couples did not qualify for inclusion in this study. Married mixed-citizenship couples, engaged couples applying for a fiancé(e) visa, and divorced individuals formerly in a mixed-citizenship marriage were included in the project.

6. I interviewed one of these couples, Lucy and Javier, in 2012 when they were engaged and again in 2016 after they married. I followed the other couple, Karen and Jo, through their fiancée visa application, which they ultimately abandoned.

7. In two instances, the spouses were interviewed separately because they were unable to find a time in which they were both available to interview together. In four other interviews, I was ultimately able to interview only one spouse.

8. I acknowledge that individuals' responses were potentially affected by the presence of their spouse in the interview, but I felt that this arrangement would be most conducive for the study. An assessment of interviews I conducted for my preliminary research, some of which were with both spouses and others with the US citizen spouse only, revealed that respondents often gave richer and more complete descriptions of their experiences when interviewed together. To ensure that both spouses had the opportunity to express themselves, I designed the interview schedule in a way to enable both spouses to share their own opinions and give each other the opportunity to discuss their personal experiences. In instances in which both spouses were asked for their individual responses to the same question, I began with the noncitizen spouse, whose experience was likely to be most different from my own.

9. I formally re-interviewed seven of those couples again between 2016 and 2018. I kept in touch and followed up with (but did not formally re-interview) four more couples from the 2012–13 interviews. I did not have any additional contact beyond the 2012–13 interview with the final four couples. For all four of the couples I was unable to re-interview, the noncitizen spouse already had long-term legal status in the US, including three spouses that had naturalized prior to our 2012–13 interview.

10. These couples were excluded from this project because the noncitizen spouse was from a Latin American country (e.g., Brazil, Argentina) that was excluded from the final project design (which I limited to families with a non-US citizen spouse from Mexico, Guatemala, and El Salvador, as described at the beginning of this appendix).

11. While I discuss my own experience only in the preface and epilogue, I believe my familiarity with many of the unique opportunities and challenges mixed-citizenship couples encounter helped me to gain access to families and to contextualize their responses during the interviews. To ensure I did not project my experience in a mixed-citizenship marriage onto other couples, I made an extra effort to recognize that our experiences could differ (and often have differed) greatly and not to assume to be familiar with their experiences. Whenever possible, I asked participants to elaborate on their responses or to clarify their answers to ensure that I received the clearest possible picture of their experiences and to avoid projecting my experiences onto them.

12. For example, Abrego 2014; Dreby 2015; Gonzales 2015; Gomberg-Muñoz 2016.

13. I also engaged several research assistants—including two students in mixed-citizenship marriages—in recoding the interviews to ensure that I did not overlook any important themes.

14. I used this as a guide with each semi-structured, open-ended interview, although I often asked follow-up and other questions *not* included on this list depending on interviewees' responses. Although most interviews lasted between 90 and 120 minutes, we were often unable to cover all of the questions in this interview guide. I did ensure that I asked some key questions in every interview, including questions about their backgrounds, belonging (in their families, hometowns, countries), family nationality, what the border means to them, their experience applying for family reunification (if applicable), and their thoughts on how US immigration policy could change to better support mixed-citizenship couples.

Bibliography

Laws Cited
California Dream Act (2010)
Illegal Immigration Reform and Immigrant Responsibility Act (1996)
Immigration Marriage Fraud Amendments (1986)
Immigration Reform and Control Act (1986)
Immigration and Nationality Act (1952)
Act of May 14, 1937 (the "Gigolo Act")

Legal Cases Cited
Baumgartner v. United States, 322 U.S. 665 (1944)
In re *Chung Toy Ho and Wong Choy Sin*, 42 F. 398 (D. Or. 1890)
Kerry v. Din, 576 U.S. 86 (2015)
Lutwak v. United States, 344 U.S. 604 (1953)
Ng Fung Ho v. White, 259 U.S. 276 (1922)
O'Bannon v. Town Court Nursing Center, 447 U.S. 773, 788 (1980)
Obergefell v. Hodges, 135 S.Ct. 2071 (2015)
Plyler v. Doe, 457 U.S. 202 (1982)
Ramirez v. Brown, 852 F.3d 954 (9th Cir. 2017).

Abrams, Kerry. 2007. "Immigration Law and the Regulation of Marriage." *Minnesota Law Review* 91: 1625–709.
Abrams, Kerry. 2009. "Becoming a Citizen: Marriage, Immigration, and Assimilation." In *Gender Equality: Dimensions of Women's Equal Citizenship*, edited by Linda McClain and Joanna Grossman, 39–59. Cambridge: Cambridge University Press.
Abrams, Kerry. 2013. "What Makes the Family Special?" *University of Chicago Law Review* 80: 7–27.
Abrego, Leisy J. 2006. "'I Can't Go to College Because I Don't Have Papers': Incorporation Patterns of Latino Undocumented Youth." *Latino Studies* 4: 212–31.
Abrego, Leisy J. 2008. "Legitimacy, Social Identity, and the Mobilization of Law: The Effects of Assembly Bill 540 on Undocumented Students in California." *Law & Social Inquiry* 33(3): 709–34.

Abrego, Leisy J. 2011. "Legal Consciousness of Undocumented Latinos: Fear and Stigma as Barriers to Claims-Making for First- and 1.5-Generation Immigrants." *Law & Society Review* 45(2): 337–69.

Abrego, Leisy J. 2014. *Sacrificing Families: Navigating Laws, Labor, and Love across Borders*. Stanford, CA: Stanford University Press.

Abrego, Leisy J. 2019. "Relational Legal Consciousness of U.S. Citizenship: Privilege, Responsibility, Guilt, and Love in Latino Mixed-Status Families." *Law & Society Review* 53(3): 641–70.

Abrego, Leisy J., Mat Coleman, Daniel E. Martínez, Cecilia Menjívar, and Jeremy Slack. 2017. "Making Immigrants into Criminals: Legal Processes of Criminalization in the Post-IIRIRA Era." *Journal on Migration and Human Security* 5(3): 694–715.

Abrego, Leisy J., and Roberto G. Gonzales. 2010. "Blocked Paths, Uncertain Futures: The Postsecondary Education and Labor Market Prospects of Undocumented Latino Youth." *Journal of Education for Students Placed at Risk* 15(1–2): 144–57.

Agius Vallejo, Jody, and Lisa A. Keister. 2020. "Immigrants and Wealth Attainment: Migration, Inequality, and Integration." *Journal of Ethnic and Migration Studies* 46(18): 3745–61.

Alba, Richard. 2005. "Bright vs. Blurred Boundaries: Second-Generation Assimilation and Exclusion in France, Germany, and the United States." *Ethnic and Racial Studies* 28: 20–49.

Alba, Richard D., John R. Logan, Brian J. Stults, Gilbert Marzan, and Wenquan Zhang. 1999. "Immigrant Groups in the Suburbs: A Reexamination of Suburbanization and Spatial Assimilation." *American Sociological Review* 64(3): 446–60.

Alba, Richard D., John R. Logan, and Brian J. Stults. 2000. "The Changing Neighborhood: Contexts of the Immigrant Metropolis." *Social Forces* 79(2): 587–621.

Alba, Richard, and Victor Nee. 1997. "Rethinking Assimilation Theory for a New Era of Immigration." *International Migration Review* 31(4): 826–74.

Alba, Richard, and Victor Nee. 2003. *Remaking the American Mainstream: Assimilation and Contemporary Immigration*. Cambridge, MA: Harvard University Press.

Aleinikoff, T. Alexander. 1986. "Theories of Loss of Citizenship." *Michigan Law Review* 84: 1471–503.

Allison, Juliann Emmons, Joel S. Herrera, Jason Struna, and Ellen Reese. 2018. "The Matrix of Exploitation and Temporary Employment: Earnings Inequality among Inland Southern California's Blue-Collar Warehouse Workers." *Journal of Labor and Society* 21(4): 533–60.

Amuedo-Dorantes, Catalina, and Francisca Antman. 2017. "Schooling and Labor Market Effects of Temporary Authorization: Evidence from DACA." *Journal of Population Economics* 30: 339–73.

Anderson, Elizabeth. 1999. "What Is the Point of Equality?" *Ethics* 109(2): 287–337.

Arar, Rawan Mazen. 2016. "How Political Migrants' Networks Differ from Those of Economic Migrants': 'Strategic Anonymity' among Iraqi Refugees in Jordan." *Journal of Ethnic and Migration Studies* 42(3): 519–35.

Arriaga, Ximena B., Christopher R. Agnew, Nicole M. Capezza, and Justin J. Lehmiller. 2018. "The Social and Physical Environment of Relationship Initiation: An Interdependence Analysis." In *The Handbook of Relationship Initiation*, edited by Susan Sprecher, Amy Wenzel, and John Harvey, 197–216. New York: Psychology Press.

ASPE (Office of the Assistant Secretary for Planning and Evaluation). 2016. *Poverty Guidelines.* Washington, DC: U.S. Department of Health and Human Services. Retrieved May 15, 2018. https://aspe.hhs.gov/poverty-guidelines.

Auyero, Javier. 2011. "Patients of the State: An Ethnographic Account of Poor People's Waiting." *Latin American Research Review* 46(1): 5–29.

Auyero, Javier. 2012. *Patients of the State: The Politics of Waiting in Argentina.* Durham, NC: Duke University Press.

Ayón, Cecilia. 2009. "Shorter Time-Lines, Yet Higher Hurdles: Mexican Families' Access to Child Welfare Mandated Services." *Children and Youth Services Review* 31(6): 609–16.

Baker, Bryan, and Nancy Rytina. 2013. *Estimates of the Unauthorized Immigrant Population Residing in the United States: January 2012.* Washington, DC: Office of Immigration Statistics, Department of Homeland Security.

Baum, Sandy, and Stella Flores. 2011. "Higher Education and Children in Immigrant Families." *The Future of Children* 21(1): 171–93.

Bean, Frank D., and Gillian Stevens. 2003. *America's Newcomers and the Dynamics of Diversity.* New York: Russell Sage Foundation.

Bergquist, Kathleen Ja Sook. 2007. "Right to Define Family: Equality under Immigration Law for U.S. Inter-Country Adoptees." *Georgetown Immigration Law Journal* 22(1): 1–20.

Bernstein, Nina. 2010. "Do You Take This Immigrant?" *New York Times,* June 11.

Bhabha, Jacqueline. 2004. "The 'Mere Fortuity' of Birth? Are Children Citizens?" *Differences* 15(2): 91–117.

Bloemraad, Irene. 2006. "Becoming a Citizen in the United States and Canada: Structured Mobilization and Immigrant Political Incorporation." *Social Forces* 85: 667–95.

Bloemraad, Irene, and Els de Graauw. 2011. "Immigrant Integration and Policy in the United States: A Loosely Stitched Patchwork." *Working Paper Series.* Berkeley, CA: Institute for Research on Labor and Employment.

Bloemraad, Irene, and Alicia Sheares. 2017. "Understanding Membership in a World of Global Migration: (How) Does Citizenship Matter?" *International Migration Review* 51(4): 823–67.

Boehm, Deborah A. 2012. *Intimate Migrations: Gender, Family, and Illegality among Transnational Mexicans*. New York: New York University Press.

Bonacich, Edna. 1973. "A Theory of Middleman Minorities." *American Sociological Review* 38(5): 583–94.

Bonjour, Saskia, and Betty de Hart. 2020. "Intimate Citizenship: Introduction to the Special Issues on Citizenship, Membership and Belonging in Mixed-Status Families." *Identities*. https://doi.org/10.1080/1070289X.2020.1737404.

Bouchard, Genevieve. 2000. "Field Officer Discretion in the Implementation Process: Immigration Policy in Canada, Quebec, and the United States." PhD diss., McMaster University. https://macsphere.mcmaster.ca/handle /11375/7208.

Bredbenner, Candice Lewis. 1998. *A Nationality of Her Own: Women, Marriage, and the Law of Citizenship*. Berkeley: University of California Press.

Brigham, John. 2009. "Seeing Jurisdiction: Some Jurisprudential Issues Arising from Law Being '. . . All Over.'" *Law & Policy* 31(4): 381–404.

Broder, Tanya, Avideh Moussiavian, and Jonathan Blazer. 2015. *Overview of Immigrant Eligibility for Federal Programs*. National Immigration Law Center, December 2015. www.nilc.org/wp-content/uploads/2015/12/overview -immeligfedprograms-2015-12-09.pdf.

Brubaker, Rogers. 1992. *Citizenship and Nationhood in France and Germany*. Cambridge, MA: Harvard University Press.

Brubaker, Rogers. 2001. "The Return of Assimilation? Changing Perspectives on Immigration and Its Sequels in France, Germany, and the United States." *Ethnic and Racial Studies* 24(4): 531–48.

Bunting, Annie. 2015. "Domains of Policy: Law and Society Research on the Family." In *The Handbook of Law and Society*, edited by Austin Sarat and Patricia Ewick, 199–211. Chichester, UK: Wiley Blackwell.

Bureau of Consular Affairs. 2015. *U.S. Visas*. Washington, DC: U.S. Department of State. Retrieved May 15, 2018. https://travel.state.gov/content/dam /visas/VisaFlyer_B1B2%20March%202015.pdf.

Bureau of Consular Affairs. 2018. "Report of the Visa Office 2018." https://tra vel.state.gov/content/travel/en/legal/visa-lawo/visa-statistics/annual-reports /report-of-the-visa-office-2018.html.

Burke, Peter J. 1991. "Identity Processes and Social Stress." *American Sociological Review* 56: 836–49.

Butler, Judith. 2020. *The Force of Non-Violence*. New York: Verso.

Caldwell, Beth. 2019. *Deported Americans: Life after Deportation to Mexico*. Durham, NC: Duke University Press.

Cardoso, Jodi Berger, Erin Randle Hamilton, Nestor Rodriguez, Karl Eschbach, and Jacqueline Hagan. 2014. "Deporting Fathers: Involuntary Transnational Families and Intent to Remigrate among Salvadoran Deportees." *International Migration Review* 50(1): 197–230.

Carens, Joseph. 2000. *Culture, Citizenship, and Community: A Contextual Exploration of Justice as Evenhandedness*. Oxford: Oxford University Press.

Carron, Anna. 2015. "Marriage-Based Immigration for Same-Sex Couples after DOMA: Lingering Problems of Proof and Prejudice." *Northwestern University Law Review* 109(4): 1021–52.

Castañeda, Heide. 2019. *Borders of Belonging: Struggle and Solidarity in Mixed-Status Immigrant Families*. Stanford, CA: Stanford University Press.

Center for Poverty Research. 2016. "What Are the Annual Earnings for a Full-Time Minimum Wage Worker?" University of California, Davis. Retrieved May 15, 2018. http://poverty.ucdavis.edu/faq/what-are-annual-earnings-full-time-minimum-wage-worker.

Chacón, Jennifer M. 2007. "Loving across Borders: Immigration Law and the Limits of Loving." *Wisconsin Law Review* 2007: 345–78.

Chauvin, Sébastien, and Blanca Garcés-Mascareñas. 2014. "Becoming Less Illegal: Deservingness Frames and Undocumented Migrant Incorporation." *Sociology Compass* 8(4): 422–32.

Chavez, Leo R. 2012. *Shadowed Lives: Undocumented Immigrants in American Society*. Boston: Cengage Learning.

Cho, Esther Yoona. 2017. "Revisiting Ethnic Niches: A Comparative Analysis of the Labor Market Experiences of Asian and Latino Undocumented Young Adults." *Russell Sage Foundation Journal of the Social Sciences* 3(4): 97–115.

Cianciarulo, Marisa S. 2015. "Seventeen Years since the Sunset: The Expiration of 245(i) and Its Effect on U.S. Citizens Married to Undocumented Immigrants." *Chapman Law Review* 18(2): 451–79.

Colon-Navarro, Fernando. 2007. "Familia e Inmigración: What Happened to Family Unity?" *Florida Journal of International Law* 19: 491–509.

Coonan, Terry. 1998. "Dolphins Caught in Congressional Fishnets—Immigration Law's New Aggravated Felons." *Georgetown Immigration Law Journal* 12: 589–620.

Coontz, Stephanie. 2006. *Marriage, a History: How Love Conquered Marriage*. New York: Penguin.

Cott, Nancy F. 1998. "Marriage and Women's Citizenship in the United States, 1830–1934." *American Historical Review* 103: 1440–74.

Cowan, Dave. 2004. "Legal Consciousness: Some Observations." *Modern Law Review* 67(6): 928–58.

Crul, Maurice and Jens Schneider. 2010. "Comparative Integration Context Theory: Participation and Belonging in New Diverse European Cities." *Ethnic and Racial Studies* 33(7): 1249–68.

Darian-Smith, Eve. 2015. "The Constitution of Identity: New Modalities of Nationality, Citizenship, Belonging and Being." In *The Handbook of Law and Society*, edited by Austin Sarat and Patricia Ewick, 351–66. Chichester, UK: Wiley Blackwell.

Das Gupta, Monisha. 2014. "'Don't Deport Our Daddies': Gendering State Deportation Practices and Immigrant Organizing." *Gender & Society* 28(1): 83–109.

de Graauw, Els, and Irene Bloemraad. 2017. "Working Together: Building Successful Policy and Program Partnerships for Immigrant Integration." *Journal on Migration and Human Security* 5(1): 105–23.

De Hart, Betty, Wibo Van Rossum, and Iris Sportel. 2013. "Law in the Everyday Lives of Transnational Families: An Introduction." *Oñati Sociol-Legal Series* 3(6): 991–1003.

Degtyareva, Victoria. 2011. "Defining Family in Immigration Law: Accounting for Nontraditional Families in Citizenship by Descent." *Yale Law Journal* 120(4): 862–909.

Delgado, Tatyana E. 2009. "Leaving the Doctrine of Consular Absolutism Behind." *Georgetown Immigration Law Journal* 24(1): 55–76.

Demleitner, Nora V. 2003. "How Much Do Western Democracies Value Family and Marriage: Immigration Law's Conflicted Answers." *Immigration and Nationality Law Review* 24: 351–90.

Dreby, Joanna. 2012. "The Burden of Deportation on Children in Mexican Immigrant Families." *Journal of Marriage and Family* 74: 829–45.

Dreby, Joanna. 2015. *Everyday Illegal: When Policies Undermine Immigrant Families*. Berkeley: University of California Press.

Ellis, Mark, Richard Wright, and Virginia Parks. 2006. "The Immigrant Household and Spatial Assimilation: Partnership, Nativity, and Neighborhood Location." *Urban Geography* 27(1): 1–19.

Enchautegui, Maria E., and Cecilia Menjívar. 2015. "Paradoxes of Family Immigration Policy: Separation, Reorganization, and Reunification of Families under Current Immigration Laws." *Law & Policy* 37(1–2): 32–60.

Enriquez, Laura. 2015. "Multigenerational Punishment: Shared Experiences of Undocumented Immigration Status within Mixed-Status Families." *Journal of Marriage and Family* 77(4): 939–53.

Enriquez, Laura. 2017a. "A 'Master Status' or the 'Final Straw': Assessing the Role of Immigration Status in Latino Undocumented Youths' Pathways Out of School." *Journal of Ethnic and Migration Studies* 43(9): 1526–43.

Enriquez, Laura. 2017b. "Gendering Illegality: Undocumented Young Adults' Negotiation of the Family Formation Process." *American Behavioral Scientist* 61(10): 1153–71.

Enriquez, Laura. 2020. *Of Love and Papers: How Immigration Policy Affects Romance and Family*. Berkeley: University of California Press.

Enriquez, Laura E., Martha Morales Hernandez, Daniel Millán, and Daisy Vasquez Vera. 2019. "Mediating Illegality: Federal, State, and Institutional Policies in the Educational Experiences of Undocumented College Students." *Law & Social Inquiry* 44(3): 679–703.

Ewick, Patricia, and Susan S. Silbey. 1998. *The Common Place of Law: Stories from Everyday Life*. Chicago: University of Chicago Press.

Faber, Jacob, and Terri Friedline. 2018. *The Racialized Costs of Banking*. Washington, DC: New America. https://community-wealth.org/sites/clone

.community-wealth.org/files/downloads/The_Racialized_Costs_of_Banking _2018-06-20_205129.pdf.

Favell, Adrian. 1998. *Philosophies of Integration: Immigration and the Idea of Citizenship in France and Britain*. New York: St. Martin's Press.

FitzGerald, David S., and David Cook-Martín. 2014. *Culling the Masses: The Democratic Origins of Racist Immigration Policy in the Americas*. Cambridge, MA: Harvard University Press.

Fix, Michael, and Wendy Zimmerman. 2001. "All under One Roof: Mixed-Status Families in an Era of Reform." *International Migration Review* 35(2): 397–419.

FRED Economic Data. N.d. "Real Personal and Family Income by Census Region, Annual." Federal Reserve Bank of St. Louis. https://fred.stlouisfed .org/release/tables?rid=249&eid=259593#snid=259616.

Friedland, Bernard, and Valerie Epps. 1996. "The Changing Family and the U.S. Immigration Laws: The Impact of Medical Reproductive Technology on the Immigration and Nationality Act's Definition of the Family." *Georgetown Immigration Law Journal* 11(3): 429–60.

Fuentes, Juan Andres. 2003. "Chasing a Dream: The Tourist Visa in Peru." *Cardozo Public Law, Policy, and Ethics Journal* 1: 199–206.

Gabriel, Ryan. 2016. "A Middle Ground? Residential Mobility and Attainment of Mixed-Race Couples." *Demography* 53(1): 165–88.

Gabriel, Ryan. 2018. "Mixed-Race Couples, Residential Mobility, and Neighborhood Poverty." *Social Science Research* 73: 146–62.

Gans, Herbert J. 1979. "Symbolic Ethnicity: The Future of Ethnic Groups and Cultures in America." *Ethnic and Racial Studies* 2(1): 1–20.

García, Angela S. 2014. "Hidden in Plain Sight: How Unauthorized Migrants Strategically Assimilate in Restrictive Localities in California." *Journal of Ethnic and Migration Studies* 40(2): 1895–914.

García, Angela S. 2019. *Legal Passing: Navigating Undocumented Life and Local Immigration Law*. Berkeley: University of California Press.

García, Michael John. 2006. *Immigration-Related Document Fraud: Overview of Civil, Criminal, and Immigration Consequences*. Congressional Research Service Report RL32657. www.fosterglobal.com/policy_papers /CRSImmigrationFraud.pdf.

Gibson, Campbell, and Kay Jung. 2002. *Historical Census Statistics on Population Totals by Race, 1790 to 1990, and by Hispanic Origin, 1970 to 1990, for the United States, Regions, Divisions, and States*. Population Division Working Paper no. 56. Washington, DC: U.S. Census Bureau. www .census.gov/content/dam/Census/library/working-papers/2002/demo/POP -twps0056.pdf.

Gibson, Margaret A. 1988. *Accommodation without Assimilation: Sikh Immigrants in an American High School*. Ithaca, NY: Cornell University Press.

Glazer, Nathan, and Daniel Patrick Moynihan. 1970. *Beyond the Melting Pot: The Negroes, Puerto Ricans, Jews, Italians, and Irish of New York City*, 2nd ed. Cambridge, MA: MIT Press.

Gleeson, Shannon. 2010. "Labor Rights for All? The Role of Undocumented Immigrant Status for Worker Claims Making." *Law & Social Inquiry* 35(3): 561–602.

Glick Schiller, Nina. 1999. "Transmigrants and Nation-States: Something Old and Something New in the U.S. Immigrant Experience." In *The Handbook of International Migration: The American Experience*, edited by Charles Hirschman, Philip Kasinitz and Josh DeWind, 94–119. New York: Russell Sage Foundation.

Golash-Boza, Tanya Maria. 2015. *Deported: Immigrant Policing, Disposable Labor, and Global Capitalism*. New York: New York University Press.

Golash-Boza, Tanya, and Pierrette Hondagneu-Sotelo. 2013. "Latino Migrant Men and the Deportation Crisis: A Gendered Racial Removal Program." *Latino Studies* 11(3): 271–92.

Gomberg-Muñoz, Ruth. 2015. "The Punishment / El Castigo: Undocumented Latinos and U.S. Immigration Processing." *Journal of Ethnic and Migration Studies* 41(14): 2235–52.

Gomberg-Muñoz, Ruth. 2016. "The Juárez Wives Club: Gendered Citizenship and U.S. Immigration Law." *American Ethnologist* 43(2): 339–52.

Gomberg-Muñoz, Ruth. 2017. *Becoming Legal: Immigration Law and Mixed-Status Families*. Oxford: Oxford University Press.

Gonzales, Roberto G. 2011. "Learning to be Illegal: Undocumented Youth and Shifting Legal Contexts in the Transition to Adulthood." *American Sociological Review* 76: 602–19.

Gonzales, Roberto G. 2015. *Lives in Limbo: Undocumented and Coming of Age in America*. Berkeley: University of California Press.

Gonzales, Roberto G., and Edelina M. Burciaga. 2018. "Segmented Pathways of Illegality: Reconciling the Coexistence of Master and Auxiliary Statuses in the Experiences of 1.5-Generation Undocumented Young Adults." *Ethnicities* 18(2): 178–91.

Gordon, Milton M. 1964. *Assimilation in American Life: The Role of Race, Religion, and National Origins*. Oxford: Oxford University Press.

Grabell, Michael. 2017. "Exploitation and Abuse at the Chicken Plant." *New Yorker*, May 8.

Guendelsberger, John. 1988. "Implementing Family Unification Rights in American Immigration Law: Proposed Amendments." *San Diego Law Review* 25(2): 253–80.

Hagan, Jacqueline, Karl Eschback, and Nestor Rodriguez. 2008. "U.S. Deportation Policy, Family Separation, and Circular Migration." *International Migration Review* 42(1): 64–88.

Hagan, Jacqueline, Nichola Lowe, and Christian Quingla. 2011. "Skills on the Move: Rethinking the Relationship between Human Capital and Immigrant Economic Mobility." *Work and Occupations* 38(2): 149–78.

Haller, William, Alejandro Portes, and Scott M. Lynch. 2011. "Dreams Fulfilled, Dreams Shattered: Determinants of Segmented Assimilation in the Second Generation." *Social Forces* 89(3): 733–62.

Harris, Tina M., and Pamela J. Kalbfleisch. 2010. "Interracial Dating: The Implications of Race for Initiating a Romantic Relationship." *Howard Journal of Communications* 11: 49–64.

Harvard Law Review. 1986. "Notes: The Constitutionality of the INS Sham Marriage Investigation Policy." *Harvard Law Review* 99: 1238–54.

Hawthorne, Monique Lee. 2007. "Family Unity in Immigration Law: Broadening the Scope of 'Family.'" *Lewis and Clark Law Review* 11(3): 809–32.

Hayes, Helene. 2001. *U.S. Immigration Policy and the Undocumented: Ambivalent Laws, Furtive Lives.* Westport, CT: Praeger.

Haynes, Eloisa. 2017. "Mixed-Status Families and the Threat of Deportation." *Journal of Sociology and Social Welfare* 44(1): 99–118.

Henderson, Nia-Malika. 2014. "Seven Charts That Explain the Undocumented Migrant Population." *Washington Post,* November 21.

Herzog, Ben. 2011. "Revocation of Citizenship in the United States." *European Journal of Sociology* 52: 77–109.

Hirsch, Jennifer. 2003. *A Courtship after Marriage: Sexuality and Love in Mexican Transnational Families.* Cambridge: Cambridge University Press.

Hirsh, Elizabeth, and Christopher J. Lyons. 2011. "Perceiving Discrimination on the Job: Legal Consciousness, Workplace Context, and the Construction of Race Discrimination." *Law & Society Review* 44(2): 269–98.

Hull, Kathleen. 2006. *Same-Sex Marriage: The Cultural Politics of Love and Law.* Cambridge: Cambridge University Press.

Hwang, Maria Cecilia, and Rhacel Solazar Parreñas. 2010. "Not Every Family: Selective Reunification in Contemporary U.S. Immigration Laws." *International Labor and Working-Class History* 78(Fall): 100–109.

Iceland, John, and Kyle Anne Nelson. 2008. "Hispanic Segregation in Metropolitan America: Exploring the Multiple Forms of Spatial Assimilation." *American Sociological Review* 73: 741–65.

Immigration Marriage Fraud: Hearing Before the Subcommittee on Immigration and Refugee Policy. 1985. U.S. Senate, 99th Cong. 1, July 26. Washington, DC: U.S. Government Printing Office.

Jiménez, Tomás R. 2010a. *Replenished Ethnicity: Mexican Americans, Immigration, and Identity.* Berkeley: University of California Press.

Jiménez, Tomás R. 2010b. "Affiliative Ethnic Identity: A More Elastic Link between Ethnic Ancestry and Culture." *Ethnic and Racial Studies* 33(10): 1756–75.

Jiménez, Tomás R. 2017. *The Other Side of Assimilation: How Immigrants Are Changing American Life.* Berkeley: University of California Press.

Jiménez, Tomás R., and David FitzGerald. 2007. "Mexican Assimilation: A Temporal and Spatial Reorientation." *DuBois Review* 4(2): 337–54.

Joppke, Christian. 1998. "Immigration Challenges the Nation State." In *Challenge to the Nation-State: Immigration in Western Europe and the United States,* edited by Christian Joppke, 5–46. Oxford: Oxford University Press.

Joppke, Christian. 2010. *Citizenship and Immigration, Volume 2.* Cambridge: Polity.

Kandel, William A. 2018. "U.S. Family-Based Immigration Policy (Updated)." *Current Politics and Economics of the United States, Canada, and Mexico* 20(1): 27–73.

Kanstroom, Daniel. 2007. *Deportation Nation: Outsiders in American History.* Cambridge, MA: Harvard University Press.

Kasinitz, Philip, John H. Mollenkopf, Mary C. Waters, and Jennifer Holdaway. 2008. *Inheriting the City: The Children of Immigrants Come of Age.* New York and Cambridge, MA: Russell Sage Foundation and Harvard University Press.

Kazal, Russell A. 1995. "Revisiting Assimilation: The Rise, Fall, and Reappraisal of a Concept in American Ethnic History." *American Historical Review* 100(2): 437–71.

Kelly, Claudia Smith, and Sonia Dalmia. 2011. "Immigration Reforms, Marriage and Legal Permanent Residence Status." *Journal of Applied Business and Economics* 12(2): 64–79.

Keyes, Corey Lee M. 1998. "Social Well-Being." *Social Psychology Quarterly* 61(2): 121–40.

Kight, Stef W. 2020. "The Real Impact of Trump's 'Public Charge' Immigration Rule." *Axios,* February 23.

Kim, Claire Jean. 1999. "The Racial Triangulation of Asian Americans." *Politics Society* 27: 105–38.

King, Shani M. 2010. "U.S. Immigration Law and the Traditional Nuclear Conception of Family: Toward a Functional Definition of Family That Protects Children's Fundamental Human Rights." *Columbia Human Rights Law Review* 41(2): 509–68.

Kobayashi, Karen M,. Laura Funk, and Mushira Mohsin Khan. 2017. "Constructing a Sense of Commitment in 'Living Apart Together' (LAT) Relationships: Interpretive Agency and Individualization." *Current Sociology* 65(7): 991–1009.

Krikorian, Mark. 2007. "Shortfalls of the 1996 Immigration Reform Legislation." *Hearing Before the Subcommittee on Immigration, Citizenship, Refugees, Border Security, and International Law.* U.S. House of Representatives, 110th Cong. 1, April 20.

Kulk, Friso, and Betty De Hart. 2013. "Mixed Couples and Islamic Family Law in Egypt: Legal Consciousness in Transnational Social Space." *Oñati Socio-Legal Series* 3(6): 1057–69.

Kymlicka, Will. 1995a. *Multicultural Citizenship: A Liberal Theory of Minority Rights.* Oxford: Clarendon Press.

Kymlicka, Will, ed. 1995b. *The Rights of Minority Cultures.* Oxford: Oxford University Press.

Lara, Argelia, and Pedro E. Nava. 2018. "Achieving the Dream, Uncertain Futures: The Postbaccalaureate Decision-Making Process of Latinx Undocumented Students." *Journal of Hispanic Higher Education* 17(2): 112–31.

Larsen, Luke J., and Nathan P. Walters. 2013. *American Community Survey Briefs: Married-Couple Households by Nativity Status, 2011.* Washington, DC: U.S. Department of Commerce.

Lee, Catherine. 2013. *Fictive Kinship: Family Reunification and the Meaning of Race and Nation in American Migration.* New York: Russell Sage Foundation.

LeMay, Michael C. 2007. *Illegal Immigration.* Santa Barbara, CA: ABC-CLIO.

Levitt, Peggy. 2009. "Roots and Routes: Understanding the Lives of the Second Generation Transnationally." *Journal of Ethnic and Migration Studies* 35(7): 1225–42.

Levitt, Peggy, and Deepak Lamba-Nieves. 2011. "Social Remittances Revisited." *Journal of Ethnic and Migration Studies* 37(1): 1–22.

Light, Ivan. 1984. "Immigrant and Ethnic Enterprise in North America." *Ethnic and Racial Studies* 7(2): 195–216.

Lipsky, Michael. 1980. *Street-Level Bureaucracy: Dilemmas of the Individual in Public Services.* New York: Russell Sage Foundation.

Lofgren, Zoe. 2005. "A Decade of Radical Change in Immigration Law: An Inside Perspective." *Stanford Law & Policy Review* 16(2): 349–78.

Logan, John R., Wenquan Zhang, and Richard D. Alba. 2002. "Immigrant Enclaves and Ethnic Communities in New York and Los Angeles." *American Sociological Review* 67(2): 299–322.

López, Ian Haney. 1997. *White by Law: The Legal Construction of Race.* New York: New York University Press.

López, Jane Lilly. 2015. "'Impossible Families': Mixed-Citizenship Status Couples and the Law." *Law & Policy* 37(1–2): 93–118.

López, Jane Lilly. 2017a. "Redefining American Families: The Disparate Effects of IIRIRA's Automatic Bars to Reentry and Sponsorship Requirements on Mixed-Citizenship Couples." *Journal on Migration and Human Security* 5(2): 236–51.

López, Jane Lilly. 2017b. "'Til Deportation Do Us Part: The Effect of U.S. Immigration Law on Mixed-Status Couples' Experience of Citizenship." In

Within and Beyond Citizenship, edited by Nando Sigona and Roberto Gonzales, 53–67. Abingdon-on-Thames: Routledge.

López, Jane Lilly. 2020a. "Together and Apart: Transnational Life in the U.S.-Mexico Border Region." *Journal of Ethnic and Migration Studies* 46(1): 242–59.

López, Jane Lilly. 2020b. "Congress Does Not 'Care' about My American Family." *The Appeal*, April 24.

López, Maria Pabón. 2008. "A Tale of Two Systems: Analyzing the Treatment of Non-Citizen Families in State Family Law Systems and under the Immigration System." *Harvard Latino Law Review* 11: 229–46.

López-Sanders, Laura. 2017. "Navigating Health Care: Brokerage and Access for Undocumented Latino Immigrants under the 2010 Affordable Care Act." *Journal of Ethnic and Migration Studies* 43(12): 2072–88.

Los Angeles Almanac. 2020. "Typical Home Values for Southern California by County 1996–2020." Retrieved May 2, 2020. www.laalmanac.com/economy/ec37.php.

Luibhéid, Eithne. 2002. *Entry Denied: Controlling Sexuality at the Border.* Minneapolis: University of Minnesota Press.

Luibhéid, Eithne, Rosi Andrade, and Sally Stevens. 2017. "Intimate Attachments and Migrant Deportability: Lessons from Undocumented Mothers Seeking Benefits for Citizen Children." *Ethnic and Racial Studies* 41(1): 17–35.

Lundstrom, Kristi. 2013. "The Unintended Effects of the Three- and Ten-Year Unlawful Presence Bars." *Law & Contemporary Problems* 76(3–4): 389–412.

Lynskey, Eileen P. 1987. "Immigration Marriage Fraud Amendments of 1986: Till Congress Do Us Part." *University of Miami Law Review* 41: 1087–116.

Make the Road New York. 2011. *Immigrant Worker Health & Safety: A Guide.* New York: Make the Road New York. Retrieved April 27, 2020. www.osha.gov/sites/default/files/2018–11/fy10_sh-20830-10_Advocate_Guide.pdf.

Marrow, Helen B. "Assimilation in New Destinations." *Daedalus* 142(3): 107–22.

Marshall, Anna-Maria, and Scott Barclay. 2003. "In Their Own Words: How Ordinary People Construct the Legal World." *Law & Social Inquiry* 28(3): 617–28.

Marshall, T.H. [1949] 1998. "Citizenship and Social Class." In *Citizenship Debates*, edited by Gershon Shafir, 93–111. Minneapolis: University of Minnesota Press.

Martin, Nathalie. 2015. "Giving Credit Where Credit Is Due: What We Can Learn from the Banking and Credit Habits of Undocumented Immigrants." *Michigan State Law Review* 2015(3): 989–1042.

Martínez de Castro, Clarissa. 2013. "Strong Families: An Economic and Social Imperative for Successful Immigration Reform." *Hearing Before the Ju-
diciary Subcommittee on Immigration and Border Security*, U.S. House of
Representatives, 113th Cong. 1, March 14.

Martinez, Lisa M. 2014. "Dreams Deferred: The Impact of Legal Reforms
on Undocumented Latino Youth." *American Behavioral Scientist* 58(14):
1873–90.

Massey, Douglas S., and Nancy A. Denton. 1985. "Spatial Assimilation as a Socioeconomic Outcome." *American Sociological Review* 50(1): 94–106.

Massey, Douglas S., and Nancy A. Denton. 1993. *American Apartheid: Segregation and the Making of the Underclass*. Cambridge, MA: Harvard University Press.

Mathema, Silvia. 2017. "State-by-State Estimates of the Family Members of
Unauthorized Immigrants." Center for American Progress, March 16. Retrieved May 9, 2020. www.americanprogress.org/issues/immigration/news
/2017/03/16/427868/state-state-estimates-family-members-unauthorized
-immigrants/.

Mazzucato, Valentina. 2008. "The Double Engagement: Transnationalism and
Integration: Ghanaian Migrants' Lives between Ghana and The Nether-
lands." *Journal of Ethnic and Migration Studies* 34(2): 199–216.

McConnell, Eileen Diaz. 2015. "Hurdles or Walls? Nativity, Citizenship, Legal Status and Latino Homeownership in Los Angeles." *Social Science Research* 53: 19–33.

Meng, Xin, and Robert G. Gregory. 2005. "Intermarriage and the Economic
Assimilation of Immigrants." *Journal of Labor Economics* 23(1): 135–74.

Menjívar, Cecilia. 2006. "Liminal Legality: Salvadoran and Guatemalan Immigrants' Lives in the United States." *American Journal of Sociology* 111(4):
999–1037.

Menjívar, Cecilia. 2011. "The Power of the Law: Central Americans' Legality
and Everyday Life in Phoenix, Arizona." *Latino Studies* 9(4): 377–95.

Menjívar, Cecilia, and Leisy J. Abrego. 2012. "Legal Violence: Immigration
Law and the Lives of Central American Immigrants." *American Journal of
Sociology* 117: 1380–421.

Menjívar, Cecilia, Leisy J. Abrego, and Leah C. Schmalzbauer. 2016. *Immigrant Families*. Cambridge: Polity.

Menjívar, Cecilia, and Cynthia Bejarano. 2004. "Latino Immigrants' Perceptions of Crime and Police Authorities in the United States: A Case Study
from the Phoenix Metropolitan Area." *Ethnic and Racial Studies* 27(1):
120–48.

Mercer, Julie. 2008. "Comment: The Marriage Myth: Why Mixed-Status Marriages Need an Immigration Remedy." *Golden Gate University Law Review* 38: 293–325.

Merry, Sally Engle. 1990. *Getting Justice and Getting Even: Legal Conscious-ness Among Working-Class Americans.* Chicago: University of Chicago Press.

Migration Policy Institute. 2016. "Unauthorized Immigrant Population Pro-files." Washington, DC: Migration Policy Institute. Retrieved May 15, 2018. www.migrationpolicy.org/programs/us-immigration-policy-program-data-hub/unauthorized-immigrant-population-profiles.

Migration Policy Institute. N.d. "Profile of the Unauthorized Population: United States." Retrieved May 9, 2020. www.migrationpolicy.org/data/un authorized-immigrant-population/state/US.

Molina, Natalia. 2014. *How Race Is Made in America: Immigration, Citizen-ship, and the Historical Power of Racial Scripts.* Berkeley: University of California Press.

Motomura, Hiroshi. 1995. "The Family and Immigration: A Roadmap for the Ruritanian Lawmaker." *American Journal of Comparative Law* 43(4): 511–44.

Muriá, Magalí, and Sergio Chávez. 2011. "Shopping and Working in the Bor-derlands: Enforcement, Surveillance and Marketing in Tijuana, Mexico." *Surveillance & Society* 8(3): 355–73.

Muro, Jazmin A., and Lisa M. Martinez. 2016. "Constrained Desires: The Ro-mantic Partner Preferences of College-Educated Latinas." *Latino Studies* 14: 172–91.

Muro, Jazmin A., and Lisa M. Martinez. 2017. "Is Love Color-Blind? Racial Blind Spots and Latinas' Romantic Relationships." *Sociology of Race and Ethnicity* 4(4): 527–40.

Murray, Sara. 2013. "Many People in U.S. Illegally Overstayed Their Visas." *Wall Street Journal,* April 7.

Ng, Kwai Hang. 2009. "'If I Lie, I Tell You, May Heaven and Earth Destroy Me': Language and Legal Consciousness in Hong Kong Bilingual Common Law." *Law & Society Review* 43(2): 369–404.

Ngai, Mae M. 2004. *Impossible Subjects: Illegal Aliens and the Making of Modern America.* Princeton, NJ: Princeton University Press.

Nielsen, Laura Beth. 2000. "Situating Legal Consciousness: Experiences and Attitudes of Ordinary Citizens about Law and Street Harassment." *Law & Society Review* 34: 1055–90.

Nock, Steven L. 2005. "Marriage as a Public Issue." *Future of Children* 5(2): 13–32.

Novak, Kenneth J., and Mitchell B. Chamlin. 2012. "Racial Threat, Suspicion, and Police Behavior: The Impact of Race and Place in Traffic Enforcement." *Crime & Delinquency* 58(2): 275–300.

O'Neil, Meghan M. 2018. "Race, Ethnicity, and the Great Recession: A Na-tional Evaluation of Mortgages and Subprime Lending, 2004–2010." State University of New York at Albany. https://search.proquest.com/openview

/fcd66d34cd737ff98f82828975facf18/1?pq-origsite=gscholar&cbl=18750& diss=y.

Osei-Twumasi, Olivia, and Guadalupe Lopez-Hernandez. 2019. "Resilience in the Face of Adversity: Undocumented Students in Community Colleges." In *Immigrant-Origin Students in Community College: Navigating Risk and Reward in Higher Education*, edited by Carola Suarez-Orozco and Olivia Osei-Twumasi, 46–62. New York: Teachers College Press.

Papadakis, Yiannis. 2018. "Borders, Paradox, and Power." *Ethnic and Racial Studies* 41(2): 285–302.

Park, Robert E., and Ernest W. Burgess. [1921] 1969. *Introduction to the Science of Sociology*, 3rd ed. Chicago: University of Chicago Press.

Parks, Malcolm R. 2017. *Personal Relationships and Personal Networks.* Abingdon-on-Thames: Routledge.

Pasquetti, Silvia. 2013. "Legal Emotions: An Ethnography of Distrust and Fear in the Arab Districts of an Israeli City." *Law & Society Review* 47(3): 461–92.

Pear, Robert. 1986. "In Bureaucracy, Aliens Find Another Unprotected Border." *New York Times*, October 19.

Portes, Alejandro, and Min Zhou. 1993. "The New Second Generation: Segmented Assimilation and Its Variants." *Annals of the American Academy of Political and Social Science* 530: 74–96.

Portes, Alejandro, and Robert D. Manning. 1986. "The Immigrant Enclave: Theory and Empirical Examples." In *Competitive Ethnic Relations,* edited by Susan Olzak and Joane Nagel, 47–68. New York: Academic Press.

Portes, Alejandro, and Rubén G. Rumbaut. 2001. *Legacies: The Story of the Immigrant Second Generation.* Berkeley: University of California Press.

Portes, Alejandro, and Rubén G. Rumbaut. 2006. *Immigrant America: A Portrait,* 3rd ed. Berkeley: University of California Press.

Qian, Zhenchao, and Jose A. Cobas. 2004. "Latinos' Mate Selection: National Origin, Racial, and Nativity Differences." *Social Science Research* 33(2): 225–47.

Qian, Zhenchao, Daniel T. Lichter, and Dmitry Tmin. 2018. "Divergent Pathways to Assimilation? Local Marriage Markets and Intermarriage among U.S. Hispanics." *Journal of Marriage and Family* 80(1): 271–88.

Radford, Jynnah. 2019. "Key Findings about U.S. Immigrants." Washington DC: Pew Research Center. Published June 17, 2019. Accessed July 14, 2020. www.pewresearch.org/fact-tank/2019/06/17/key-findings-about-u-s -immigrants/.

Rae, Karen L. 1988. "Alienating Sham Marriages for Tougher Immigration Penalties: Congress Enacts the Marriage Fraud Act." *Pepperdine Law Review* 15: 181–205.

Rawls, John. 1971. *A Theory of Justice.* Cambridge, MA: Harvard University Press.

Reiter, Keramet, and Susan Bibler Coutin. 2017. "Crossing Borders and Criminalizing Identity: The Disintegrated Subjects of Administrative Sanctions." *Law & Society Review* 51(3): 567–601.

Reyes Lola, Christine E. 2017. "Low-Wage Workers and Bullying in the Workplace: How Current Workplace Harassment Law Makes the Most Vulnerable Invisible." *Hastings International and Comparative Law Review* 40(2): 231–54.

Richins, Nancy K. 1988. "Comment: The Marriage Viability Requirement: Is It Viable?" *San Diego Law Review* 18: 89–106.

Riger, Stephanie, and Paul J. Lavrakas. 1981. "Community Ties: Patterns of Achievement and Social Interaction in Urban Neighborhoods." *American Journal of Community Psychology* 9(1): 55–66.

Rincon, Alejandra. 2020. "Immigrants' Efforts to Access Public Schools and Higher Education in the United States." In *Handbook on Promoting Social Justice in Education*, edited by Rosemary Papa, 2137–64. Berlin: Springer.

Rodriguez, Cassaundra. 2016. "Experiencing 'Illegality' as a Family? Immigration Enforcement, Social Policies, and Discourses Targeting Mexican Mixed-Status Families." *Sociology Compass* 10(8): 706–17.

Salcido, Olivia, and Cecilia Menjívar. 2012. "Gendered Paths to Legal Citizenship: The Case of Latin-American Immigrants in Phoenix, Arizona." *Law & Society Review* 46: 335–68.

Sánchez, George J. 1993. *Becoming Mexican American: Ethnicity, Culture, and Identity in Chicano Los Angeles, 1900–1945*. Oxford: Oxford University Press.

Sapiro, Virginia. 1984. "Women, Citizenship, and Nationality: Immigration and Naturalization Policies in the United States." *Politics & Society* 13(1): 1–26.

Sarat, Austin. 1990. "The Law Is All Over: Power, Resistance and the Legal Consciousness of the Welfare Poor." *Yale Journal of Law and the Humanities* 2: 343–79.

Schachar, Ayelet, and Ran Hirschl. 2007. "Citizenship as Inherited Property." *Political Theory* 35(3): 253–87.Schaeffer, Felicity Amaya. 2012. *Love and Empire: Cybermarriage and Citizenship across the Americas*. New York: New York University Press.

Schueths, April M. 2012. "'Where Are My Rights?': Compromised Citizenship in Mixed-Status Marriage—A Research Note." *Journal of Sociology & Social Welfare* 39(4): 97–109.

Schueths, April M. 2015. "Barriers to Interracial Marriage? Examining Policy Issues Concerning U.S. Citizens Married to Undocumented Latino/a Immigrants." *Journal of Social Issues* 71(4): 804–20.

Silbey, Susan. 2008. "Legal Consciousness." In *New Oxford Companion to Law*, edited by Peter Crane. Oxford: Oxford University Press.

Singer, Audrey. 2004. "Welfare Reform and Immigrants: A Policy Review." In *Immigrants, Welfare Reform, and the Poverty of Policy*, edited by Kalyani Rai, 21–34. Westport, CT: Praeger.

Skinner, Allison L., and Caitlin M. Hudac. 2017. "'Yuck, You Disgust Me!' Affective Bias against Interracial Couples." *Journal of Experimental Social Psychology* 68: 68–77.

Skrentny, John D., and Jane Lilly López. 2013. "Obama's Immigration Reform: The Triumph of Executive Action." *Indiana Journal of Law and Social Equity* 2(1): 62–79.

Smith, J.D. Rebecca. 2012. "Immigrant Workers and Worker's Compensation: The Need for Reform." *American Journal of Industrial Medicine* 55(6): 537–44.

Smith, Robert C. 2006. *Mexican New York: Transnational Lives of New Immigrants*. Berkeley: University of California Press.

Snel, Erik, Godfried Engbersen, and Arjen Leerkes. 2006. "Transnational Involvement and Social Integration." *Global Networks* 6(3): 285–308.

Soederberg, Susanne. 2012. "The U.S. Debtfare State and the Credit Card Industry: Forging Spaces of Dispossession." *Antipode* 45(2): 493–512.

South, Scott J., Kyle Crowder, and Erick Chavez. 2005a. "Geographic Mobility and Spatial Assimilation among U.S. Latino Immigrants." *International Migration Review* 39(3): 577–607.

South, Scott J., Kyle Crowder, and Erick Chavez. 2005b. "Migration and Spatial Assimilation among U.S. Latinos: Classical Versus Segmented Trajectories." *Demography* 42(3): 497–521.

Soysal, Yasemin Nuhoğlu. 1994. *Limits of Citizenship: Migrants and Postnational Membership in Europe*. Chicago: University of Chicago Press.

Spörlein, Christoph, Ted Mouw, and Ricardo Martinez-Schuldt. 2017. "The Interplay of Spatial Diffusion and Marital Assimilation of Mexicans in the United States, 1980–2011." *Journal of Ethnic and Migration Studies* 43(3): 475–94.

Sprecher, Susan, Amy Wenzel, and John Harvey, eds. 2018. *The Handbook of Relationship Initiation*. New York: Psychology Press.

Swidler, Ann. 2001. *Talk of Love: How Culture Matters*. Chicago: University of Chicago Press.

Taylor, Paige. 2009. "The Good, the Bad, and the Ugly: A Survey of Selected Fifth Circuit Immigration Cases." *Texas Tech Law Review* 41: 989–1011.

Telles, Edward E., and Vilma Ortiz. 2008. *Generations of Exclusion: Mexican Americans, Assimilation, and Race*. New York: Russell Sage Foundation.

Terriquez, Veronica. 2014. "Trapped in the Working Class? Prospects for the Intergenerational (Im)Mobility of Latino Youth." *Sociological Inquiry* 84(3): 382–411.

Thronson, David B. 2006. "You Can't Get Here from Here: Toward a More Child-Centered Immigration Law." *Virginia Journal of Social Policy & the Law* 14: 58–86.

Torpey, John. 1997. "Coming and Going: On the State Monopolization of the 'Legitimate Means of Movement.'" *Sociological Theory* 16(3): 239–59.

Trucios-Haynes, Enid. 1998. "'Family Values' 1990's Style: U.S. Immigration Reform Proposals and the Abandonment of the Family." *Brandeis Journal of Family Law* 36: 241–50.

U.S. Census Bureau. 2016a. *Figure 1: Real Median Household Income by Race and Hispanic Origin: 1967–2015*. Washington, DC: U.S. Census Bureau. Retrieved May 15, 2018. www2.census.gov/programs-surveys/demo /visualizations/p60/256/figure1.pdf.

U.S. Census Bureau. 2016b. *Figure 2: Female to Male Earnings Ratio and Median Earnings of Full-Time, Year-Round Workers 15 Years and Older by Sex: 1960–2015*. Washington, DC: U.S. Census Bureau. Retrieved May 15, 2018. www2.census.gov/programs-surveys/demo/visualizations/p60/256/fig ure2.pdf.

U.S. Census Bureau. 2016c. "Income and Poverty in the United States: 2015." Washington, DC: U.S. Census Bureau. Retrieved May 15, 2018. www.cen sus.gov/library/publications/2016/demo/p60–256.html.

U.S. Census Bureau. 2019. "Real Median Personal Income in the United States [MEPAINUSA672N]." August 30. FRED, Federal Reserve Bank of St. Louis. https://fred.stlouisfed.org/series/MEPAINUSA672N.

U.S. Code §1182. https://uscode.house.gov/view.xhtml?req=granuleid%3AUSC -prelim-title8-section1182&num=0&edition=prelim.

USCIS. 2013. "Affidavit of Support." Washington, DC: U.S. Department of Homeland Security. Retrieved May 15, 2018. www.uscis.gov/green-card /green-card-processes-and-procedures/affidavit-support.

USCIS. 2016. "Maintaining Permanent Residence." Last updated February 17, 2016. Retrieved October 21, 2019. www.uscis.gov/green-card/after-green -card-granted/maintaining-permanent-residence.

USCIS. 2018. *USCIS Policy Manual*. Washington, DC: U.S. Department of Homeland Security. Retrieved April 19, 2018. www.uscis.gov/policymanual /Print/PolicyManual-Volume8-PartK.html.

USCIS. 2019. "USCIS Highlights Legal Responsibilities of Sponsors of Aliens." Last updated September 27, 2019. Retrieved April 28, 2020. www.uscis.gov /news/alerts/uscis-highlights-legal-responsibilities-sponsors-aliens.

USCIS. 2020. "Public Charge Fact Sheet." Last updated March 10, 2021. Retrieved April 22, 2021. www.uscis.gov/news/fact-sheets/public-charge-fact -sheet.

USCIS. 2021. "Form I-864P, 2020 HHS Poverty Guidelines for Affidavit of Support." Last updated April 1, 2021. Retrieved April 22, 2021. www.uscis .gov/i-864p.

USCIS Fraud Referral Sheet. 2004. (Obtained January 2010 by *New York Times*.) Retrieved May 15, 2018. http://graphics8.nytimes.com/packages /pdf/nyregion/USCIS_Fraud_Referral_Sheet.pdf.

USDA. 2019. *WIC Fact Sheet: The Special Supplemental Nutrition Program for Women, Infants, and Children (WIC Program)*. U.S. Department of

Agriculture Food and Nutrition Service. Published February 14, 2019. Retrieved April 27, 2020. https://fns-prod.azureedge.net/sites/default/files/wic/wic-fact-sheet.pdf.

Vasquez, Jessica M. 2015. "Disciplined Preference: Explaining the (Re)Production of Latino Endogamy." *Social Problems* 62(3): 455–75.

Vasquez-Tokos, Jessica. 2017. *Marriage Vows and Racial Choices*. New York: Russell Sage Foundation.

Volpp, Leti. 2006. "Divesting Citizenship: On Asian American History and the Loss of Citizenship through Marriage." *UCLA Law Review* 53: 405–83.

Waldinger, Roger. 1996. *Still the Promised City? African-Americans and New Immigrants in Postindustrial New York*. Cambridge, MA: Harvard University Press.

Waldinger, Roger. 2015. *The Cross-Border Connection: Immigrants, Emigrants, and Their Homelands*. Cambridge, MA: Harvard University Press.

Warren, Robert, and Donald Kerwin. 2017. "The 2,000 Mile Wall in Search of a Purpose: Since 2007 Visa Overstays Have Outnumbered Undocumented Border Crossers by a Half Million." *Journal on Migration and Human Security* 5(1): 124–36.

Waters, Mary C. 1999. *Black Identities: West Indian Immigrant Dreams and American Realities*. New York: Russell Sage Foundation.

Waters, Mary C., and Tomás R. Jiménez. 2005. "Assessing Immigrant Assimilation: New Empirical and Theoretical Challenges." *Annual Review of Sociology* 31: 105–25.

Wright, Richard, Serin Houston, Mark Ellis, Steven Holloway, and Margaret Hudson. 2003. "Crossing Racial Lines: Geographies of Mixed-Race Partnering and Multiraciality in the United States." *Progress in Human Geography* 27(4): 457–74.

Yoshikawa, Hirokazu. 2011. *Immigrants Raising Citizens: Undocumented Parents and Their Children*. New York: Russell Sage Foundation.

Zhou, Min. 1997. "Segmented Assimilation: Issues, Controversies, and Recent Research on the New Second Generation." *International Migration Review* 31(4): 975–1008.

Zhou, Min, and Carl L. Bankston III. 1998. *Growing Up American: How Vietnamese Children Adapt to Life in the United States*. New York: Russell Sage Foundation.

Zolberg, Aristide R. 1999. "Matters of State: Theorizing Immigration Policy." In *The Handbook of International Migration: The American Experience*, edited by Charles Hirschman, Philip Kasinitz, and Josh DeWind, 71–93. New York: Russell Sage.

Index

Printed in the USA
CPSIA information can be obtained
at www.ICGtesting.com
LVHW030753060823
754365LV00003B/303